THE BEST IN TELEVISION

50 Years of Emmys

Publisher: W. Quay Hays
Editorial Director: Peter L. Hoffman
Editors: Steve Baeck, Dana Stibor
Art Director: Chitra Sekhar
Production Director: Trudihope Schlomowitz
Prepress Manager: Bill Castillo
Production Artist: Bill Neary
Production Assistants: David Chadderdon, Russel Lockwood,
   Marc Music, Bob Penczar
Copy Editor: Dianne Woo
Indexer: Bruce Tracy

The Publisher would like to thank Meryl Marshall, Craig Mathew, David
Michaels, and Hank Rieger for all of their assistance.

For information:

General Publishing Group, Inc.
2701 Ocean Park Boulevard, Suite 140
Santa Monica, CA 90405

Library of Congress Cataloging-in-Publication Data

Gelman, Morrie
   The best in television : 50 years of Emmys / by

THE BEST IN TELEVISION
50 Years of Emmys

By Morrie Gelman & Gene Accas

Introductions by Betty White and Bob Newhart

General Publishing Group
Los Angeles

TABLE OF CONTENTS

ACKNOWLEDGMENTS

Our deep appreciation to Meryl Marshall, Dr. James Loper, and the staff of the Academy of Television Arts & Sciences, especially Hank Rieger, a friend for 30 years. You all made this project possible. Many thanks for your encouragement, counsel, and patience.

Thanks, too, to all at the Academy who unlocked the doors to the archives and endured the grating sounds of Emmy Awards telecast tapes being fast-forwarded and reversed over long hours.

Special appreciation to Harlan Böll, who, with good cheer and diligence, made possible many of the 65 interviews that provided a great deal of the substance of this book, and to those in the TV industry who granted the interviews.

Our great regard for David Michaels and TV Cares, which, through the Academy, promotes responsible programming in the areas of awareness, education, and fundraising for the ongoing struggle against HIV/AIDS.

The Emmys all started with Syd Cassyd, a gentle, caring, creative man who truly loves television. He always thought of television as a lighted lamp on high, a star in everybody's sky. He's a friend and inspiration.

To the men and women of the television industry, most of whom are straight shooters.

Keep dodging the slings and arrows.

BETTY WHITE

"Oh, it's such an honor just to be nominated. That's the best thrill of all."

As classic clichés go, that one has to be high on the list. I'm sorry to say I have uttered it on more than one occasion—and meant it. But it is almost true, and after all, what is a cliché but the truth overused? I can only speak personally, but for me being nominated is almost the best. For one thing it's always a lovely surprise, and should it happen, you can enjoy being a contender up to the time the butterflies take over on Emmy night. Of course, the operative word in all of the above is "almost." Trust me, winning's even better.

On a certain day in July each year the Emmy nominations are announced on the early morning news. You pretend to yourself that you've forgotten what day it is; God forbid you listen to the broadcast. No, you wait for the moment a dear friend calls to congratulate you—or doesn't.

Admittedly, Emmy is a colossal ego trip for the actor or actress involved, but it is something else as well. It is a sweet antidote for the low times: the canceled series, the part you would die for and didn't get, the performance that you didn't quite nail.

It was in 1952 that I won my first Emmy, and I was too new to the game even to be very nervous. Actually, I went to the ceremony more or less as a spectator. True, I was nominated (for my first series, *Life With Elizabeth*) but Zsa Zsa Gabor was a shoo-in for her series *Bachelor's Haven*. It was exciting for me just to hear my name read as a nominee. When they read it again as the winner, my brain went into slo-mo, like one of those dream sequences. Everyone else was as shocked as I, including Zsa Zsa. We've laughed about it since.

It would be 22 years before I would hear the magic words again—this time uttered by my good buddy, Ed Asner. "Winner for Best Supporting Actress in a Comedy Series, from *The Mary Tyler Moore Show*..." And the following year that rotten Sue Ann Nivens lucked out again.

In 1983, I won Emmy No. 4 for a short-lived game show called *Just Men*. We were on for only 13 weeks, and up to that time hosting a game show had been strictly male territory. The Daytime Emmy Awards ceremony was held in New York, and I didn't make the trip because, once again, my chances were somewhere between zero and zilch. Imagine my astonishment when they called that night to say I had won. It was a gender-oriented choice, I'm sure, but I wasn't about to argue.

No favoritism intended, but Miss Emmy No. 5 was the most exciting. This time it was for Best Actress in a Comedy Series, which was *The Golden Girls*. There were four of us "girls"— Bea Arthur, Rue McClanahan, Estelle Getty, and me, and we were a unit. Each performance was so interdependent on the other three that an award for one of us was an award for all of us. In trying to make this point in an unprepared acceptance speech, I must have sounded like I was Rose Nyland. The voters took care of the situation by choosing another one of us each year until we all had Golden Emmy Girls of our own.

The unexpected frosting on the cake was a guest actress Emmy for *The John Larroquette Show* in 1995–96. Was it still exciting? Were the butterflies still there? An unqualified yes!

Time has slipped by since that thrilling first win in 1952, and Emmy has grown up in the meantime. She's a big girl now, with a telecast of her own each year that goes worldwide via satellite.

These days, on Emmy night myriad stars step out of long black limousines that are lined up for blocks. Glittering in their very finest, a bit ridiculous since it's still a sunshiny California afternoon when they first arrive, they wave to the fans cheering them on from the bleachers across the street. Then comes the hard part, as they turn and make their way through the wall of cameras and microphones lining the steps into the theater. Many make a slight detour to exchange greetings with famed *Daily Variety* columnist Army Archerd, an Emmy tradition in his own right.

Fifty years in the television business is cause for celebration, and I deeply appreciate the privilege. The Academy of Television Arts & Sciences has been miraculously kind to me, with six wins and 12 nominations. With the millennium approaching, I want to wish all the future contenders the very best, and I urge them to enjoy and taste every moment. Being nominated is as good as it gets. Almost.

BOB NEWHART

In 1959, *The Tonight Show* with Jack Paar was getting enormous ratings in Chicago. But the late night movies that WMAQ, the NBC outlet in Chicago, aired following Paar were not holding the audience he delivered. NBC decided to put in a variety show starring Dan Sorkin, a very popular disc jockey. I was hired by Dan to be an on-screen performer and writer. The show was eminently unsuccessful. Our director Dave Baumgarden said, "If you stick your head out the window at midnight, you could hear an audible click caused by people turning off their sets by the thousands all over Chicago."

Dan and I continued to stay in touch after the show was canceled. When Warner Bros. Records executives Jim Conkling and Jimmy Hilward came to Chicago to press the flesh of the top DJs to hopefully get them to play some of their artists, Dan mentioned he knew someone in Chicago they should record, namely me. At the time, comedy records were enjoying some success with Mike Nichols and Elaine May, Shelley Berman, Mort Sahl, and Lenny Bruce. They said they would be glad to listen to a tape. Dan hurriedly called me up and told me to put some of my routines on tape. I borrowed a tape recorder from a friend and recorded "Abe Lincoln's PR Man," "The Driving Instructor," and "The Submarine Commander." They were impressed, or perhaps, because of Dan, they said they were impressed. They said, "Okay, we'll record you at your next nightclub appearance." I said, "I've never played a nightclub, only small dates around Chicago." They said, "We'll book you into a nightclub," which they did.

The club was called the Tidelands, in Houston, Texas. I was the opening act for Ken and Mitzi Welch, who went on to write most of the special material for Carol Burnett. At that point, I think I had a total of 18 minutes of stand-up material, and I needed another 18 minutes to have a complete album. Either that, or issue the first album without a B-side, which probably wouldn't have been a very commercial idea. I remember one night coming off stage after the first show. The material had been well received, and as I passed by the maitre d' station, he said, "Go back. They're still applauding." I said, "That's all I have." He said, "Go back anyway." So I returned to the stage, and with all the naïveté of a budding stand-up comic asked, "Which one would you like to hear again?"

After two weeks of trying out new material, I came up with enough material to fill up the other side of the album, and it was recorded. I thought of the album as an adjunct to a stand-up career. I continued to play a number of small clubs, Mister Kelly's in Chicago, the Rancho something in Winnipeg, the Elmwood Casino in Windsor, Canada, and so on.

It had been a couple of months since I had recorded the album, but I'd heard nothing from Warner Bros. about its release. Dan called me inquiring about the album because he wanted to play it on his program in Chicago to try and get something going. I called Warner Bros. and asked what happened to the album. They said a disc jockey in Minneapolis named Howard Viken had "opened" it, and they were sending every available copy to Minneapolis because the stores couldn't keep it in stock.

About that time I was booked for two weeks in a Minneapolis nightclub called Freddie's. My money "soared" from $300 a week at the Tidelands to $400 a week at Freddie's. It was during that engagement that I got a call from Bob Finkel, who was producing the 1960 Emmy Awards. He asked me if I could do the "Abe Lincoln" routine on the show. Naturally, I was floored, but before I could accept his offer I had to check with Pete Corallis, who owned Freddie's, to see if he would let me off for two days. He agreed, and I flew out to Burbank, arriving the morning of the show. At the rehearsal, I was introduced to Steve Allen, Don Knotts, Tom Poston, and Louis Nye, who were doing a comedy bit on the Emmy show. At rehearsal, I was shown where I would enter, where my marks were, and where the cue cards would be if I needed them. I said, "No thank you, I think I know it."

Mike and Elaine were also on the show, and I was going to share a dressing room with Mike. I was watching Mike and Elaine on the dressing room monitor rehearsing their routine. They were doing a very funny routine on shampoos. All of a sudden, the rehearsing stopped and the stage went quiet as Bob Finkel conversed with Mike and Elaine. After about 15 minutes, I would guess, the door to the dressing room opened and Bob and Ed Simmons, the head writers on the Emmy show, came into the room. It turned out one of the sponsors of the Emmy show was a well-known shampoo and had objected to the material. Mike and Elaine were adamant about being censored and would not be doing the show. Bob and Ed wanted to know if I had another routine about six minutes long dealing with Television, which was the theme of the show. I said I had another routine, but it really didn't have anything to do with Television. Ed Simmons said do it for him, and they would figure out the blend into the Television theme. So, for an audience of two, I did "The Submarine Commander." Afterward, Ed came up with a rather tenuous blend to fit the theme of the show. I wound up doing the two routines on national television. To me, doing the Emmy show was a long way, in a short five months, from doing an 18-minute act at the Tidelands. Late that night, I returned to Minneapolis and Freddie's, and to a lot more people in the club's audience than when I had left two days earlier.

That was my introduction to the power of television.

In January 1949, the first Emmy presentation was held in Hollywood. Six awards, covering the 1948 calendar year, were presented—one to a performer, two to programs (one live, the other film), one to a local Los Angeles station, one technical award, and a special award to Louis McManus for designing the Emmy statuette. In the years since, the Emmy has become universally recognized and accepted as television's most distinguished and respected honor. The winners and nominees comprise a virtual history of the growth of the medium. When Emmy debuted there were only 16 television stations and 190,000 television homes across the country. Fifty years later, there are now a total of 1,500 TV stations and 98 million TV households.

1948-59

No trumpets were blaring and no klieg lights were searching the skies over Hollywood when the Academy of Television Arts & Sciences was born. The announcement was buried in the "On the Air" column of the *Hollywood Reporter* issue of November 15, 1946. It read: "Seven people interested in video, and called together by Syd Cassyd, who produced in the medium in New York, met here last night to form an Academy of Television Arts & Sciences. The plan is to set up an organization similar to the American Television Society in the East and seek affiliation with that group when membership warrants. They'll hold another meet on the 26th."

I Love Lucy was the definitive sitcom of the '50s, and topped the ratings for most of its 1951–57 run on CBS. Of the principals in the cast—Lucille Ball, Desi Arnaz, Vivian Vance, and William Frawley—the men never won an individual Emmy. The show, however, won an Emmy as Best Situation Comedy in 1952.

Emmy's Roots
From Mexico With Love

Emmy had a Texas Ranger for a grandfather. Or at least Luis Manuel McManus did, and he was the man who designed the Emmy statuette. Emmy was an important player in a touching love story.

Dorothy Harris was a promising pianist who accompanied guitarist Vincente Gomez in "Concierto Flamenco" on Decca Records in the early 1960s. She married McManus after he sent her love letters, each accompanied by a small, exquisite painting. Dorothy was the model for Emmy, the female figure depicted holding the symbol of the atom and standing on a globe.

McManus was born and educated in Mexico City. His paternal grandfather served as the U.S. Consul to Mexico in the state of Chihuahua. McManus' father was born in the consulate. The family fled Mexico in 1916 during a revolution. An artist throughout his life, McManus had several one-man exhibits in the Los Angeles area and sold many paintings during his career.

He and his two brothers went into the motion picture business. Daniel worked for the Walt Disney Studios for more than 30 years. Mario, known as Bob, was with Pacific Title. After getting his start at the Mack Sennett Studios and then at Disney— he was at Disney during the production of *Fantasia*—Louis (who Americanized his name after leaving Mexico) spent some 30 years with the Hal Roach Studios. His happiest years were with Roach during the Laurel and Hardy era.

"It was a very special time in his life," his wife later recalled. In 1947, requests went out for design submissions for a television award. A friend suggested that McManus come up with an idea. He used the love of his life as his inspiration and model. A special award was given during the first Television Academy Awards Presentations to McManus for his design of the Emmy statuette. Though his design was selected over more than 100 other sketches, McManus was unwilling to accept a monetary reward for his artistic effort. Instead, the Academy gave him a lifetime gold membership card and, of course, an eternal monument to his artistry, the symbol of its highest achievement, an Emmy.

In presenting the Emmy to McManus, Academy President Charles Brown said prophetically, "Louis, here is our baby. She will be here long after we're gone."

After McManus died in 1968 at age 70, his wife spent her years living in the Pacific Northwest close to two of her daughters and six grandchildren. The love Louis and Dorothy McManus had for each other was expressed in their special song. It was Claude Debussy's "Claire de lune."

The founders wanted a membership organization that would "advance the arts and sciences of television." Soon a more defined, more targeted purpose emerged: to recognize outstanding achievements in the television industry by conferring annual awards of excellence. The objective was to provide an incentive for achievement within television and to focus public attention on cultural, educational, and technological achievements in the industry.

In relatively short order, the Academy's now world-recognized symbol, the Emmy, was created.

Syd Cassyd, then a trade journalist with *Film World* and *TV World* magazines, was the organizer, first member, and first chairman pro tempore of the new television group. He became the Academy's fourth president after serving as recording secretary.

In 1949, former KFI radio station manager Charles Brown, the Academy's second president (succeeding ventriloquist Edgar Bergen), said he felt certain that the Academy already was "well-organized," "solid," and a "constructive force in television." Brown was confident, he continued, that the scene had been set "for a long and successful history."

As third president, Harry R. Lubcke, a pioneer in the technology of video, fired the first shot in what was to become an ongoing battle with the television community in New York. He declared Hollywood "the logical television center of the world."

The beginnings of the Academy were small and localized. The formal date of birth is 1947, and the Emmy Awards were first presented in 1949 for the calendar year 1948.

The awards for 1948 marked the beginning not only of the Academy, but of television itself. The Station Award went to KTLA Los Angeles, the first commercial television station west of the Mississippi, for Outstanding Overall Achievement. A Technical Award was presented to engineer Charles Mesak of Don Lee Television for the introduction of TV camera technology. Louis McManus, designer of the Emmy Award statuette, received a special award.

The Most Outstanding Television Personality Award went to a UCLA student working at KTLA, Shirley Dinsdale, and her puppet, Judy Splinters. The Best Film for Television was a half-hour adaptation of Guy de Maupassant's classic short story, "The Necklace." Mike Stokey's *Pantomime Quiz* was Most Popular Television Program.

Emmy Awards for the calendar years 1949 and 1950 increased in number to 8 (plus three special awards) and 13 (plus two special

Milton Berle was television's first clown, known the world over as "Uncle Miltie." Berle's television career dates back to 1948 when his *Texaco Star Theater* debuted on NBC.

Gian-Carlo Menotti's mighty *Amahl and the Night Visitors*, first broadcast on December 24, 1951, won a Peabody Award and became an annual NBC Christmas special. Though it didn't fit any of the seven Emmy categories that year, the movie was the first in the *Hallmark Hall of Fame* dramatic series, which would go on to win 78 Emmys over its 47-year (and counting) run.

awards), respectively. However, because no coast-to-coast network transmission existed, only Hollywood-produced and Los Angeles–area telecast programs were recognized.

Nonetheless, from the very start of the Emmy presentations, the Academy looked beyond its local borders. "The Necklace," from Grant-Realm Productions, and Stokey's *Pantomime Quiz*, while produced and initially telecast in the L.A. area, in time were shown in other markets as well.

Emmy Awards for 1949 went to such New York–based stars as Milton Berle and Ed Wynn, among others, and to "the show that sold TV sets," Berle's *Texaco Star Theater*.

By 1951, the Emmys already was a major entertainment industry event, and 600 persons crowded the Ambassador Hotel's Cocoanut Grove in Los Angeles. Comedy was king in television then (as now), confirmed by the naming of Imogene Coca and Sid Caesar as Best Actress and Actor in television. The duo beat out such distinguished dramatic performers as Helen Hayes, Margaret Sullavan, Charlton Heston, Walter Hampden, and Robert Montgomery.

Early TV's Leaning Tower of Comedy: Carl Reiner, Sid Caesar, and Howard Morris.

Imogene Coca and Sid Caesar first teamed in 1949 in the *Admiral Broadway Revue*, but they began winning Emmys with NBC's classic series *Your Show of Shows*. They were voted Best Actress and Best Actor in 1951's Best Variety Show. After *Your Show of Shows* left the air in 1954, Caesar and Coca pursued separate careers. An attempt to reunite in 1958 on

The starring vehicle for Coca and Caesar, *Your Show of Shows*, also won the Emmy in the Best Variety Show classification, and Red Skelton won as Best Comedian or Comedienne over a powerhouse list of nominees that included not only Caesar and Coca but Lucille Ball, Jimmy Durante, and the popular team of Martin (Dean) and Lewis (Jerry).

The 1951 Emmys established that television was not just about entertainment. A special achievement award went to Senator Estes

Sid Caesar Invites You was unsuccessful. Caesar, a member of the TV Academy's Hall of Fame, won a 1956 Emmy for his *Caesar's Hour* series. In 1967, *The Sid Caesar, Imogene Coca, Carl Reiner, Howard Morris Special* won Emmys as the Outstanding Variety Special and for Outstanding Writing Achievement in Variety.

Emmy's Genesis
A Catalyst Named Cassyd

The Academy of Television Arts & Sciences (ATAS) was formed in 1946, little more than five years after commercial television operations officially began on July 1, 1941. The catalyst to forming the Academy was an energetic trade journalist named Syd Cassyd. In 1946, he brought together six other men in Hollywood who had little in common, other than that they were acquaintances of Cassyd's.

In addition to Cassyd, others at the founding meeting were S.R. Rabinof, head of American Television Laboratories; Orville Engstrom, a teacher from the Los Angeles bedroom community of Glendale; cartoon producer Morrie Goldman; Sam Nathanson, president of Meridian Pictures, a distributor for 16-millimeter films; radio station owner Harmon Stevens, owner of WHLS, a radio station in Michigan; and special effects technician Russel Furse. Two others, Harry R. Lubcke and Klaus Landsberg, who were not part of the founding meeting, helped give birth to the Academy. Both would figure prominently in the early history of television.

Lubcke, a brilliant engineer, had many television "firsts" under his belt, starting as assistant director of research at the Philo T. Farnsworth laboratories in San Francisco (an inventor, Farnsworth was the "boy wonder" of television). At the time Cassyd and his friends were forming ATAS, Lubcke was director of television for the Don Lee Broadcasting System in Hollywood, in charge of previously experimental station W6XAO, then KTSL, subsequently KNXT, and currently KCBS-TV. As president of the Society of Television Engineers in Hollywood, Lubcke (who would himself be honored by the Academy in 1990–91 for Lifetime Technical Achievement) suggested that the award for excellence in television be called "Emmy," explaining that it was the feminine version of "Immy," the nickname of the image-orthicon tube that was to early black-and-white television cameras what the microphone was to radio. The name stuck.

Landsberg, a German refugee who, at the age of 16, built the most effective shortwave receiver yet conceived, was vice president of Paramount Television Productions Inc. and general manager of experimental station W6XYZ, Hollywood, later KTLA. Besides many technical innovations, he produced and directed dozens of the earliest remote telecasts.

In October 1946, Cassyd, with the help of Landsberg, held the Academy's founding meeting at the American Television Laboratories at 5600 Sunset Boulevard. It was Landsberg who, armed with a list of Southern California owners of television sets, had asked that these owners submit by mail symbols that "best exemplified the spirit, meaning, and purpose of television as an instrument of entertainment, information, and education." This solicitation inspired the design for the Emmy Award.

Cassyd—whose wife, Myriam, was the first full-time paid executive secretary of the Academy—produced the third Emmy Awards event in 1950 and became the organization's fourth president (succeeding Lubcke). For many years he was the West Coast editor of *Box Office* magazine, the trade journal of theater owners since 1919. He was the recipient of three Emmys (Governors Awards). In 1991, the Academy established the Syd Cassyd Founders Award and named him as its first recipient.

Cassyd's vision was for the Academy to be a place for people to present ideas. "The purpose of our constitution was to hold forums and not to give out awards," he once said. Cassyd saw television as a tool for enlightenment and education.

1948—The Coming of Television

Total U.S. TV sets: 300,000

Total U.S. radio sets: 66,000,000

Total U.S. radio households: 37,000,000

Average price of home TV sets: $400

Price range of home TV sets: $169.50–$2,495

Installation fee price range: $45–$300

Average capital investment for a TV station: $375,000

Total number of U.S. TV sets manufactured in 1948
(est.): 600,000

Total number of U.S. TV sets manufactured prior to
1946: 10,000

Total number of U.S. TV sets manufactured in 1946:
6,500

U.S. commercial TV markets (March 1, 1948): 13

Commercial TV stations per market (March 1, 1948):
New York (3), Philadelphia (3), Washington, D.C. (3),
Baltimore (2), Los Angeles, Chicago, Cincinnati,
Detroit, Cleveland, St. Louis, Milwaukee,
Schenectady, N.Y., Minneapolis–St. Paul (1 each)

Total number of U.S. TV sets manufactured (through
March 1, 1948): 279,000
New York City area (including northern New Jersey
and southern Connecticut): 127,000
Philadelphia: 22,000
Los Angeles: 15,700
Chicago: 15,300
Washington, D.C.: 8,000
Detroit: 6,400
Baltimore: 5,000
St. Louis: 4,000

Cincinnati: 3,000
Cleveland: 2,300
Schenectady, N.Y.: 1,800
Milwaukee: 1,300

Commercial TV stations on the air: 20

Construction permits granted: 87

Construction applications pending: 178

Total TV advertising expenditures,1948 (est.):
$10,000,000

Total radio advertising expenditures, 1947:
$447,000,000

NBC time sales, 1947: $800,000

NBC time sales, 1948 (est.): $3,000,000

R.J. Reynolds (Camels) weekly expenditures "Fox
Movietone News," NBC, nightly: $650,000 ($350,000
programming; $300,000 station charges)

1947 telecasting deficit (NBC): $1,700,000

1947 telecasting deficit (DuMont): $ 900,000

Paramount Pictures investment in television (since
1938, and including 30 percent interest in DuMont):
$3,000,000

Major TV advertisers (1947–48): Ford (major-league
baseball rights around the country), General Foods,
Gillette (including $100,000 for Joe Louis vs. Jersey
Joe Walcott return fight), Atlantic Refining, R.J.
Reynolds ("Fox Movietone News")

Source:
Fortune **magazine, May 1948**

TV Academy's First President
Edgar Bergen

Edgar Bergen, star of NBC Radio's *Chase & Sanborn Hour*, was the first president of the Academy of Television Arts & Sciences. He was a gentle, soft-spoken man of Swedish descent who came out of the Midwest and entered show business as a ventriloquist. His alter ego was a wooden dummy named Charlie McCarthy. A critic of the time described Charlie as "completely fresh, impudent, and know-it-all, constantly bragging." During the heyday of network radio, Bergen's Sunday night program, originating from Hollywood with Don Ameche as announcer and W.C. Fields as frequent guest, was consistently among the most popular evening broadcasts. Listening to the clever, rapid, often racy repartee between Charlie, Bergen, and such guests as Mae West became a weekly American pastime.

Cascade Pictures, located at the Hal Roach Studios in Culver City, was a major factor in the establishment of the Academy. Its administration included Charles Brown, destined to become second president of the Academy. He was former manager of KFI, NBC's flagship station on the West Coast, and had worked with Bergen while there. Russel Furse, one of the seven founding fathers of the Academy, was director of television operations at Cascade Pictures. Furse suggested that the Academy of Television Arts & Sciences needed a personality with a name so that efforts to get the word out about the organization would be properly publicized. Brown said he knew Edgar Bergen and suggested that a meeting be arranged with him.

Brown, Bergen, and Furse met at the Hollywood Athletic Club. According to Furse, Bergen said, "I don't know much about television but would be honored to serve." After the meeting, Bergen drove Furse back to his apartment and they further discussed the matter en route. At the next meeting, it was agreed to ask Bergen to serve. Once he was aboard, the Academy began to get the exposure that eventually led to its successful establishment. Bergen was convinced he was chosen because he owned the two requisites for the job: a large room where meetings could be held, and a 32-cup percolator for making coffee.

"There were big problems discussed at our Academy meetings," Bergen recalled in an interview. "There were such questions as whether or not an audience would laugh at our jokes when we did television without an in-studio audience [prior to the introduction of laugh tracks]. There was talk about having to use green makeup for color cameras, and what kind of lighting would we need to film a program. The whole idea of going to a studio to film before an audience just rocked us."

Bergen didn't kid himself that he was a TV star. Never bitter about his lack of success on television, he once told a reporter how he felt when radio was fading and a new star was rising in the media firmament. "I became frightened of television," Bergen admitted. He figured the wooden dummy was a Frankenstein monster, explaining that on radio, "Charlie would drive a car, a motorcycle, or fly a plane." The wild, fast-moving, active Charlie McCarthy on radio could only sit and talk on what Bergen referred to as "the glass furnace" that was TV. He explained to an interviewer that "TV always wants to get right up into your face, and a ventriloquist's act was not meant for a tight close-up." Instead, he pointed out, the act needs a little distance to maintain the illusion and not have a TV camera constantly zoom in on a carved, painted block of wood. As television developed, Bergen, seeing there would be a mortality rate, decided to let the new medium "shake down." He finally came on the air with a quiz show called *Do You Trust Your Wife?* He fronted it for two seasons. (It later became *Who Do You Trust?* with Johnny Carson as host.)

His daughter, Candice, a future multiple Emmy Award winner, grew up in show business. Bergen had her on his top-rated radio show when she was six years old. Not wanting her to step on his lines, he reminded: "It isn't polite to talk when people are laughing." When they got off stage, she said, "Gee, Dad, I had to wait the longest time on my laughs."

Candice did a walk-on part on ABC-TV's *Hollywood Palace* when her father was guest hosting. She had three or four lines, and by all accounts wasn't good at all. Afterward, Bergen said, "Candy, let me be the first to tell you, you have nothing to give the theater." He later saw her in the motion picture *T.R. Baskin*, doing a crying scene on the telephone and a laughing scene, and declared both of them "pure Academy Award stuff."

On September 30, 1978, while in Las Vegas for a series of farewell performances capping a more than 50-year career, Bergen suffered a heart attack. He died at age 75.

Fifty Years Ago in TV

Fifty years ago, when Emmy was born, commercial TV in New York featured such programs as wrestling, Bob Smith's *Puppet Playhouse* on NBC, starring Howdy Doody (opposite, top), Jon Gnagy in *You Are an Artist* on DuMont, and Douglas Edwards reading the news on CBS.

As of April 1, there were 20 television stations on the air in 13 cities, with three each in New York, Philadelphia, and Washington, D.C. A total of 285 additional stations was authorized by the Federal Communications Commission and applied for as of April 1, 1948. Of this total, only 62 had non–radio station ownership interests (but did have interests in movies, newspapers, radio and television set manufacturing, and department store retailing). The average capital investment for a TV station was about $375,000, although WPIX in New York and WGN-TV in Chicago were estimated to have spent more than $1 million for transmitter towers, studios, and remote units.

There were only about 300,000 television receivers in the nation, three-fourths of them in eastern cities and at least half in the New York area alone. The average price of home sets was $400, with prices ranging from $169.50 to $2,495 (plus installation fees of $45 to $300).

Total advertising expenditures in television for 1948 were projected at $10 million (NBC estimated $3 million alone). Major national advertisers included American Tobacco, General Foods, Gillette, Atlantic Refining, R.J. Reynolds Tobacco (Camels), and 20th Century Fox. TV rights to the Joe Louis–Joe Walcott heavyweight championship fight went for $100,000. All home baseball games of the Yankees, Giants, and Dodgers were televised in New York at a cost to the advertisers of about $700,000 total. Prime-time rates for NBC's New York station, WNBT, started from a base of $750 an hour plus $1,000 for use of station facilities.

NBC estimated it lost $1.7 million in television in 1947, but its RCA parent company had record profits of $18.8 million (some of which came from selling transmitting and production equipment as well as TV receivers).

Paramount Pictures, with a minority interest in the DuMont Network, operator of the sole TV commercial station in Los Angeles, and a $3 million investment in TV as of 1948, forecast that up to half of all TV programming eventually would be on film (citing the advantages of economy, editing, repeat performance, and the integration of motion picture techniques with video). The consensus at the time was that whether current, full-length Hollywood feature films would ever be available for home television was doubtful—despite surveys showing that TV viewers would like to see current movie features on television. It was thought unlikely that any sponsor could pay the price of a good Hollywood feature film.

(Left) The Clown Prince of TV Comedy, Red Skelton, whose career spanned six decades, made his TV debut with an NBC weekly live show in 1951, for which he won Emmys as Best Comedian and Best Comedy Show. The TV Academy awarded him its prestigious Governors Award in 1986 and inducted him into the TV Academy Hall of Fame two years later.

Trivia

Can You Spell "Pantomine"?

When Mike Stokey's *Pantomime Quiz* won the biggest Emmy of the evening, Most Popular Television Program, at the inaugural awards ceremony on January 25, 1949, Stokey was a hot TV producer. He had a second show—*Armchair Detective*, a weekly whodunit—in the running for the same prize. Stokey remembers thinking to himself that this would be the first of many, many Emmys. "I never saw another," he acknowledged in a recent interview.

Having name recognition in those early days of television, Stokey was asked by TV Academy founder Syd Cassyd to run for president of the organization. Stokey was the Academy's fifth president and presided at the fourth annual Emmy Awards celebration at the Ambassador Hotel's Cocoanut Grove, telecast locally on February 14, 1952, by ABC's KECA-TV, Channel 7 in Los Angeles.

Since there was no coast-to-coast network that evening, a novel feature of the awards program was the contact of winners in New York by long-distance telephone. Conversations between the hosts in L.A. and award winners in New York were heard by those assembled at the Cocoanut Grove and local viewers.

Actress Eve Arden telephoned Sid Caesar in New York to tell him that he had won the Emmy for Best Actor on television. Caesar, Stokey remembers, said, "What's an Emmy?"

Primitive was the operative word for the time, according to Stokey. The Academy had inscribed "Pantomine" on the base of the statuette he won for *Pantomime Quiz*. Several years ago, Stokey, noticing that his by then more than 40-year-old Emmy needed refurbishing, sent it back to the Academy for repairs. Instead, the Academy offered him a replacement Emmy, but with corrected spelling. Stokey accepted the substitute Emmy but on one condition, that they leave the spelling error intact.

His family was appalled that he gave away the original statuette.

Short Story Yields Tall Reward

Stanley Rubin had no idea of the historical significance of receiving the first Emmy for a film made for television. He didn't even own a tuxedo in 1949, and he went to the first Emmy presentation at the Hollywood Athletic Club on the night of January 25 in a dark suit and black tie. He was there as both the writer/producer of "The Necklace" (*Your Show Time* series), the winning film, and as representative of Marshall Grant/Realm Productions, the companies responsible for the production.

Rubin had been a motion picture story reader (later called story analyst) before World War II. He worked for Marshall Grant, head of the story department at Universal Pictures. Grant promoted Rubin, taking him from the story department to write some of his first pictures. In 1942, Rubin enlisted and was assigned to the U.S. Army Air Corps. In the last few months of his time in the service, toward the end of '45, Rubin was working with Joel Malone, a member of the motion picture unit who had been a radio writer. Malone got Rubin a job writing for *The Whistler* radio series. "It was just a way to make some money, frankly, a way to make a living," Rubin recalls.

Subsequently, Rubin was signed to a writing contract at Columbia Pictures, where he worked in 1946–47. He was teamed with another writer, Lou Lantz. When their contract was not renewed, Lantz and Rubin, as the latter describes it, were "footloose and fancy free."

Rubin's fancy was to create a show for television, which was just beginning to have an impact. "Somebody ought to do a television series on film," he figured. With Lantz, he decided to do a pilot.

"The concept of a pilot was not known," Rubin reminds. "Another concept that wasn't known to us, but was to become very important, was residual values." The big question in Rubin's mind was what would happen in television programming? Would weekly episodes be 15 minutes long, or would they be 30? He never thought about an hour. The decision was made to produce a long 15 minutes so, if that turned out to be the most popular length, it would be relatively easy to cut program content to accommodate advertising. If the prevailing length of television entertainment was a half hour, it would not be difficult to stretch the "long" 15 minutes to 26 minutes.

More important, Rubin and Lantz needed to find a story for which they did not have to buy the rights. They thought of dramatizing short stories, yet couldn't afford to pay for rights to contemporary short stories. So they came up with the idea for *The World's Greatest Short Stories*, which would present stories that were in the public domain. For the pilot they wrote an adaptation of Guy de Maupassant's "The Necklace." Immediately afterwards, they began searching for other public domain short stories that would translate well into the new medium.

Rubin and Lantz found a financing partner named Norman Elzer—a businessman whose family owned a glass company. Elzer funded "The Necklace." Rubin and Lantz then brought in Sobey Martin, a director who'd also been a head film editor for MGM in Europe, as a partner.

A company, Realm Productions, was formed. Realm came from the initial of the last name of each partner—Rubin, Elzer, Lantz, and Martin—with an "a" added to make a word.

The partners figured they needed some stability, somebody with a business background. They enlisted Marshall Grant, who was at loose ends after International bought Universal. Marshall Grant Productions joined Realm Productions as a partner in the TV film project.

Gil Ralston, a writer/producer, was brought aboard as agent/salesman. He took "The Necklace" pilot to the advertising agency Foote, Cone & Belding. The project was quickly sold to American Tobacco Co. through the agency.

Ralston made a deal for 26 half hours. The partners wanted to call their series *The Book Shop Man*, but American Tobacco decided on *Your Show Time* as the umbrella title.

Arthur Shields, brother of Academy Award–winning actor Barry Fitzgerald (both came out of the Abbey Theater in Dublin), was chosen as host and narrator. He would play a man in a bookstore who was in love with books and stories. In each episode, he would lead viewers into the story of the week.

Shields also served another function. As the host/narrator, he was able to bridge scenes that the writers/producers could not afford to stage. Stage space and offices were rented at the Hal Roach Studios in Culver City on Washington Boulevard. The deal with American Tobacco called for 26 episodes at $8,500 per half hour.

The partners got busy finding adaptable short stories and writers, hiring friends to find great stories and write the adaptations. One was Walter Doniger, who later took up directing and became the lead director on *Peyton Place* at Fox. Another was Bess Taffle, who had sold an original story to RKO.

Marshall Grant/Realm Productions shot two half hours of *Your Show Time* per week. The cast would read the script first thing Monday morning, after which the crew would begin to shoot. Filming would be completed by noon on Wednesday; after lunch, work would start on the second half hour of the week. "Sometimes we would be shooting until Friday midnight before we would finish," Rubin remembers.

Each show ran 26 minutes and 30 seconds with titles and credits. Among the episodes in development were great short stories by Russians like Fyodor Dostoyevski and Aleksandr Pushkin. "They were public domain and we had writers who were eager to write adaptations," says Rubin. But someone specifically discouraged Rubin: "No Russian short stories." He was told it was because of the Communism scare of the time. "We said," he remembers, "'what does this have to do with politics? These are classics. They're recognized as classics.'"

According to Rubin, the partners fought but lost. "It was tragic, but funny, too, now that you look at it." The producers paid scale, $55 a day, to actors such as Alan Napier, Melville Cooper, Edgar Barrier, Jeanne Cagney, Sterling Holloway, Marjorie Lord, Robert Warwick, Hurd Hatfield, Robert Alda, J. Edward Bromberg, Reginald Denny, Dan O'Herlihy, John Beal, Pedro de Cordoba, Leif Erickson, Eva Gabor, Stanley Andrew, Ray Teal, Jan Clayton, and Eric Blore.

The half hours were shot motion picture–style, or as mini-movies, because the hired hands all had film backgrounds. Major motion pictures had been shot at Hal Roach Studios, and, within limitations, Rubin and his partners could use parts of leftover sets because they were unrecognizable on TV as being from theatrical features.

The Emmy Award–winning pilot, "The Necklace," starred John Beal, Maria Palmer, Fay Baker, and Stanley Andrews. Rubin remembers when *Life* magazine featured a strikingly beautiful young actress on its front page: "When we won the Emmy we were hoping to get the cover but Joy Lansing got the cover instead." Winners of the first Emmy Awards were relegated to the inside of the magazine.

Rubin, who had been in the entertainment business since getting out of UCLA at the age of 19, knew live television productions could not be repeated because the kinescopes of the time were terrible in quality. He had in mind that his films would have residual values. But after several episodes, production manager Rudy Abel and the accountant did a breakdown and came to the producers with very long faces. They said, "Listen fellows. We're getting $8,500 per show and these shows are costing us $11,500. So the great news we have to tell you, we're losing $3,000 a show."

"We created deficit financing," Rubin recalls ruefully. The producers asked Ralston to go back to the ad agency and ask for more money. The agency increased the weekly license fee to $9,000, allowing the producers to complete production for the season.

The agency offered to pick up another 26 half hours. But because the producers were losing about $2,500 per week, they went to banks seeking a loan. "We must have gone to six banks," Rubin remembers. "We talked residual values, but could not borrow a nickel, even though these programs were on film and we said they are going to be reused. The banks wanted to know where they were going to be reused, and we didn't know. 'They're going to be replayed and we're going to get more money for them,' we told the banks. 'You could have them as collateral.'"

The pickup for the second season initially was for $9,500 per week, as Rubin remembers. The agency offered to go as high as $10,500. The partners decided they couldn't go on doing these pictures and losing more money with each one. They turned down the pickup for 26 more shows, consequently losing a very valuable asset. The series eventually did go into syndication through Ziv Television Programs (the leading syndication company of the time) and the half-hour pictures returned a substantial amount of money, which was divided among the partners. As part of the deal Grant/Realm made with Ziv, the syndicator would pay off the deficit immediately and in turn receive the larger percentage of distribution revenues.

"It didn't help my fortunes to win an Emmy, but it didn't hurt me," Rubin says. "It definitely gave me added prestige and worked to my benefit. It helped me, and helped my agent, get me into RKO as a writer/producer."

Kefauver of Tennessee, who investigated organized crime nationwide and opened his hearings to the television audience. Noteworthy, too, was an impressive turnout of stars, including such top personalities of the time as Lucille Ball, Eve Arden, Susan Ball, Zsa Zsa Gabor, Adele Jergens, Ed Wynn, Charles Ruggles, Alan Young, and William Demarest.

By the time of the fifth annual Emmy Awards, with the location shifted to the downtown Los Angeles Statler Hotel, Lucille Ball was on the top rung of TV's ladder of celebrities. The *I Love Lucy* star received thunderous applause as she mounted the stage to accept her two gold statuettes for Best Situation Comedy and Best Comedienne.

Some who experienced the early years of television look back on 1953 as the medium's seminal year. "It was a year replete with promise and, as it turned out, problems, too," a trade publication reported. The year marked the beginning of the golden age of television's live, anthology drama programs. The "gold" was perhaps best represented by NBC's Sunday night *Television Playhouse*, an anthology program sponsored on alternate weeks by Philco and Goodyear and produced by the highly talented Fred Coe. Every week there were such quality, live dramatic

Future TV Academy Hall of Famer Fred Coe chats with British actress Cathleen Nesbit, the star of Paddy Chayevsky's "The Mother," which aired on the *Philco TV Playhouse* on April 4, 1954.

CBS program executive and 1958–59 TV Academy President Harry Ackerman with the network's crown *I Love Lucy* jewels: Lucille Ball, Desi Arnaz, and Vivian Vance (Ethel Mertz).

Blue Shirt or Not, Edwards Was a Winner

Ralph Edwards was the creator of two American TV classics: *Truth or Consequences* and *This Is Your Life*. He won Emmys for both.

Truth or Consequences won a 1950 Emmy, the first ever given in the game/audience participation show category. Its competition was *Kay Kyser's Kollege of Musical Knowledge*, *Life With Linkletter*, *Pantomime Quiz*, and *You Bet Your Life*. *This Is Your Life* on NBC was nominated in 1952, but CBS' *What's My Line?* won the Emmy. The next year, *This Is Your Life* shared the award with the CBS game show but won the Emmy solo for the category in 1954.

Edwards, a veteran of radio when television came along, conceived and sold *Truth or Consequences* as a radio show in 1940, and created *This Is Your Life* as a live surprise biography show for radio in 1948.

In the pioneering days of television, those who proved most adept on the small screen were veterans of radio, such as Jack Benny, Bob Hope, Martha Raye, and particularly Milton Berle.

Edwards had been a radio announcer in San Francisco as far back as 1935, and a CBS staff announcer in New York before the start of World War II. Ad-libbing in front of an open mike was second nature to him.

It was hot and muggy on the night of January 23, 1951, under the lights of local Los Angeles station KLAC-TV inside the Ambassador Hotel when Edwards was presented with his Emmy for *Truth or Consequences*. It was "with great humidity," Edwards said, that he accepted the award.

On-camera people, in those beginning days of the medium, were taught that because the television signal forms varying lines of light, it was imperative to wear clothes of color to avoid blending into the scene being televised. Knowing this, of course, Edwards was no less glib when accepting his first *This Is Your Life* Emmy at the sixth annual awards presentation.

"I'll tell you how surprised I was," he told the audience at the Hollywood Palladium, "I didn't even wear a blue shirt." It must have slipped his mind. He didn't need his blue shirt. There was no telecast that year.

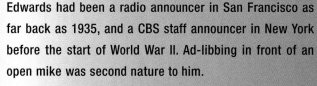

Off the Airwaves
They Could Have Been Contenders

Television wasn't for everybody. Some of radio's biggest shows and stars couldn't make the successful transition. Emmy Award–winning producer Harry Ackerman once revealed in an interview his experience as a CBS programming executive trying to turn network radio's famous *Lum 'N' Abner* comedy show into a TV property.

"I always thought of Lum [Chester Lauck] and Abner [Norris Goff] in radio days as enormously funny hillbilly characters," he recalled. CBS tried the comedy team in several pilots but, according to Ackerman (TV Academy president, 1960–61), "they just never seemed to work visually." One of the most popular radio shows of all time, *Fibber McGee and Molly*, also never made the successful switch to television. Again, several pilots were produced, both with the original cast and with new faces. A version with Bob Sweeney and Cathy Lewis replacing the original Fibber McGee and Molly (Jim and Marion Jordan) aired on NBC but lasted less than a season.

A particularly tragic example was Fred Allen (below, with Jack Benny pictured left), arguably the most brilliant

radio comedian of them all. He could never find the right niche in television. He served as the master of ceremonies of a short-lived NBC quiz show called *Judge for Yourself*, and in brief stints in such comedy variety shows as *The Colgate Comedy Hour* and *Chesterfield Sound Off Time*. When *The George Burns and Gracie Allen Show* came to CBS in 1950, with Burns (above, with Gracie Allen) stepping out of the situation comedy set to talk directly to the audience as narrator, Allen remarked to a colleague, "Now that's what I should have done. I need that kind of freedom."

Just the Facts
Dragnet's Jack Webb

Jack Webb and *Dragnet* go together, as the song lyric has it, like "a horse and carriage…You can't have one without the other."

Dragnet premiered on January 3, 1952, as a biweekly half-hour series, then went weekly and lasted until 1959 as a highly rated audience show. It was a three-time winner of the Emmy Award, 1952–54. The category was Best Mystery, Action, or Adventure Program.

As producer, director, and star of *Dragnet*, Webb was one of the first of television's triple-threats. Webb, who began his career as a radio announcer, moved up as the star of *Pat Novak for Hire* on a San Francisco radio station in 1946. He, together with James Moser and Richard Breen, first put *Dragnet* on NBC Radio in June 1949. The series moved to the NBC television network for its entire run.

From its outset on radio, *Dragnet*'s semidocumentary police-drama style, the terse and technical cop talk such as "Just the facts, ma'am" and the "dum-de-dum-dum" musical theme, became part of the popular culture. The theme was composed by Walter Schumann.

Adapted from actual cases in Los Angeles Police Department files dealing with investigation, tracking, and apprehension of criminal suspects, *Dragnet* featured Jack Webb as Sgt. Joe Friday doing voice-over narrations of stories that were devoid of gimmicks and emphasized everyday detective work.

Webb was a perfectionist, involving himself in all aspects of the show, including set design, wardrobe, makeup, sound recording, and film editing. After voluntarily closing down *Dragnet* in 1959, Webb brought the series back for a revival that began in 1967 and lasted 96 episodes.

Webb once told a reporter of his last moments with his good friend Dick Breen, who began as a freelance radio writer upon graduating from college. The two were associated later in TV and feature films, with Breen writing the screenplay for *Pete Kelly's Blues*, starring Webb, which made the transition from a radio series to feature film.

In February 1967, Breen was in St. Joseph Hospital in Burbank, California, dying of a ruptured aorta. Webb came for a last visit. Breen said something, but Webb couldn't hear him. He bent down, putting his ear close to Breen's lips. He heard Breen, halting after each syllable of each word, whisper, "Take…more…vacations." Webb didn't pay heed. He died of a heart attack at age 62.

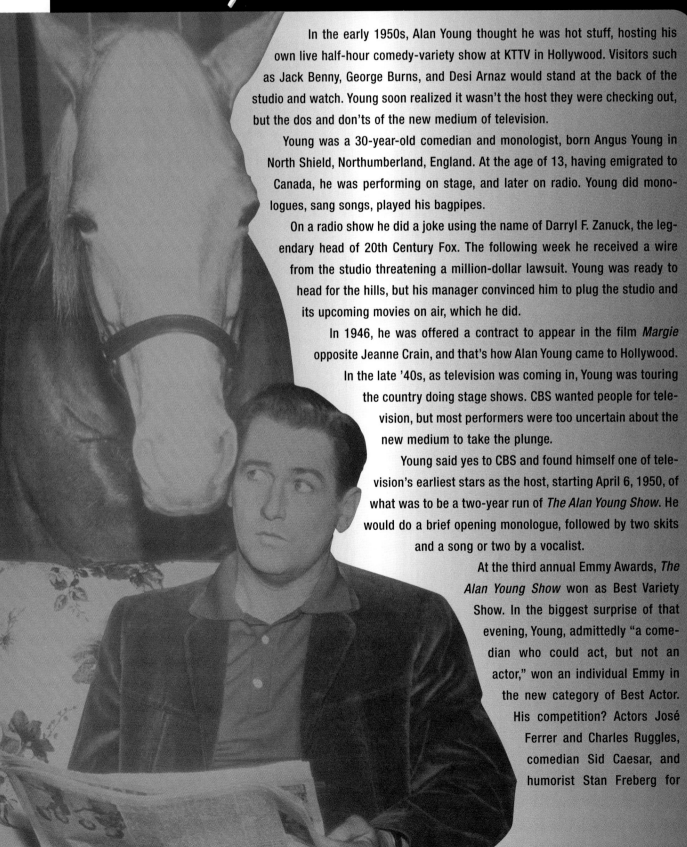

Emmys, Mister Ed:
Thank Darryl F. Zanuck

In the early 1950s, Alan Young thought he was hot stuff, hosting his own live half-hour comedy-variety show at KTTV in Hollywood. Visitors such as Jack Benny, George Burns, and Desi Arnaz would stand at the back of the studio and watch. Young soon realized it wasn't the host they were checking out, but the dos and don'ts of the new medium of television.

Young was a 30-year-old comedian and monologist, born Angus Young in North Shield, Northumberland, England. At the age of 13, having emigrated to Canada, he was performing on stage, and later on radio. Young did monologues, sang songs, played his bagpipes.

On a radio show he did a joke using the name of Darryl F. Zanuck, the legendary head of 20th Century Fox. The following week he received a wire from the studio threatening a million-dollar lawsuit. Young was ready to head for the hills, but his manager convinced him to plug the studio and its upcoming movies on air, which he did.

In 1946, he was offered a contract to appear in the film *Margie* opposite Jeanne Crain, and that's how Alan Young came to Hollywood. In the late '40s, as television was coming in, Young was touring the country doing stage shows. CBS wanted people for television, but most performers were too uncertain about the new medium to take the plunge.

Young said yes to CBS and found himself one of television's earliest stars as the host, starting April 6, 1950, of what was to be a two-year run of *The Alan Young Show*. He would do a brief opening monologue, followed by two skits and a song or two by a vocalist.

At the third annual Emmy Awards, *The Alan Young Show* won as Best Variety Show. In the biggest surprise of that evening, Young, admittedly "a comedian who could act, but not an actor," won an individual Emmy in the new category of Best Actor. His competition? Actors José Ferrer and Charles Ruggles, comedian Sid Caesar, and humorist Stan Freberg for

his voice-over performance in the puppet show *Time for Beany*.

Not only did Alan Young go into the books as the first Best Actor winner, but he also became the third double winner in Emmy history. The previous year, Milton Berle and Ed Wynn won dual Emmys: Berle for Best Kinescope Show (*Texaco Star Theater*) and for the Most Outstanding Kinescope Personality; Wynn for Best Live Show (*The Ed Wynn Show*) and for Outstanding Live Personality. Subsequently, Young became one of TV's most enduring stars, playing Wilbur Post, the architect who discovers a talking horse in the CBS classic sitcom *Mister Ed*, now a syndicated evergreen.

Young didn't think a great deal about the historic significance of his Emmys at the time. He had his own popular TV series and was young, married, a recent father, and, generally, sitting on top of the world. His exposure led him to a contract with Howard Hughes' RKO Pictures and a role in *Androcles and the Lion*, top-billed in a stellar cast of motion picture "names" that included Jean Simmons, Victor Mature, Robert Newton, Maurice Evans, Elsa Lanchester, Alan Mowbray, and Gene Lockhart.

"It all started," Young remembered many years later, "because I thought Darryl F. Zanuck was a funny name."

Fran Allison was the live performer working with the company of puppets created by Burr Tillstrom in NBC's clever and popular series *Kukla, Fran and Ollie*, which won a 1953 Emmy for Best Children's Series.

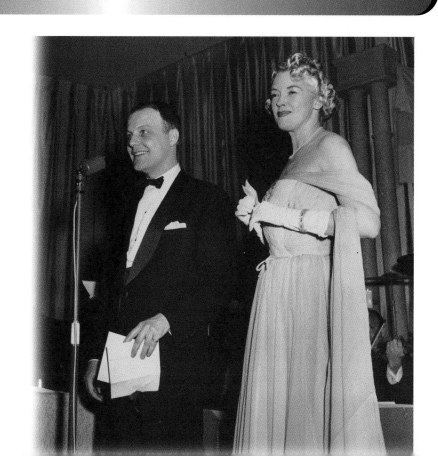

Loretta Young
More Than an Actress

Loretta Young, three-time Emmy Award winner in the '50s for her NBC dramatic anthology series, *The Loretta Young Show*, was more than an actress. She was a movie star doing television at a time when most of the film industry shunned it. She was a wife, mother, and community leader. She was also a fashion figure. When her show started in 1953, her husband, Tom Lewis, a former ad agency executive turned writer-producer, decided to have Young appear as much like her real-life self as possible.

Asked by a reporter why this decision was made, Lewis replied, "The audience doesn't want this standoffish thing on television. They want somebody to be their friend." He had Young's mother, a decorator, reproduce the Lewis' living room as the set at the opening of each episode. Young's designer was told to come up with a different fashion each week for her to wear when she glided into the living room to introduce the night's play. He had her turn around after the intro and glide to the door of the room before closing it and departing. It became the show's trademark.

"It was a miniature fashion show," Lewis explained about the famous opening. About the program itself, Lewis said, it amounted to nothing more than a glossy soap opera. "If you didn't know what you saw, at the end she'd tell you." The series, originally titled *Letter to Loretta*, started with a mistaken concept. Young's clothes at first were too elaborate, Lewis later acknowledged. "No matter how much clothes cost, if they are simple enough so that the woman who is watching thinks she can copy it, you're in," he said. *The Loretta Young Show* was "in" for eight years (1953–61).

programs as *Studio One*, *Playhouse 90*, *Kraft Television Theatre*, *Robert Montgomery Presents*, and the *U.S. Steel Hour*.

The geometric expansion of television households and the consequent multiplication of advertisers' TV budgets, coupled with the economic advantage of film over live production, inevitably meant this golden age was to be a short one. Live drama was missing entirely from network TV's prime-time schedule by the 1960–61 season.

The first Emmy Awards telecast across the nation aired in 1954. NBC carried the program, paying $45,000 for the rights. That fee

A Self-Made Man

When Delbert Mann was piloting a B-24 Liberator bomber during World War II, he knew nothing of television. Stationed near London, he saw more than 50 theatrical productions, including Laurence Olivier's staging of *Peer Gynt*. The experience inspired him to enroll in Yale Drama School to pursue a life in the theater. But by 1949, TV, a young, hungry contender, was challenging theater and even movies for audiences. The theatrical neophyte found himself directing for the *Philco TV Playhouse* under legendary producer Fred Coe.

Mann carved a place for himself among the directors, writers, producers, and performers who molded the 1950s into the golden age of television drama. He directed such acclaimed productions as Tad Mosel's first tele-play, "Ernie Barger Is 50," and J.P. Miller's "The Rabbit Trap." His career, spanning five decades, was capped by 1979's "All Quiet on the Western Front," yet Mann never won an Emmy.

Ironically, when Mann turned to motion pictures, he won an Academy Award his first time out with his com-passionate directing of *Marty*, Paddy Chayefsky's study of human relationships. *Marty* was the first of what was to become a wave of filmed teleplays to make it to the big screen. The original version of "Marty" for television, also directed by Mann, lost to the CBS production of writer Reginald Rose's "Twelve Angry Men" as Best Individual Program of the Year in 1954. Then, two years after *Marty* won an Academy Award as Best Picture, *Twelve Angry Men* was nominated for a Best Picture Oscar but didn't win.

Shooting From the Hip at the Emmys
"You Had to Be a Little Insane"

Producer-director Bob Finkel, who specialized in variety programs, produced more Emmy telecasts than any-one else. Finkel remembers back to 1954, before Emmy went network and he was directing (not producing) from the Statler Hotel for KLAC-TV, a local Los Angeles station providing the coverage. Character actor Charles Ruggles was president of the Academy that year and during the telecast handed the gavel to fellow actor Don DeFore. Radio-TV personality Art Linkletter was the host.

"You had to be a little insane to begin with because not only were you doing a live show, you were doing a live show that hadn't even been rehearsed," Finkel says. "You were shooting from the hip the entire show. But I loved it."

Nervousness is a by-product of live telecasts, Finkel knew. He sensed the crew was jittery and the performers were tentative about what they were to do. To relieve the tension, he dressed in a suit and tie. "It had a calming effect when I went into the truck, dressed like that," he was later to recall. "The crew looked at me and said, 'Hey, this is a party for him, so I guess it must be for us.' It calmed people down."

Finkel went on to produce the Emmys in 1959, 1963, and 1964, then again in 1972, 1973, 1974, and 1975. He also produced two Oscar telecasts and 14 People's Choice Awards, and helped create the Prime Time Golden Globe Awards as well as many other award specials.

(Above) John Conte hosted NBC's daytime *Matinee Theatre*, Pat Weaver and producer Al McCleery's ambitious attempt to do quality afternoon drama. In 1955, the show won an Emmy for Best Contribution to Daytime Programming.

(Above, right) Jack Benny and actress Jane Wyatt both won their first Emmys in 1957; he for his continuing comedy performance on *The Jack Benny Show*, and she for her role as Margaret Anderson in *Father Knows Best*. Benny, who took seven years to win his first Emmy, also won a TV Academy Trustees Award that year.

(Right) *The Ed Sullivan Show*, one of the most popular in television history, was a Sunday-night tradition for 23 years. The show was named Best Variety Series in 1955, and Sullivan received a Trustees Award in 1971.

helped bail the Academy out of debt, and the national exposure provided welcomed prestige and publicity.

In 1955, New York became the Academy's second chapter. Two years later, in June 1957, the Los Angeles and New York chapters formed the National Academy of Television Arts and Sciences. Ed Sullivan, a syndicated newspaper columnist and the host of his own CBS weekly variety series, was elected president of the now-national organization.

By the 10th annual Emmy Awards, the Academy's prestige and national recognition were second only to those of the Oscar organization, the Academy of Motion Picture Arts and Sciences. Masters of ceremonies for the event were big TV names: Phil Silvers in the East and Danny Thomas in the West. Sponsors for the national telecast were among the leading TV advertisers: Procter & Gamble and the Pontiac Division of General Motors Corporation.

Presenters for the 10th annual awards (telecast by NBC from the Cocoanut Grove and the network's New York studios) included the principal members of TV's performing community: Steve Allen, Eve Arden, Jack Benny, Gertrude Berg, Milton Berle, Red Buttons, Eddie Cantor, Art

Behind the Scenes at the Emmys
March 17, 1956

It's Saturday, March 17, 1956. There are 30 million television homes in America and 2,000 Academy of Television Arts & Sciences members. You are in Southern California, and that night the television industry evaluates and pays tribute to itself.

The eighth annual prime-time Emmy Awards is scheduled, with a total of 40 awards to be presented. The first 24 presentations will be telecast nationally for 90 minutes by NBC from two origination points. One is the newly renovated Pan Pacific Auditorium in Hollywood. The other is the Grand Ballroom of the Waldorf-Astoria Hotel in New York City. Master of ceremonies at the Pan Pacific is audience participation show host Art Linkletter (right). Newsman and panel show personality John Daly conducts the proceedings from the Waldorf-Astoria.

Presenters of the first 24 Emmys will include comedian George Gobel (below), of *The George Gobel Show*, actor Bob Cummings (*My Hero*), and Jimmy Durante (*The Jimmy Durante Show*) in Hollywood. In New York, presenters are humorist Sam Levenson (*The Sam Levenson Show*), quiz show host Hal March (*The $64,000 Question*), and Phil Silvers (*The Phil Silvers Show*).

Immediately behind and above the stage at the Pan Pacific Auditorium is a 9 x 12-foot rear-projection screen that shows events as they occur either in the Pan Pacific or in the Grand Ballroom at the Waldorf. Two additional screens are hung on the north and south walls. There are also four 28-inch viewing monitors. A raised 5-foot platform near the east wall of the Pan Pacific (normally used for college basketball games and ice-skating pageants) is the main stage, with an area of some 9,000 square feet. It is encircled on the front two sides by a raised platform to accommodate more than 200 nominees. Flanking center stage are two working fountains, 12 feet in diameter, with an orchestra pit directly in front of the stage. Two ramps lead from the platform where the nominees sit to the stage. Winners are escorted to the stage to receive their Emmys.

There is seating in the Hollywood auditorium for 2,460 Academy members and guests. They occupy a floor area of about 37,000 square feet. The audience is to be seated at

circular tables spaced at intervals throughout the auditorium. The balance of the auditorium is closed off by 20-foot rayon satin drapes in gray, yellow, and maroon. Ten 12 x 122-foot shag rugs in red, gray, and green are spaced throughout the floor area, as much for sound absorption as for aesthetics.

At the main entrance of the Pan Pacific is a 9-foot gold-colored plastic replica of the Emmy award. It's set in front of a 20-foot curved backing. There's more to this statue than decoration. It's screening a 12-foot scaffold tower erected on the other side to support two TV cameras. These are used to cover the stage action some 125 feet away. Accenting the floor and wall decorations are three truckloads of shrubs that are distributed along the main stage and draperies. On stage, Linkletter and the various presenters work from a lectern equipped with a special TV monitor. A quick glance at the monitor and Linkletter or the others can see exactly what's going out over the air.

Working press arrives at the Pan Pacific at 5 P.M. for cocktails. They are met by ATAS members and public relations representatives of the Ettinger Co. and NBC. The press is seated at special "ringside" tables, where space has been set aside for post-award interviews. Photographers using flash equipment must operate backstage. Newsreel crews are assigned to positions at the back of the auditorium or work backstage in a special room. After the prime-time telecast, dinner will be served (during which the remaining 16 national awards are presented, viewed only by those present at the Pan Pacific and the Waldorf).

The televised event begins with a shot of glamorous Zsa Zsa Gabor arriving at the Pan Pacific in a gleaming white Oldsmobile. Olds is sole sponsor of the national telecast. William Bennington is directing in Hollywood and Dick Schneider in New York. Both are working under William Kayden, who is producing backstage at the Pan Pacific. Actor Don DeFore, president of the Academy, delivers a state-of-the-organization report, noting that this is the second year of national awards. He focuses on the formation of a New York chapter and making the Academy "a truly national organization."

Ed Sullivan, host of *The Ed Sullivan Show* and chairman of the New York Chapter, takes a bow in front of the audience at the Waldorf. He voices conciliatory words about the East Coast/West Coast rivalry of the past. "We're all in the same industry" and no more bickering becomes the theme of this night's get-together. Musical director Gordon Jenkins and his orchestra take over in Hollywood with a fanfare, and the show begins.

Best Children's Series is the first category announced, and *Lassie*, the story of a young boy and his collie, is the first winner. Tommy Rettig (above, with costar Jan Clayton and actor Lloyd Nolan), who plays the boy, Jeff Miller, is in the audience, beaming with delight. Producer Al McCleery, a television

visionary, later goes on stage to accept an Emmy for NBC's *Matinee Theatre* for Best Contribution to Daytime Programming. He praises two "courageous bosses," top NBC executives Pat Weaver and Bob Sarnoff. The legendary Edward R. Murrow of CBS is cited as Best News Commentator, but to the disappointment of all he's a no-show. CBS gets another Emmy for its atomic bomb test coverage in the Best Special Event or News Program category.

There are some technical glitches. Smoke mysteriously drifts up from the stage at the Waldorf. Everyone looks bewildered, but this turns out to be an instance of smoke, but no fire. The projection screen at the Pan Pacific blacks out briefly, confusing Linkletter at the lectern. When Bob Cummings reads the nominees in the Best Action or Adventure Series category, there is a memorable reaction shot of the famed director in the audience when his *Alfred Hitchcock Presents* series is named. Hitchcock loses out to *Disneyland*, ABC's first major hit program. Actress-comedienne Nanette Fabray weeps tears of happiness while accepting her Emmy in New York as Best Actress in a Supporting Role for *Caesar's Hour*. Dinah Shore clutches her Emmy as Best Female Singer and tells the television audience "there's two indispensable words on our program—Bob Banner" [producer of *The Dinah Shore Show*]. Perry Como accepts his Emmy as Best M.C. or Program Host from the stage of the Century Theater in New York, where he's rehearsing.

Bachelor Phil Silvers, hoisting aloft his Emmy as Best Comedian, points out all the other winners are happily married and he isn't. "Until that happy day," he says, "this is the most cherished possession I have." Later, winning his second Emmy of the night (for Best Comedy Series), Silvers explains that a television show is a collaborative effort. "The only thing you handle alone is anxiety," he tells the audience. Easily the star of the night, Silvers wins a third Emmy as Best Actor—Continuing Performance for playing Sgt. Bilko in *You'll Never Get Rich* (renamed *The Phil Silvers Show*). George Gobel, on stage at the Pan Pacific as a presenter and noticeably wilting under the heat of the lights, makes it known "anyone who wants to boil an egg can start with me."

The roll of winners keeps unfurling. Lucille Ball receives a roar of approval when announced as Best Actress—Continuing Performance for *I Love Lucy*, but she's not there to hear the plaudits. Writer Madelyn Pugh accepts on her behalf. Mary Martin (above), star of the *Producers' Showcase* production of "Peter Pan," wins as Best Actress–Single Performance. She, too, is absent. Her young daughter, Heller Halliday, serves as her mother's stand-in. Surprisingly, with rock 'n' roll impacting the land, *Your Hit Parade*, a nostalgic throwback to the heyday of radio, is named Best Music Series. Ed Sullivan, Walt Disney, producers Fred Coe and Franklin Schaffner, and writers Rod Serling and Nat Hiken are all Emmy winners this night. Some are destined to be linked forever with television's so-called golden age and, three decades later, others are chosen for television's Hall of Fame.

After dinner, a crew of 45 men dismantle and truck away all traces of the Emmy event. It took 1,832 man-hours to set the stage for Emmy. It takes eight hours of hammering and heavy lifting to again transform the Pan Pacific back into a basketball arena.

Versatile actor Art Carney, who won a total of five Emmys, took home a Golden Lady in 1955 for his hilarious take as Jackie Gleason's sidekick Ed Norton, the sewer worker, in the CBS comedy classic *The Honeymooners*.

Carney, Jill Corey, Arlene Francis, James Garner, Dave Garroway, George Gobel, Ida Lupino, Gisele MacKenzie, Garry Moore, Louis Nye, Paul Winchell, Jane Wyatt, Ed Wynn, Loretta Young, Morey Amsterdam, Jerry Lester, Cliff Norton, Arnold Stang, Mel Allen, Frank Blair, Walter Cronkite, Alex Dreier, Douglas Edwards, Don Goddard, Chet Huntley, John Secondari, Bob Trout, and Eric Sevareid.

No question—the TV Academy and the Emmys had come of age. *TV Guide*, in a March 16, 1957, editorial, rhapsodized: "When the Emmy Awards were started by the Academy of Television Arts & Sciences, they had no more importance than any of a dozen or so other plaques, scrolls, and statuettes being doled out to television performers.... This year for the first time, the Emmy Awards finally have achieved the stature of the movie Oscars. Certainly everyone in television feels that the Emmy is the highest honor in the industry."

The 1950s was a decade marred by "the junior senator from Wisconsin," as CBS news commentator Ed Murrow dubbed Joseph McCarthy. "McCarthyism," the use of unsubstantiated accusations in an attempt to expose Communist subversion, led to a blacklist of, among others, persons in the TV industry. *Blacklisting* became a fearful term in television. As a result, the careers of many of the most talented and admired were destroyed or at least interrupted.

Early in the same decade, the American Broadcasting Co. (ABC) merged with Paramount theaters. Leonard Goldenson, the architect of

Emmy Memories
Polly Bergen

"The night of the Emmys, I remember the master of ceremonies was Phil Silvers. When they started to name all the nominees, I was seated next to Perry Como. He was on one side, and Freddie [Fields, Bergen's husband, and a noted TV executive] the other. I lowered my head and Phil said, 'The winner is...' I thought he said, 'Helen Hayes [one of the other nominees for Best Actress, along with Julie Andrews, Piper Laurie, and Teresa Wright],' so I didn't hear my name. And the applause started. I'm waiting for that ghastly moment to be over so I can look up, bravely smile, and applaud Helen Hayes, and Perry nudged me. 'Polly, he called your name.' But I never heard it.

"I got up and did everything you don't do. I went running up the aisle, sobbing like an idiot, babbling like a total maniac. Phil, of course, was thrilled. He was one of our best friends. He was crying by the time I got up there."

—Polly Bergen, on winning an Emmy in 1957 for "The Helen Morgan Story"

About six weeks later, Bergen's agent got a call from Las Vegas, where she had headlined in small, second-rate hotels for $3,500 a week. She was offered $50,000 a week to open at the Riviera, with the very same act.

The Crusading Defense Lawyer Was a Champ Among Champions

It has been said that Erle Stanley Gardner, creator of the Perry Mason character and author of the many novels featuring the crusading defense lawyer, personally selected Raymond Burr as the lead for the TV series.

The question is, why? In many of his movie roles, the heavyset Burr played the bad guy. He certainly was menacing in his most famous role as the murderer Jimmy Stewart sees in *Rear Window*, Alfred Hitchcock's 1954 film.

Whatever Gardner's reason, it was prescient. As television's Perry Mason, Burr portrayed a celebrated "good guy" character in a role that lasted 27 years. *Perry Mason* became TV's longest-running and most successful lawyer series, lasting for nine seasons on CBS from 1957 through 1966, followed by years of syndicated reruns.

Subsequently, in December 1985, NBC aired "Perry Mason Returns" as a made-for-TV movie, under the aegis of former network executive turned independent producer Fred Silverman. For more than seven years, Burr starred in an average of three new Perry Mason telefilms annually, the 26th and final installment, "Perry Mason: The Case of the Killer Kiss," airing only a few weeks after Burr died in 1993.

Burr won two Emmys for his work in the series, as Best Actor in a Leading Role in a Dramatic Series in 1959, and two years later for Outstanding Performance by an Actor in a Series. Barbara Hale, who played Perry

Mason's devoted secretary, Della Street, also won an Emmy in 1959 in the Best Supporting Actress in a Dramatic Series category.

"Perry Mason went on the air when people were first buying television sets," Burr said in an Associated Press interview the year of his death. "A lot of people in this country didn't know what their legal system was all about. I'm sure just from the people who have watched the show over the years, particularly the minorities, they found out the system of justice was for them."

James McEachin, who played Lt. Ed Brock in the NBC Perry Mason movies, said about his TV antagonist in an interview: "When the history of television is written, Raymond Burr has to be among the absolute forerunners. When you talk about someone who has changed the color and face of television, I think he did it. He was just a champ among champions."

NBC published a full-page memorial in the Hollywood trades with a small photo of Burr. The memorial read: "A Television Legend. A Valued Colleague. A Good Friend. Raymond Burr 1917–1993." Below these words were Perry Mason's battered briefcase on a courtroom table next to a legal pad. The banner on top of the page simply said: "The Defense Rests."

Barbara Hale, Charles Bronson, Abby Dalton, Robert Stack, and Don Knotts at the 1957 Emmys. Hale, who played Della Street in *Perry Mason*, won a Best Supporting Actress award for the 1958–59 season; Stack won a Best Actor award in 1960 for *The Untouchables*. Knotts would go on to win four Emmys. Dalton costarred in *The Jonathan Winters Show*, and Bronson was set to star as the *Man With a Camera* for ABC.

A youthful Leonard Bernstein in an appearance on CBS' *Omnibus*.

this deal, had a film industry background and turned to Hollywood seeking answers to third-ranked ABC's programming problems.

In 1954, a little more than a year after the merger, ABC and Walt Disney signed a long-term deal calling, initially, for 26 hours of television programming a year. This agreement was a breakthrough not only because major studios considered television "the enemy," but also because, despite a few exceptions, there was no real tradition of filmed production for television. TV series, in large part, were born of radio and Broadway theatrical presentations.

Advertisers were drawn to the mass audience made possible as set ownership grew. Film on television came into its own. Live TV production put heavy demands on performers, while filmed programming provided the security of retakes and editing and, more important, offered an economic boon: repeats of programs or syndication after network runs. The ABC–Disney agreement lured another one of the majors, Warner Bros., to the ABC negotiating table, and an ABC–Warner contract was drawn for the production of series for the 1955–56 season.

But the television transformation of

The Night Uncle Milty Preempted the History of Television

Producer and network executive Perry Lafferty's first experience with Emmy was a nightmare. He had been hired by the TV Academy as a consultant to the 10th annual Emmy Awards. It was April 15, 1958, and the telecast over the NBC-TV network was from the Seventh Regiment Armory National Guard in New York and the Cocoanut Grove of the Ambassador Hotel in Los Angeles.

Ed Sullivan, the national president of what was then the National Academy of Television Arts & Sciences, came on first with the introduction. Phil Silvers was master of ceremonies in New York and Danny Thomas his counterpart in Los Angeles. Presenters included Steve Allen, Eve Arden, Jack Benny, Gertrude Berg, Milton Berle, Red Buttons, Eddie Cantor, Art Carney, Arlene Francis, James Garner, Dave Garroway, George Gobel, Ida Lupino, Garry Moore, Jane Wyatt, Ed Wynn, and Loretta Young.

Berle was the fly in the ointment. Lafferty, producer Bill Kayden, and various Academy staff people had put together a "cavalcade" of television in keeping with the 10th anniversary telecast. "We worked for three months building a film clip package, a beautiful presentation, which ran about 15 minutes. It was to be scattered throughout the program," Lafferty later recalled. "In those days you had to be off the air on time. There was no running over," he pointed out. "We worked so hard and we got this wonderful chronology and then Berle came on and did what he always did in those days, 20 minutes when he was supposed to do two minutes. We had to cut everything. Everything we did [in the clips] was thrown out."

Danny Thomas, who previously was guilty of telling a three-minute-long anecdote, was steamed. He noted that Berle "had accomplished the impossible," cutting out "our cavalcade." The elder statesman of radio-TV comedy, Jack Benny, was reduced to merely announcing *Playhouse 90* as the Best Dramatic Anthology Series and handing an Emmy to producer Martin Manulis.

Eventually Berle got the message. "I won't bore you anymore with Art Linkletter material," he quipped.

"I sat in my living room watching Berle's spot stretch and knew that all of our work for three months was going down the drain. It was heartbreaking at the time," said Lafferty.

Better days were ahead. Lafferty produced *The Danny Kaye Show* for CBS and at the end of the program's first season, 1963–64, it was nominated for Best Variety Show and Kaye for Best Variety Performer.

The show and Kaye both won Emmys in 1964. Lafferty, experiencing "unbelievable elation," accepted the Emmy as producer. Kaye was performing at the Desert Inn in Las Vegas, so Lafferty picked up his Emmy.

The telecast was live on the East Coast but tape-delayed on the West Coast. Los Angeles–based Lafferty drove home, had a couple of drinks and dinner, and then sat with his family and watched the West Coast feed. It was an added thrill to see himself on television before all the distinguished people of his industry.

"The Emmys get an awful lot of criticism from everybody all the time, and I could be included right on top of the parade," he acknowledged in an interview. "The Emmys take a lot of abuse until you get nominated," he added. "Then they're not so bad. And then when you win, they're great."

48

(Above) British journalist Alistair Cooke, the charming emcee of *Omnibus* and later host of *Masterpiece Theatre*.

(Right) Hal March was the host and psychologist Dr. Joyce Brothers was the guest in the onstage "isolation booth," where contestants answered *The $64,000 Question*, TV's first big money game show. It won an Emmy in 1955 for Best Audience Participation Series.

Hollywood was not an overnight phenomenon. In 1955, for example, about 54 percent of the three-network Sunday through Saturday prime-time schedules were filmed productions. That year, a *New York Times* survey reported Hollywood was turning out more than 10 times as many films for TV as for theatrical exhibition. As much as 30 to 40 percent of the average TV station's daily schedule was on film.

The economics of filmed programming and the growing need for film production talent and studio space drove programming west. Demand for programming was virtually insatiable. Small, independent producers and syndicators cranked out an ever-increasing stream of inexpensive, quickly made series, which became necessary and popular as the number of stations and their schedules expanded.

Out of the transition to film came *Cheyenne,* originally one of three rotating hourlong dramas from Warner Bros. for ABC. In July 1958, Westerns claimed more than a quarter of network prime time.

The 1950s ended with television's dirtiest linen revealed: the "rigging" of certain quiz shows exposed for government and public scrutiny. The scandal—which involved producers of such highly popular giveaway shows as *Twenty One* and *The $64,000 Question* providing some contestants with answers prior to airtime—led to the networks taking greater control over programming and diminished the ability and power of advertisers to produce and deliver their own shows. The quiz scandal, combined with the ever-escalating costs of TV commercial time, all but marked the end of sole or even dual sponsorship of series programming.

By this time, little more than a decade after the coming of the TV set into America's homes, the nation was so hooked on the tube that it was difficult to recall what life was like before television.

THE BEST IN TELEVISION *50 Years of Emmys*

"Gunsmoke"
Twenty Years, Hard to Top

As Marshal Matt Dillon of Dodge City, James Arness usually got his man, but he never got an Emmy. As Kitty Russell, owner of the Longbranch Saloon, Amanda Blake had a winning way about her, but she never won an Emmy either. The vehicle they rode for 20 seasons, *Gunsmoke*, gained a total of 15 Emmy nominations, but only five of them "got the gold."

When *Gunsmoke* debuted on CBS-TV September 10, 1955, it set off a stampede of "adult" Westerns. That same 1955–56 prime-time network season saw *Frontier*, a Sunday night anthology, begin on NBC, as well as *Cheyenne*, starring Clint Walker, and *The Life and Legend of Wyatt Earp*, a half hour introducing Hugh O'Brian to stardom, both on ABC (the latter starting the same week as *Gunsmoke*).

By the 1959–60 season, there were 25 Westerns in prime time—10 on ABC, 8 on NBC, and 7 on CBS. *Gunsmoke* was the king. It was the top-rated program for four consecutive seasons, 1957–61.

Gunsmoke was not only the longest-running Western ever (1955–75), but its 20-season run is longer than any other prime-time series with continuing characters. Despite these and other

achievements, *Gunsmoke* won but two Supporting Actor Emmys (Dennis Weaver, 1959; Milburn Stone, 1968), a Sound Editing Emmy, and another for Best Editing of a Film for Television. The big Emmy for *Gunsmoke* was as Best Dramatic Series with Continuing Characters in 1957.

The program's star, James Arness, was nominated for Best Actor in a Dramatic Series in 1956, 1957, and for the 1957–58 season. He lost twice to Robert Young in *Father Knows Best* and once to Raymond Burr in *Perry Mason*. Costar Amanda Blake also was nominated in the 1958–59 season competition but lost to another *Perry Mason* performer, Barbara Hale.

PROD. NO.
PRESIDENT KENNEDY
SCENE
1
TAKE
SOUND
2
DIRECTOR
CAMERAMAN
DATE
7/3/63
EXT.
INT
PRODUCED BY

1960-69

There was once a series on NBC called *That Was the Week That Was*. It was different—precocious, irreverent, confrontational to those in high and mighty places. Dressed as a musical production, the program was political satire, entertainment with an edge. Appropriately, it appeared in the '60s because "That Was the Decade That Was."

The annual Emmy telecast, which recognizes excellence in entertainment and information, found itself constantly challenged to be more than an awards show because television, in its best moments during the 1960s, reflected momentous world events. It was a decade of confusion in the cities of America and, especially, in many universities. There was citizen and student unrest over issues of race and the growing armed conflict in a far-off region of the world, Vietnam. There were outbreaks of violence and

John F. Kennedy was the first president to make use of the new medium of television. His televised debates with Richard Nixon in 1960 are widely believed to have won him the election. In 1963, the Academy presented Kennedy with a Trustees Award, "for news conferences and in honor of his continued recognition of television's importance to a free society."

demonstrations by hundreds of thousands of people. Riots, police bullying, and brutality marked the 1968 Democratic National Convention in Chicago. Television was in the middle, sometimes a bloodied participant as well as an observer.

Television during this decade also covered the shocking assassinations of President John F. Kennedy, his brother, Sen. Robert Kennedy, and two charismatic leaders, the Rev. Martin Luther King Jr. and Malcolm X.

As television evolved into a window of history, the Emmys recognized and rewarded these changes. NBC's "The Tunnel," described as "a gripping documentary of a desperate flight to freedom under the Berlin Wall," was named Program of the Year at the 15th annual Emmy Awards in 1963. It was the first time in the history of the TV Academy that a documentary was voted the top award in the annual event.

The following season, another documentary, ABC's "Making of the President 1960," won the coveted Program of the Year Emmy. Based on Theodore H. White's Pulitzer Prize–winning book, the program was produced by the independent David Wolper organization. NBC's

Best known for his long-running music series *American Bandstand* on ABC, Dick Clark (below, during a July 9, 1960, taping) won a 1979 Emmy as Best Host in a Game or Audience Participation Show for *The $20,000 Pyramid*. He followed with another Emmy in 1983 for the best children's entertainment special, "The Woman Who Killed a Miracle."

David Susskind, a multiple Emmy winner who produced hundreds of dramas and specials, interviews Richard Nixon for one of his *Open End* talk shows.

"So far, Fred Astaire has been on camera more than I have."

—Joey Bishop (below), host in New York of the 13th annual Emmy Telecast, after Fred Astaire's special "Astaire Time" on NBC had won two Emmys, and he'd also won for Outstanding Performance in a Variety or Musical Program or Series for the same variety program, 1961

"It's almost embarrassing, I've almost been on more than you have, Joe."

—Producer George Schaefer to New York emcee Joey Bishop after his production of "Macbeth" for *Hallmark Hall of Fame* on NBC won five Emmys at the 13th Annual Emmy Telecast, including Program of the Year, 1961

two-part "American White Paper" investigation of the Bay of Pigs and the Cuban missile crisis also was an Emmy winner in 1964.

In 1966, writer Millard Lampell, a 10-year victim of the McCarthy blacklist, was another sobering reminder of the world beyond television as he accepted an Emmy for "Eagle in a Cage," a play he wrote for NBC's *Hallmark Hall of Fame*.

The 1960s also witnessed the first live television transmission from space, followed by the first satellite-transmitted Olympics, originating from Tokyo. John Glenn's orbital space flight in 1962 was seen by 135 million viewers, and a year later astronaut Gordon Cooper sent the first TV pictures from space. By 1969, as the decade's closing act, the world watched live as astronaut Neil Armstrong walked on the moon, in what many observers still consider television's greatest feat.

As bookends to the space coverage, in 1962 the Academy's Board of Trustees voted to honor the heads of the news departments of the three networks specifically for their coverage of Glenn's space flight, and they ended the decade honoring the Apollo VII, VIII, IX, and X space missions with the Trustees Award. Perhaps what best symbolized the finest of television in the 1960s was the citation that went with the award: "For sharing

Memorable Moments
Newhart's First Impression

It was June 6, 1960, the evening of the 12th annual Academy of Television Arts & Sciences Awards show. Bob Finkel was executive producer for the telecast, and Bob Henry was producer-director. The site on the West Coast was NBC's Burbank Studios, where Fred Astaire was the host, with Arthur Godfrey cohosting at the Ziegfeld Theatre in New York. Immediately before the telecast, there was an announcement that the comedy team of Mike Nichols and Elaine May, scheduled to do one of their celebrated comedy spots, had withdrawn because "they were not satisfied with the material." A virtually unknown comedy performer, Bob Newhart, agreed to fill in. Following is one of the two monologues performed by Newhart on that telecast:

"This is called a headset, and it's used by telephone operators, but it's also used by TV directors, and through it they talk to their crew and they also listen to the crew. Now, in a TV studio they have a series of TV cameras, which the director watches. They also have what's known as a camera run-through and this is where they kinda walk through what they're gonna do and iron the bugs out. Now, this was especially true of the Khrushchev [who visited President Dwight Eisenhower shortly before the telecast] landing. A lot of people don't know, but Khrushchev landed a day ahead of time...and he kinda walked through what he was gonna do, so they could set the cameras. And if you had been in the control room you would have heard something like this: 'All right, all right, Jerry...cue the plane...all right, have the plane come down...that's the...that's the way. All right, have the plane land. All right, taxi. All right, Jerry, have him stop on the chalk marks if you can. All right...that's all right. All right, camera one, get in tight on the door...get in tight on Khrushchev...in tight.... A what? A mustache? I don't think so, Jer. Jerry you're on the wrong guy. Pan around.... The fact sheet I got said he should be a short, stocky guy in a gray suit. Looks like he slept in it? That's him, that's him. That's him. All right, have him wave to the crowd. Tell him there'll be a crowd.... All right, Jerry...make a note...we're gonna have to spray the plane. I'm getting too much glare off it. All right, have him walk down the ramp.... All right...cue the flower girl.... All right, where's the little creep with the flowers, huh? Why do we always have to use somebody's little kid? Why can't we use midgets? Huh? All right...have him get back in the plane. All right...you got the flower kid? All right...hang on to her, will you? All right...go in tight on the...Jerry...hang on to the flower kid.... She's running up the ramp.... She's supposed to be at the foot of the ramp.... All right...let her go. Tell Khrushchev he's gonna have to watch the door. He's gonna bang...he banged the kid with the door! Oh, come on, come on... All right, all right...have him wave to the crowd. Have him wave his hat. Make a note, Jer...we're gonna have to spray his head. All right...have him take the flowers from the kid.... All right...tell him to kiss the kid. All right...have him walk down the ramp. Don't have him skip like the kid, Jerry...it looks ridiculous. All right...all right...have him walk over towards Ike. All right, somebody cue Ike. Somebody take the putter from Ike, huh? All right...have him shake hands with Ike. All right...have him shake hands with Herter [American Secretary of State].... Not Ike shake hands with Herter, have Khrushchev shake hands with Herter. All right...rest of the diplomatic corps...all right...walk back to the microphones. All right, have him start the speech. Jerry, tell him not to do the whole speech...we don't have time, Jer...Jer, he's doing the whole speech. Tell him not to do the speech...No, not ever...he'll do the whole speech tomorrow, but we don't have time now, Jer. I got *Guiding Light* [one of TV's longest-running soap operas] right behind me. All right, he finishes the speech. All right, cue the official cars.... Have them get in the cars. Not all of them in the same car, Jer. They ought to know that.... All right, have the cars pull out.... Have them pull by the camera platform. Jerry, that's Mrs. Khrushchev running alongside the car...Tell them they forgot Mrs. Khrushchev. All right...stop the car. Have her get in the car. Start the car again...now have them drive by the troops.... Have him stand and wave at the troops... (SOFTLY) Jer...don't have the troops wave back...not with their rifles and all that. Jer...all right, Jer...have Khrushchev sit down. That's good...Jer, why did he jump up again? Jer, how many times do I have to tell you...take the putter away from Ike.... All right, everybody back in the plane...We're gonna have to take it from the top.

(APPLAUSE)

The next morning Cecil Smith, entertainment editor of the *Los Angeles Times*, referred to Newhart as "a young comedy sensation," suggesting a special award should be offered to him. The newspaperman need not have worried. By the 1961–62 season Newhart had his own NBC comedy series, which won an Emmy for Outstanding Program Achievement in Humor.

Memorable Moments
Weaver's "Hamlet" Parody Steals Telecast

It was early in both his career and in the TV Academy's history that Dennis Weaver got his Emmy. His portrayal of Chester won him Best Supporting Actor in a Dramatic Series for *Gunsmoke*'s 1958–59 season.

"There wasn't as much ballyhoo, hoopla, and importance placed on it then as there is now," Weaver observed in a recent interview. "I probably didn't realize the importance of it as I would if I would win an Emmy now."

There was no mistaking, though, the sensational publicity he received when he didn't win an Emmy—he wasn't even nominated. At the 13th annual Emmy Awards in 1961, Weaver was part of the lineup of presenters assembled by executive producer Bud Yorkin. Weaver was asked to do a parody of *Hamlet* as part of the telecast.

"I'm not really into making fun of *Hamlet*," Weaver remembers saying. "I will do the parody if I'm able to approach it as though it were the real work," he said. And in doing so, Weaver made the parody funnier. At one time he even had tears in his eyes.

In dead-serious tones, Weaver recited such lines as "TV or not TV, that is the question. Whether 'tis nobler to suffer the slugs and arrows of *Bonanza*...or switch to *Perry Mason*."

One critic suggested it was time for Sir Laurence Olivier to move over. Another described Weaver's performance as "brilliant." All agreed he stole the show, even from the big Emmy winner that night, *Hallmark Hall of Fame*'s production of the real "Macbeth."

Bill Hanna and Joe Barbera, shown with some of their inimitable animated creations, made television history in 1960 when their *Huckleberry Hound* became the first cartoon series to win an Emmy.

with the American public and the rest of the world the incredible experience of the unfolding of the mysteries of outer space and the surface of the moon via live television."

The decade began with the Academy's enrollment reaching a record high 6,000 members. Television was now in 85 million homes, many of which tuned in to the four debates between presidential candidates Richard Nixon and John F. Kennedy.

The 12th annual Emmy telecast in 1960 was highlighted by four firsts:

A black performer won an Emmy: Harry Belafonte, for his music program, "Tonight With Belafonte."

A syndicated show, Hanna-Barbera's *Huckleberry Hound*, won an Emmy.

An actress, Ingrid Bergman (in *Ford Startime*'s "The Turn of the Screw") won an Emmy for her first performance on television.

An actor, Laurence Olivier (in *The Moon and Sixpence*), won an Emmy for his debut television performance.

(Above) Harry Belafonte, the first African American to win a major Emmy Award, is shown here with game show host Gene Rayburn at the 19th annual awards in 1967.

(Left) Allan "Bud" Yorkin directed and produced three Jack Benny one-hour live NBC specials in 1959. Yorkin, shown with Benny, won a best director Emmy for his work on the first one. He had previously won three Emmys for writing, directing, and producing "An Evening With Fred Astaire."

But no show that year dominated the voting. ABC's *The Untouchables* received four Emmys, three of which were technical awards. NBC's special *The Moon and Sixpence* won two Emmys. Rod Serling, in his prime at 35 but already recognized for writing such plays as *Requiem for a Heavyweight* and *Patterns* in the 1950s, won his fourth Emmy for writing various episodes of CBS' *The Twilight Zone*. CBS president Dr. Frank Stanton's indefatigable defense of television's free-press rights was recognized with a Trustees Award.

The bicoastal May 16, 1961, Emmy Awards telecast on NBC was

(Above) Robert Stack portrayed Eliot Ness, the legendary leader of a Chicago prohibition-era Treasury Department squad nicknamed "The Untouchables." The role in the hourlong ABC crime saga won Stack a 1959–60 best actor award.

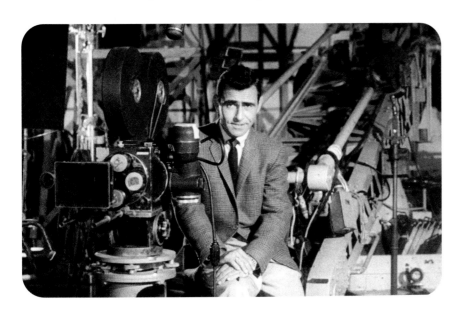

(Left) Rod Serling, writer of such classics as *Requiem for a Heavyweight* (winner of five Emmys), *The Twilight Zone* (he won two statuettes for his writing), and other TV dramas and plays, was in the second group of inductees to the Television Academy Hall of Fame. At the time, it was said that Serling "lifted television programming to a high level." He was also Academy president in 1965–66.

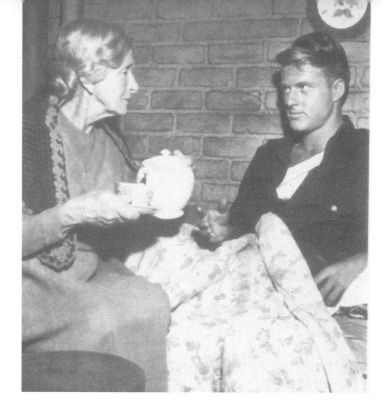

Early in his career, Robert Redford appeared in several television shows. Above, he is shown in a classic episode of *The Twilight Zone*.

dominated by Hallmark Cards, Inc. and its dramatic showcase, *Hallmark Hall of Fame*. Hallmark's production of "Macbeth" took Emmys for actors Judith Anderson and Maurice Evans and director George Schaefer, and it was named Outstanding Drama and also Program of the Year. A Trustees Award went to Hallmark president Joyce C. Hall for "his personal interest in uplifting the standards of television." Fred Astaire's "Astaire Time" was voted Outstanding Variety Show, and the song-and-dance star won an Emmy for his performance on the show. By this time, a pattern was beginning to emerge. The cream of television's talent was rising to the top and it

What the Emmy Means to Me

"The first time I won an Emmy, I honestly felt that I wasn't any better, or even as good, as the other people in my category. However, who am I to argue? Take the award and be glad someone noticed you're doing at least a credible job. In subsequent years, I've continued to feel this way."

—Carl Reiner, Emmy winner, 1956, 1957, 1961–62, 1962–63, 1963–64, 1964–65, 1965–66, 1966–67 (2), 1995

George Schaefer
Producer Extraordinaire

George Schaefer was one of the most-honored producer-directors of dramatic specials in television. Five won Emmys: "Little Moon of Alban" (1959), "Macbeth" (1961), "The Magnificent Yankee" (1965), "Elizabeth the Queen" (1968), and "A War of Children" (1973).

He also was one of the most prolific. Schaefer was responsible for some 100 productions, directing and producing 57 *Hallmark Hall of Fame* dramas. Included were live black-and-white performances of "Hamlet," "Richard II," and "Macbeth."

His career spanned six decades. It included 1979's "Blind Ambition," a four-part, eight-hour docudrama about the Watergate scandal. Schaefer died in 1997 at 76.

tended to stay there for a while, repeatedly winning awards. Astaire, Dinah Shore, and Rod Serling already had emerged. Carol Burnett, Carl Reiner, Mary Tyler Moore, *The Defenders*, and *The Dick Van Dyke Show* began to crop up consistently among Emmy nominees and winners. By the 1990s, Shore and Moore, each with eight, held the record for most Emmys won by a female performer.

Bob Newhart was master of ceremonies at the Hollywood Palladium, Johnny Carson was at the helm at New York's Astor Hotel, and NBC newsman David Brinkley emceed at the Sheraton-Park Hotel in Washington, D.C., as a total of 26 awards were presented at the 14th annual Emmy telecast in 1962. The use of film and tape clips from nominated shows was initiated that year.

The courtroom drama *The Defenders*, which debuted during the 1961–62 season, was the big winner. It won Emmys for Outstanding Drama and for its star, E.G. Marshall; writer Reginald Rose; and director Franklin Schaffner.

The Washington segment of the telecast gained the spotlight when

(Left) Julie Harris won her second Emmy in 1962 for Outstanding Single Performance by an Actress in a Leading Role for *Hallmark Hall of Fame*'s "Victoria Regina," which was also voted The Program of the Year. Costar James Donald (left) was also nominated but lost to Peter Falk. (Right) Jackie Cooper, Fred Astaire, Ed Wynn, and Danny Kaye at the 13th annual Emmys in 1961. Cooper was nominated for *Hennesey* that year but lost to Raymond Burr. Astaire's NBC special, "Astaire Time," won two Emmys. At the second Emmy ceremony, Wynn was honored not only for having the best live show, but for being the best "live" personality. Kaye would go on to win in 1964 for Outstanding Performance in a Variety or Musical Program or Series for his award-winning *The Danny Kaye Show* on CBS.

a special Trustees Award was given to Jacqueline Kennedy for her CBS-TV tour of the White House. The award was presented by U.S. Supreme Court Justice William O. Douglas and accepted by Lady Bird Johnson. Presidential Press Secretary Pierre Salinger and Sen. Warren Magnuson also got into the Washington act, presenting Emmys in the news and public affairs categories.

The 15th annual awards presentation in 1963 again was a three-way Hollywood–New York–Washington, D.C., ceremony, and again *The Defenders* was the most-honored program, with five Emmys. Making its presence felt, *The Dick Van Dyke Show* captured three awards in the field of comedy. Both Don Knotts of *The Andy Griffith Show* and Carol Burnett became three-time winners. Rod Serling

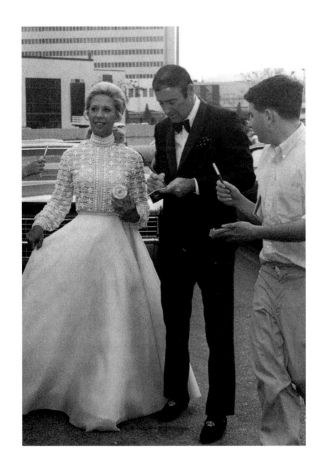

Dinah Shore, arriving for one of her many Emmy appearances in the '60s, won the golden lady eight times.

Winning an Emmy for Outstanding Writing Achievement in Drama for *The Twilight Zone*, Rod Serling accepts his 1961 award from Connie Stevens and Troy Donahue.

picked up his sixth Emmy in as many years for writing. First-time winners included Broadway's Kim Stanley, British actor Trevor Howard, and movie screen veteran Glenda Farrell.

The Texas Pavilion of the New York World's Fair joined the Hollywood Palladium as the site for the 16th annual awards, presented May 25, 1964, and telecast by NBC. Top awards went to *The Dick Van Dyke Show* with five Emmys. Mary Tyler Moore won for Best Actress for the series, and Dick Van Dyke took home the Best Actor award. It was his first Emmy, while his show was honored for the third time.

A variety series, *The Danny Kaye Show*, was also a multiple winner with four awards. Kaye, who was playing an engagement in Las Vegas, taped an introduction to the Emmy telecast in which he appeared in many guises.

The telecast opened in New York. Actor

Casey vs. Kildare

Two medical dramas, ABC's *Ben Casey* and NBC's *Dr. Kildare*, premiered in the 1961–62 season, competing for audiences. At the Emmy Awards presentation for the following season, stage star Kim Stanley won an Emmy for Outstanding Single Performance by an Actress in a Leading Role for her portrayal in "A Cardinal Act of Mercy," a *Ben Casey* two-parter. But Stanley was a no-show, which maybe was just as well. The presenters were Richard Chamberlain and Raymond Massey, costars of rival *Dr. Kildare*.

Innovative comedian Ernie Kovacs, one of the first to see the visual possibilities of television, won an Emmy in 1962 for Outstanding Achievement in Electronic Camera Work for ABC's *The Ernie Kovacs Show*. Earlier, he did a half-hour comedy special for NBC without words. Upon his induction into the Academy Hall of Fame, it was noted that Kovacs "depended on the eye to evoke laughter as well as his own sense of the absurd."

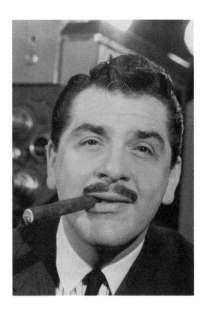

E.G. Marshall, star of *The Defenders*, which won two more awards, reminded the audience of one of the earliest experimental telecasts: President Franklin Delano Roosevelt's speech opening the 1939 World's Fair in New York.

Three programs dominated the Emmys for the 1964–65 season, accounting for 17 statuettes, more than half of the 29 presented. They were: "My Name is Barbra," six awards; "The Louvre," also six; and "The Magnificent Yankee," five.

There were more than the usual memorable moments during the 19th annual awards telecast in 1966. *The Dick Van Dyke Show*, in its fifth and final season, won four Emmys and already was being hailed as a TV classic. Bill Cosby, master of ceremonies for the CBS telecast in Hollywood (Danny Kaye was emcee in New York), won an Emmy for his costarring role in NBC's *I Spy* series.

In an ironic twist, NBC was presented an Emmy for its coverage of the U.S. Senate hearings on Vietnam. CBS, the host network for the telecast, denied airtime for live coverage of the Senate hearings because it would have meant the preemption of a rerun of *I Love Lucy*.

There was a notable first the following year, during the 19th annual awards—an Emmy for a television special combining live action and animation. "Jack and the Beanstalk," named Outstanding Children's Program, was produced by film legend Gene Kelly (for Hanna-Barbera), who also directed and starred.

The Trustees Award that year suggested television had matured to the point where it could now honor one of its most illustrious pioneers. The Emmy went to Sylvester L. (Pat) Weaver Jr., the NBC executive who introduced the concept of preempting regular series for a "special" (originally called "spectacular") as well as bracketing the weekday schedule with "Today" and "Tonight" programs.

Emmy's 20th, covering the 1967–68 season, was cohosted by

The Clampett family comes to Beverly Hills, including Jethro (Max Baer Jr.) behind the wheel, Jed (Buddy Ebsen) next to him, and Granny (Irene Ryan) and Elly May (Donna Douglas) in the backseat. Nominated for Outstanding Program Achievement in the Field of Humor for the 1962–63 season, the number one–ranked *The Beverly Hillbillies* was beaten out by *The Dick Van Dyke Show*. Despite its high ratings, the half-hour comedy never won an outstanding series award during its entire 1962–1971 run.

Presenter Lucille Ball, with Carl Reiner and Bob Newhart, at the 14th annual nighttime Emmys in 1962. Reiner won that year for writing *The Dick Van Dyke Show*. Newhart, whose telephone comedy skit stole the Emmy telecast in 1960, saw his *The Bob Newhart Show* on NBC win the Emmy for Best Program Achievement in the Field of Humor.

"The Defenders" Need No Defending When the Subject Is Quality TV

When the subject of "quality" TV series is discussed, *The Defenders* is likely to be among the top 10 cited. Using a legal setting, *The Defenders* became the public sounding board for the moral and political controversies of the 1960s.

Some of television's most-honored people worked on *The Defenders* during its 1961–65 run on CBS, most prominently Reginald Rose and Franklin J. Schaffner. Rose was one of the exceptional playwrights to emerge from what has been called the golden age of live, original dramas. He wrote for *Studio One*, *Philco TV Playhouse*, and other

dramatic anthology series. Among his notable TV plays was *The Sacco-Vanzetti Story*, a two-part NBC docudrama in 1960, directed by Sidney Lumet and starring E.G. Marshall, Peter Falk, Martin Balsam, and Steven Hill, none of whom were marquee names at the time.

Schaffner, who started with CBS in 1948, directed everything in early television from baseball to the evening news to coverage of the political conventions of 1948 and 1952. Prior to *The Defenders*, he had won Emmys for directing Rose's "Twelve Angry Men" in 1954 and "The Caine Mutiny Court-Martial" in 1955. In motion pictures he won both the Academy Award and Directors Guild Award in 1970 for his direction of *Patton*.

Rose, who created and wrote several teleplays for *The Defenders*, already had won an Emmy for "Twelve Angry Men" for CBS' *Studio One* in 1954. He won two more for *The Defenders*, one in 1962 for various episodes, and one in 1963 (with Robert Thom) for "The Madman" episode of the CBS series.

Two other acclaimed TV writers, Ernest Kinoy for "The Blacklist" and David Karp for "The 700-Year-Old Gang," won Emmys for their work on *The Defenders*. Among directors, Schaffner, Paul Bogart, and Stuart Rosenberg won individual Emmys for the series, as did star E.G. Marshall (right, with costar Ossie Davis) and guest actor Jack Klugman.

The Defenders was voted the best drama for the 1961–62, 1962–63, and 1963–64 seasons. Under the guidance of Herb Brodkin, one of television's most distinguished producers, the show left an unforgettable impression on viewers because of the quality of its writing, direction, acting, and treatment of serious themes.

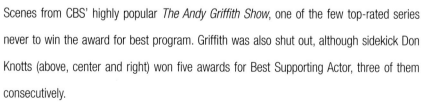

Scenes from CBS' highly popular *The Andy Griffith Show*, one of the few top-rated series never to win the award for best program. Griffith was also shut out, although sidekick Don Knotts (above, center and right) won five awards for Best Supporting Actor, three of them consecutively.

Shirley Booth
Hazel's Alter Ego

Shirley Booth was a star of stage, film, radio, and television. She won three Tony Awards for her work on Broadway, an Oscar for *Come Back, Little Sheba*, and two Emmys for playing the title role in *Hazel*, the wisecracking, know-it-all but lovable maid. Brooks Atkinson, the eminent theater critic for the *New York Times*, wrote of her: "No one in the theatre has made native decency so human, so triumphant, and so captivating."

Yet Booth was not the first choice for the role, according to Ted Key, creator of the *Hazel* television series (and of the cartoon character Hazel, which appeared for many years in the *Saturday Evening Post*). Screen tests were made with Betty Fields, Agnes Moorehead, and Bibi Osterwald, among others. The highly regarded character actress Thelma Ritter was also considered. But both Key and Bill Dozier, West Coast production chief at Screen Gems, the TV arm of Columbia Pictures, favored Booth.

Dozier flew east with a pilot script written by Peggy Chantler Dick and Bill Cowley. He met with Bill McCaffrey, Booth's manager (who also represented Mary Martin and Art Carney). "Shirley's not interested in TV," McCaffrey told Dozier.

"I flew here to talk to her, can I do that?" Dozier asked.

"It's pointless, Bill," McCaffrey replied. "She doesn't want to do TV."

"Would you just call and tell her what the project's about?" Dozier tried again. "I've got a pilot script. If she says no, I'll fly back."

McCaffrey phoned. "Shirley?" he began. "Bill Dozier's here from the Coast with a TV project. I told him how you feel about TV."

"What's the name of the project?" asked Booth.

"Hazel," said McCaffrey.

"I'll do it," she said.

The cast of the 1961–62 Emmy-nominated sitcom *Hazel*: Whitney Blake, Bobby Buntrock, Don DeFore, and Shirley Booth. Booth won two consecutive Emmys for the title role.

Booth wasn't impulsive or irrational. She was familiar with the property. In 1948, Key and a friend had written a *Hazel* comedy play for the theater. Together they had been radio writers on staff at the J. Walter Thompson advertising agency in New York. Sam Harris, producer of many George S. Kaufman comedies on Broadway, took a liking to the *Hazel* script. Booth was anxious to play the lead.

But the script needed rewrites. While the play was being written, Key commuted between Pennsylvania, where he lived, and Manhattan, where his collaborator lived. For the rewrites, Key asked his friend to commute from New York to Pennsylvania. "No way," was the response. The project languished. Some 12 years later, in 1960, Bill McCaffrey called and Shirley Booth remembered. Yet even with the famed Booth, the television launch was not without problems. The veteran character actor Edward Andrews was cast as George Baxter, Hazel's boss. Advertisers loved the pilot, but not Andrews. The pilot was reshot with Don DeFore as Baxter.

Hazel ran on NBC from 1961 to 1965 with the Ford Motor Company as the sole sponsor, and then switched to CBS for a final season. When Lee Iacocca, then a Ford executive, unveiled the Mustang, it was introduced to America on *Hazel*. In the first season, Booth won an Emmy to go alongside her Tonys and Oscar (repeating the next year against Lucille Ball and Mary Tyler Moore). Shortly after Booth died in 1992, Anthony Quinn, who costarred with her in the 1958 motion picture *Hot Spell*, said of Booth: "I've worked with good actresses, but never one with the understanding she possessed. Ingrid Bergman and Greta Garbo were beautiful, but she was a genius."

Leading Ladies
Mary Tyler Moore

For Mary Tyler Moore, the 1963–64 season was a triumphant one. As Laura Petrie on *The Dick Van Dyke Show*, she won the Emmy for best lead actress in a series. In her 1995 autobiography, *After All*, Moore (left, with Carl Reiner and Dick Van Dyke) remembered how "tears welled up, making it impossible to speak." She felt "the release" of the many "hurts, slights, and failures" she had encountered on the way to becoming a star. Moore described the feeling of being honored by her peers as the equivalent of a "momentary breakthrough with a psychiatrist." Though she has won six Emmys for lead actress during her television career, Moore admittedly has never overcome her "normal insecure self." Still, to her the Emmy amounts to a "huge compliment," and getting one "sure feels good."

Frank Sinatra in Hollywood and Dick Van Dyke in New York. One of the telecast's great moments had Sinatra, Lucille Ball, and Carol Burnett singing nostalgically, "I Remember It Well."

The following year, to the delight of the press (it made good copy), four different canceled series won either entertainment program or individual achievement Emmys: NBC's *Get Smart* and *The Ghost and Mrs. Muir*, ABC's *Judd for the Defense*, and CBS' *The Smothers Brothers Comedy Hour*.

The most controversial votes at the 21st annual awards were no-votes. No Emmy was given in three categories: Outstanding Single Performance by an Actor in a Supporting Role; Outstanding Directorial Achievement in Comedy, Variety, or Music; and Outstanding Achievement in Children's Programming.

The top-rated TV shows of the 1960s were *Gunsmoke*, *Wagon Train*, *The Beverly Hillbillies*, *Bonanza*, *The Andy Griffith Show*, and *Rowan and Martin's Laugh-In*. As an indication that audience popularity

Bill Cosby, cohost in New York (with Danny Kaye in Hollywood), provided one of the dramatic highlights of the 18th annual Emmy Awards show in 1966 when he accepted an Emmy for Outstanding Continued Performance in *I Spy*. He thanked NBC for "having guts" to put on a prime-time series costarring (with Robert Culp) a black actor. Presenting the Emmy to Cosby is fellow TV Academy Hall of Famer Carol Burnett, whose variety series won 22 Emmys.

doesn't necessarily equate with Emmy, only *Gunsmoke* and *Laugh-In* won outstanding series awards.

At the start of the decade, the new Kennedy-appointed chairman of the FCC, Newton Minow, rocked the television industry by charging that the medium for the most part was a "vast wasteland." Complaints of excessive violence on TV carried an even greater impact by the end of the decade. The industry promised that programming containing gratuitous violence (nonessential to the plot) would be eliminated. The 1969–70 season saw a decided reduction in violence on prime-time series, and, once again, as the industry moved into the 1970s, the Emmys reflected these changes.

"I want to thank a man who talks out of the side of his mouth, but who talked straight when he asked me about taking this part and I said, 'Oh sure, you call me, I won't call you.'"

—Bill Cosby, referring to *I Spy* producer Sheldon Leonard, when accepting an Emmy for Outstanding Continued Performance by an Actor in a Leading Role in a Dramatic Series, 1966

"It's been a long, long time. The last time I got it [an Emmy] I thought it was because I had a baby. That baby is now 14."

—Lucille Ball, accepting her award for Outstanding Continued Performance by an Actress in a Leading Role in a Comedy Series for *The Lucy Show*, CBS, 1967

Spotlight
"The Dick Van Dyke Show"

A few weeks before Christmas 1958, a pilot was filmed at New York's Gold Medal Studios. Produced by Stuart Rosenberg and Martin Poll and directed by Don Weis, "Head of the Family" was written and created by Carl Reiner, who also was the lead actor. Reiner was "at liberty" despite a recent Emmy Award–winning stint as performer-writer on *Caesar's Hour*.

The role of Reiner's wife, Laura, was played by Barbara Britton. Reiner's coworkers, Sally Rogers and Buddy Sorrell, were played by Sylvia Miles and Morty Gunty. The pilot script focused on TV writer Robert Petrie, who, having learned that his young son is embarrassed to tell his friends what his father does for a living, tries to convince him of the value of comedy writing.

"Head of the Family" didn't sell, but it aired on July 19, 1960, on *Comedy Spot*, a CBS anthology series. A little more than three years after the pilot was filmed, a revamped version, with Dick Van Dyke in the Reiner role, was filmed at Hollywood's Desilu Cahuenga Studios. Van Dyke had already made his mark as the star of the Broadway hit musical *Bye Bye Birdie*.

Written, created, and produced by Carl Reiner, the new pilot, "The Sick Boy and the Sitter," was directed by future TV Academy Hall of Famer Sheldon Leonard, who, with Danny Thomas, was also executive producer. Twenty-four-year-old Mary Tyler Moore, previously heard but not seen (except for her legs) in *Richard Diamond, Private Detective*, was now Laura Petrie, and Rose Marie and Morey Amsterdam were playing Sally and Buddy. Amsterdam was a veteran nightclub entertainer–comic–comedy writer. Rose Marie had made her show business debut at age three as a singing-dancing dynamo billed as Baby Rose Marie. Able actors Richard Deacon, Jerry Paris, and Ann Morgan Guilbert were also in the regular cast, as was child actor Larry Matthews.

The working title for the new pilot, "The Full House," was discarded (as were such others as "Double Trouble" and "All in a Day's Work") in favor of "The Dick Van Dyke Show." The pilot

was produced at a cost of less than $50,000, and with it in hand Sheldon Leonard sold the series concept to Procter & Gamble for a full year's sponsorship commitment. Through Lee Rich, then senior vice president in charge of media and programming at its agency, Benton & Bowles, New York, P&G offered the series to CBS.

The Dick Van Dyke Show did not exactly follow a yellow brick road straight to becoming one of the most-honored TV series of its time. It struggled to attract an audience in its first 1961–62 season. But by the following season, it was the ninth highest-ranked series, averaging a 27.1 rating, zooming to number three and a 30.3 average in 1963–64. For the concluding two seasons of its five-season run, it remained in the top 20 programs in prime time.

A bountiful crop of Emmys followed in the wake of audience approval. Carl Reiner, who in addition to being creator-producer was head writer, story editor, and "resident genius," won his first Emmy for Outstanding Writing Achievement in Comedy for *The Dick Van Dyke Show* in 1962. Reiner won two more Emmys the following year, one for Outstanding Program Achievement in the Field of Humor and another for his writing. Dick Van Dyke, Mary Tyler Moore, and Rose Marie were all nominated that year but did not win, while John Rich took an Emmy for Outstanding Directorial Achievement in Comedy. In the show's last season, 1965–66, it gained eight nominations and won four Emmys, including Mary Tyler Moore's second acting Emmy; the second award for the writing team of Bill Persky and Sam Denoff; and the fourth consecutive Emmy as the season's outstanding comedy. Those four wins established a new record for most wins as Outstanding Comedy Series, a mark subsequently tied first by *All in the Family* and later by *Cheers* and *Frasier*. In addition to the honors won by Reiner, Moore, and Persky and Denoff, Dick Van Dyke won two Emmys for his acting, and Jerry Paris, moving up from supporting actor, took an Emmy in 1964 for his directorial work.

Author Vince Waldron, in his 1994 *The Official Dick Van Dyke Show Book,* concluded that the series was a direct forerunner of *The Mary Tyler Moore Show*, unquestionably the most-honored situation comedy in television history: "The show's unique blend of wit and warmth would prove beyond any argument that a situation comedy could be sophisticated and urbane—and still deliver a sizable audience."

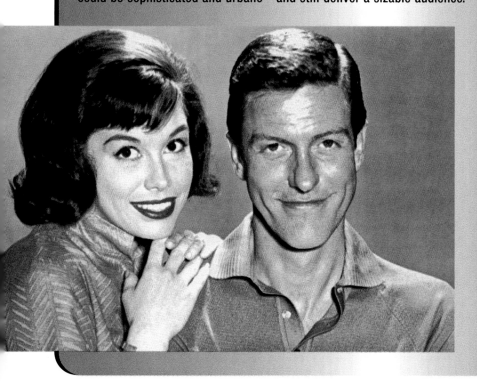

"The way my luck is running I'd go on *The Dating Game* and wind up with Tiny Tim."

—Frank Sinatra, emcee in Hollywood of the 20th annual Emmy telecast, after opening the proceedings by singing "Luck Be a Lady Tonight," 1968

"This is a shock. Out there in that vast wasteland, a lot of people love me."

—Lucille Ball, upon receiving her fourth Emmy, 1968

"You're like the Gabor sisters. You won't let anyone talk."

— Eva Gabor, presenter on the 20th annual Emmy telecast, to fellow presenter Tom Smothers, 1968

(Above) Peter Falk and Carol Burnett, mugging for the cameras, were both multiple Emmy winners.

(Below) At the 18th annual Emmy ceremony, newsman Chet Huntley presented a posthumous Emmy in New York to the late Edward R. Murrow. Bill Cosby, who won an Emmy that year for his performance in *I Spy*, was emcee at the Americana Hotel.

(Opposite page, bottom) By the late 1960s, "Good Night, Chet"..."Good Night, David" was well-recognized across America as the sign-off of NBC's high-rated evening newscast, *The Huntley-Brinkley Report*. The anchor team won Emmys consecutively from 1959–64, and the program picked up additional Emmys in 1969 and 1970.

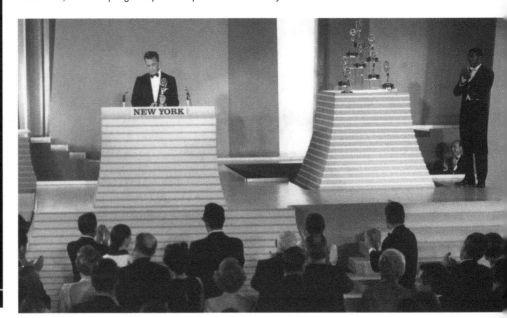

Recognizing Edward R. Murrow

The 18th annual awards ceremony, covering the 1965–66 season, was witness to a dramatic display. NBC newsman Chet Huntley presented a posthumous Trustees Emmy in New York to broadcast journalism's brightest light, Edward R. Murrow, who had died the previous year, for exemplifying "the courage, the sensitivity, and the devotion to truth and duty to which all free men aspire." Murrow had spent 40 years in broadcasting, first in radio and then in television. He became "a symbol to colleagues and the public alike of the complete broadcast journalist." The crowd at the Americana Hotel stood in ovation as Richard C. Hottelet of CBS accepted the award on behalf of Murrow's wife, Janet, and son, Casey.

"We will take this somewhat maligned and slandered young lady and try to give her a good home."

—NBC newscaster Chet Huntley, stroking the Emmy he and David Brinkley won for news reporting during the Emmy telecast boycotted by ABC and CBS, 1964

(Right) Barbara Bain, named best actress in 1967 for her role as the beautiful female member of the *Mission: Impossible* team, with producer Sheldon Leonard, accepting the second of Bill Cosby's three Emmys for *I Spy*. To the right are presenters Inger Stevens and Peter Falk. (Left) In both 1967 and 1968, the winners of the best actor and actress awards for a comedy series were Don Adams for *Get Smart* and Lucille Ball for *The Lucy Show*. Oddly, Emmys for best actor and actress in a dramatic series those two years also were repeat winners: Barbara Bain and Bill Cosby. (Below) Holding their Emmys for best comedy series, Bert Schneider and Bob Rafelson, producers of NBC's *The Monkees*, stand backstage with, from left, Mike Nesmith, Peter Tork, Davy Jones, and Mickey Dolenz of the sitcom's rock quartet, along with presenters Jimmy Durante and *Family Affair*'s Anissa "Buffy" Jones.

Memorable Moments
Little Billy's Standing Ovation

The audience at the 21st annual awards in New York's grand Carnegie Hall was upset. Billy Schulman, a retarded 12-year-old boy, was one of three nominees in the supporting actor, single performance category, for his role in the *Hallmark Hall of Fame* production of "Teacher, Teacher" on NBC. But no performance in that category was deemed worthy of an Emmy. The program, though, won as Outstanding Dramatic Program.

Producer George Lefferts, in accepting the award, complained about Billy not "being allowed to compete and to win or lose with dignity." But the last act in this little drama hadn't been played. Billy was asked to stand and, to resounding cheers of the glittering audience, was presented with a special citation, recognizing his "extraordinary achievement" of playing a retarded boy in the *Hallmark* drama. The citation pointed out that Billy had shown that "a mentally retarded person, given love and understanding, can achieve far more than anyone might have expected, and that he can indeed compete and accomplish as much or more than any youngsters his age."

Top NBC executive Sylvester L. "Pat" Weaver Jr., creative "father" of the *Today*, *Home*, and *Tonight* shows, and creator of the TV "spectacular" (later "special"), celebrates his Trustees Award at the 1967 prime-time Emmy telecast. He subsequently was awarded the sixth annual ATAS Governors Award (1983), and was inducted into the Academy's Hall of Fame two years later.

(Above) Dick Van Dyke hosted the 20th annual Emmy Awards from the Grand Ballroom of New York's Americana Hotel, and Frank Sinatra presided from the Hollywood Palladium. (Below) Three icons performing at the 20th annual Emmys: Carol Burnett, Frank Sinatra, and Lucille Ball. Sinatra's "Frank Sinatra: A Man and His Music" special for NBC won an Emmy in 1966.

"Let the message be known to bigots and racists that they don't count."

—Bill Cosby, accepting his third successive Emmy in 1968

(Middle, left) Milburn Stone won one of *Gunsmoke*'s few Emmys. Shown here at the 20th annual prime-time telecast, he accepts from presenters Sebastian Cabot and his two charges from *Family Affair*, Anissa Jones and Johnnie Whitaker. (Above) ABC's Saturday afternoon sports anthology, *Wide World of Sports*, was the springboard for series host Jim McKay and executive producer Roone Arledge (shown with Olympian Peggy Fleming). Arledge rose to become president of ABC Sports and also, subsequently, ABC News. The show won a total of 15 sports programming Emmys. (Left) Jack Haley Jr. won a 1968 Emmy for Outstanding Directorial Achievement in a Musical or Variety Series for NBC's *Movin' With Nancy*, starring Nancy Sinatra.

Susan Saint James (below, left) won a supporting actress Emmy in 1969 for her role as editorial assistant Peggy Maxwell on NBC's anthology series *The Name of the Game*. (Below, right) The 1968–69 season's Best Actor and Best Actress in a Comedy Series were Don Adams (*Get Smart*) and Hope Lange (*The Ghost and Mrs. Muir*).

Multi-Emmy winner Fred Astaire (above) is flanked at the 21st annual awards telecast by Diahann Carroll and Barbra Streisand, whose CBS special "Barbra Streisand: A Happening in Central Park" won an Emmy for Outstanding Individual Achievement in Music. Carroll, who played a nurse and single mother in the groundbreaking series *Julia*, saw her program edged out by *Get Smart* as best comedy. (Below) The comedy duo of Dan Rowan and Dick Martin hosted NBC's *Rowan and Martin's Laugh-In* from 1968–73. The show won four Emmys at the 20th annual event, including Outstanding Musical or Variety Series. It was considered a remarkable achievement for a program that first aired in January 1968 as a mid-season replacement. Dan Rowan, executive producer George Schlatter, and Dick Martin (below, right) are shown with their hands full.

Emmy's Mensch
Donald H. McGannon

Donald H. McGannon, longtime chairman and president of Group W, Westinghouse Broadcasting Co., was Emmy's *mensch*—a Yiddish expression meaning an honorable, decent person. A colleague once said of him, "He stood for something. He held deep, personal beliefs, and no matter what the fashion of the day seemed to dictate, he stuck to what he believed in."

A young reporter learned firsthand that it wasn't because he was successful, wealthy, and an industry leader that McGannon was a mensch. In the early 1960s, assigned to write a profile of the broadcaster, the reporter visited McGannon in his East 42nd Street office in New York City, equipped with a newfangled, complicated, and bulky Wollensak reel-to-reel tape recorder. It had been a hard-wrought appointment—McGannon was a busy man and the interview was intruding on an especially hectic day.

After getting 90 minutes of the executive's undivided attention, the journalist trudged back to his Madison Avenue office, triumphant in achieving his objective. He rewound the tape and leaned back in anticipation of extracting the fruits of his labor. But the tape was blank. Not a word of McGannon's analysis of such issues as local television stations' needs vs. network interests or his thoughts on recruiting minority personnel was recorded. There goes my job, thought the reporter. Swallowing his pride and summoning his courage, the young man called and confessed to McGannon. "I blew it," he said, his voice shaking. "The tape recorder didn't work and I didn't take notes."

McGannon didn't hesitate. There was not a trace of impatience in his voice. "That's OK, son," he quickly replied. "You come right back and we'll do it all over again." That's what happened. The second interview came off without a hitch. It was a virtual duplicate of the first. The young reporter had his story and never told his editor about the mishap.

In 1968, McGannon received a Trustees Award from the TV Academy. It was for his outstanding contribution to the industry, but specifically, it was for McGannon's leadership of one of the most important station groups in the country, the scope and quality of his group's public service, and for his own early recognition of broadcasting's need to train and employ minority persons. The Emmy citation used such words as "creative," "dynamic," "encouraging," and "innovating." Emmy, a lady symbolizing excellence, was honoring Don McGannon, a man of character.

"Through the Looking Glass"
Costuming's First Emmy

Television is a visual medium, yet costume design was not recognized as an Emmy category until 1967. Bob Mackie, one of the most gifted and versatile designers in America, won the first Emmy for Best Costume Design (together with Ray Aghayan) for a spectacular NBC special, "Alice Through the Looking Glass." Broadcast November 6, 1966, the musical featured Judi Robin as Alice and a star-studded cast that included Nanette Fabray, Jimmy Durante, Tom and Dick Smothers, Agnes Moorehead, Jack Palance, Ricardo Montalban, and Richard Denning.

Mackie, who had fought to have costume design recognized by the TV Academy, remembered that in the old days CBS built its first TV studios in Hollywood without dressing rooms, because television was treated like radio and thus didn't require such accommodations. "You were issued a key for a closet to hang your coat. It was almost like a locker," Mackie recalled. "But there were no dressing rooms. For years the dressing rooms were portable ones like they use on movie sets." When he worked on *The Judy Garland Show* in 1963, CBS had to put a trailer out on the balcony. "There was not a star dressing room in the entire place," said Mackie.

Ironically, Mackie wasn't present when that first Emmy for costume design was presented on June 4, 1967, at the Century Plaza Hotel in Los Angeles. He was in Europe on vacation but was "thrilled" when he heard the news.

Mackie went on to have many other opportunities to collect Emmys. He has received 15 nominations and won seven Emmys. His client list includes Cher, Carol Burnett, Diahann Carroll, Bernadette Peters, Angela Lansbury, Rosemary Clooney, Madonna, Fran Drescher, Carol Channing, RuPaul, and Julia Louis-Dreyfus.

(Clockwise from top left) Eva Gabor, the star of 1965–1971's *Green Acres*, arrives for an Emmy telecast. *Star Trek*'s Leonard Nimoy and William Shatner at the 1967 Emmy presentations. The sci-fi program, which inspired a rabid cult following, was nominated twice as best dramatic series, in 1967 and 1968. It lost to *Mission: Impossible* both times. Natalie Schafer, who played Lovey Howell on *Gilligan's Island*, with *I Dream of Jeannie*'s Hayden Rourke. Nine-time nominee Elizabeth Montgomery (five of them were for *Bewitched*). Producer Aaron Spelling and actress Carolyn Jones (his wife at the time) with Mickey Rooney. Jones was starring as Morticia Frump Addams in the macabre sitcom *The Addams Family*, based on the cartoon characters of Charles Addams. Television's sweethearts, multiple Emmy winner Betty White and husband Allen Ludden, whose role as host of ABC's *Password* earned him an Emmy. Agnes Moorehead was escorted to the 19th annual Emmys by veteran character actor Cesar Romero. Moorehead won a supporting actress award for *The Wild, Wild West*. She also was nominated that year for best actress in a leading role in a comedy series for *Bewitched* but lost to Lucille Ball.

1970-79

In the 1970s, the Emmys played out against a backdrop of increasing governmental regulation and unfolding technological evolution. The courts, Congress, and primarily the Federal Communications Commission (FCC) heavily impacted television, consequently impacting the Emmys.

Times were changing more rapidly than ever. Television put on a new face, one considerably more sensitive to politics and social awareness. Social messages began working their way into television—and inevitably also crept into Emmy telecasts.

The networks got slapped around during the 1970s, and the decade opened with shocking news. Congress passed legislation to outlaw cigarette and tobacco advertising on radio and TV, effective January 2, 1971. This ruling stripped

Ed Asner, Betty White, Mary Tyler Moore, and Ted Knight all won Emmys for *The Mary Tyler Moore Show*. The show won a total of 29 Emmys over its 1970–77 prime-time run.

David J. O'Connell and Robert Young

A Winning Combination

If producer David J. O'Connell's Emmy batting average was calculated in baseball terms, he probably wouldn't make the starting lineup. He received a single Emmy in 1970 for coproducing (with David Victor) the best dramatic series, ABC's *Marcus Welby, M.D.* But O'Connell's Emmy achievements take on a greater glow in light of the 13 Emmy nominations gained by *Marcus Welby* over its eight-year run.

In 1971, O'Connell produced (again with David Victor) *Vanished*, credited with being the first two-part TV movie, and paving the way for subsequent miniseries. This thriller, which, like *Marcus Welby*, starred Robert Young (right), earned nine Emmy nominations. That gave O'Connell, who spent 28 years with MCA and Universal Studios, a total of 22 nominations for just two television projects.

the broadcast advertising business of $250 million in billings. In what came to be known as the prime-time access rule, the FCC declared that network-affiliated stations in the top 50 markets could not accept more than three hours of network programming between 7 P.M. and 11 P.M., prohibiting those same stations from programming off-network shows in syndication one hour per day. The networks also were barred from acquiring subsidiary rights in independently produced programs. In addition, the FCC passed a number of important cable rules. One banned cross-ownership of cable and TV stations locally, and another barred the networks from owning cable systems in the United States.

The war in Vietnam grabbed much TV news attention and gobbled

(Above, left) *Sesame Street*'s lovable Big Bird and songwriter Burt Bacharach at the 1970 Emmys. Bacharach's special "The Sound of Burt Bacharach" won several awards that year. He was also a winner the following year for his special, "Singer Presents Burt Bacharach." (Above, right) Audience-participation show host Monty Hall presents Patty Duke with an Emmy as 1976–77's Outstanding Lead Actress in a Limited Series for NBC's *Captains and the Kings*. Duke had previously won in 1970 for *My Sweet Charlie*. (Below) Bill Cosby and Dick Cavett cohosted the 1970 awards presentation, Cosby from Los Angeles' Century Plaza Hotel, and Cavett from New York's Carnegie Hall.

"Brian's Song"
A Double Story

Feature films made expressly for television came to the airwaves in the late 1960s by way of NBC's two-hour *World Premiere Movies* and ABC's 90-minute *Movie of the Week*. 1971's *Brian's Song* was one of the greatest made-for-television movies. It received Emmys for Outstanding Single Program, Best Teleplay, Best Supporting Actor (Jack Warden), and Film Editing (Bud Isaacs). The film's stars, James Caan and Billy Dee Williams, were also nominated. At the time of its telecast, *Brian's Song* was the highest-rated made-for-television movie.

Gale Sayers, the sensational running back for the Chicago Bears, had written his autobiography, *I Am Third*, an excerpt of which appeared in *Collier's* magazine. Leonard Goldberg, who was then running the production end of Screen Gems/Columbia Pictures, bought the property for the studio. He assembled an all-star production team of past and future award winners, including Paul Junger Witt as producer, Buzz Kulik as director, and William Blinn as screenwriter, with music by Michel Legrand. In addition to Caan as Brian Piccolo and Williams as Sayers, Jack Warden was cast as legendary Bears coach George Halas, and Shelley Fabares as Joy Piccolo, Brian's wife.

Brian's Song told two stories. One was how Piccolo, diagnosed with cancer, persevered and continued to play for the Bears. The other was about the warm friendship between a black man and a white man at a time when such relationships were rare. The film was critically acclaimed and later released theatrically.

No to Oscar, Yes to Emmy

George C. Scott, an Oscar winner in 1970 for *Patton*, won an Emmy for his February 3, 1971, performance in "The Price" on NBC's *Hallmark Hall of Fame*. He rejected the Oscar, but called fellow nominee Jack Cassidy from a New York location and asked him to accept on his behalf during the 23rd annual Emmy Awards ceremony at the Hollywood Palladium. Cassidy was nominated for his performance in *The Andersonvile Trial*, which Scott directed. (At right is a scene from *Jane Eyre* with Scott and Susannah York. For the role, Scott received an Emmy nomination in 1972.)

Encore
Rhoda Meets Lucy, Again

Valerie Harper was "astounded" in 1971 when she was nominated for an Emmy as Outstanding Actress in a Supporting Role in a Comedy after the inaugural season of *The Mary Tyler Moore Show*. It was her first television work. She had started as a dancer in stage shows at Radio City Music Hall and worked with Second City Chicago, an improvisational comedy troupe, before appearing on Broadway in a number of musicals, including *Subways Are for Sleeping*.

Harper was concerned about what to wear to the awards ceremony. An interior designer friend took her to several shops in uptown Manhattan and Greenwich Village. They settled on a place on Eighth Street with a Spanish name meaning "light and dark." Harper bought a black halter-top gown with a white lining. She also decided to wear earrings that a friend had given her for her birthday. "I just wanted to look appropriate," Harper recalled in an interview. Harper said her hairstyle "bears forgetting," but she does remember putting it up with a lot of "sausage curls."

The envelope at the Hollywood Palladium was opened and the winner was Harper. The experience of winning was "fantastic and thrilling," she reminisced. Up on stage were two show business icons, Jack Benny and Lucille Ball. It was an "incredible" moment for her, having grown up listening to and watching these superstars perform. Harper turned to Ball and said, "Hi, Lucy, remember me?" Ball was flustered. It was obvious she didn't know Harper at all. They both had been in a 1960 Broadway show called *Wildcat*, and worked together for eight months. Lucy was the star, and Harper only a dancer in the chorus line.

"It was a terrible thing for me to do to her," Harper acknowledged. "All she could do was nod her head and smile." Later, Harper apologized. Lucy, once prompted about *Wildcat*, did remember.

As Rhoda Morgenstern, Harper won three Emmys for Outstanding Performance in a Supporting Role in a Comedy for her work on *The Mary Tyler Moore Show*. She won a fourth Emmy for best leading actress on the spinoff series, *Rhoda*.

"Oh, my God, it's George C. Scott!"

—Actress Suzanne Pleshette, opening the envelope announcing Oustanding Single Performance by a Lead Actor for "The Price," and repeating Goldie Hawn's line from the earlier Academy Awards ceremony when Scott won a Best Actor Oscar for the title role in *Patton*, 1971

"Although we were defeated, I'm tremendously proud of what we did."

—Actor Hal Holbrook, accepting an Emmy for his title role in the canceled "The Senator" segments of NBC's *The Bold Ones*, 1971

Emmy Memories
Jay Sandrich

Director Jay Sandrich's first Emmy nomination was for *He & She*, a critically acclaimed sitcom created by Leonard Stern and starring Richard Benjamin and Paula Prentiss. It had a brief 1967–68 season run on CBS, with reruns in the summer of 1970. Afterward, Stern said of this show, "It's a credit I won't mumble."

Sandrich, then in his 30s, flushed by his first big directing job, figured he had a real chance of taking home an Emmy. "I remember, when I didn't win, feeling that well, that was it, I was never going to get another shot at it. I do remember the disappointment," he recalled later.

Sandrich was a much better director than seer. He went on to win four Emmys, two each for directing *The Mary Tyler Moore Show* and *The Bill Cosby Show*. He also won a religious programming Emmy for directing the syndicated *Insight* series of Father Ellwood E. Kieser.

Sandrich keeps his Emmys on a shelf in his den. "If a big earthquake hits, I could be stabbed to death by my Emmys," he joked.

"Any writer would rather write than be president—especially this year!"

—Actor Arthur Hill, referring to Richard Nixon and the Watergate scandal, after presenting a dramatic tribute to the role of the writer in television, 1973

up budgets. More than 110 million viewers watched President Richard Nixon's August 1974 resignation in the wake of the Watergate scandal. Gasoline shortages hit, and heiress Patty Hearst was kidnapped. David O. Selznick's theatrical blockbuster *Gone With the Wind* played in two parts on NBC during the November 1976 sweeps, averaging more than a 47 rating and 65 share. The United States celebrated its bicentennial. North and South Vietnam were reunited. Israeli airborne commandos rescued 103 hostages held at Entebbe Airport in Uganda, inspiring two made-for-TV movies. Finally, in 1979, the cameras shifted to continuous coverage of the 444 days Americans were held hostage in the U.S. Embassy in Tehran, Iran.

On the technological side, Home Box Office, Time Inc.'s pay-cable subsidiary, inaugurated a satellite-distributed network; Sony unveiled its Betamax videocassette; and RCA introduced its SelectaVision home videodisc player. Once viewers began paying for programming, television was never quite the same.

No single program or personality dominated the 22nd annual Emmy Awards in 1970. The awards were distributed evenly, with Robert Young honored for *Marcus Welby, M.D.*, Hope Lange for *The Ghost and Mrs. Muir*, and William Windom for *My World and Welcome To It*. Two new ABC series—*Room 222* and *Marcus Welby*—

Switch-Hitter
Ed Asner Is Top Banana

One of television's greatest achievements, *The Mary Tyler Moore Show* started its run in September 1970. Before the comedy series concluded in 1977, Ed Asner, who played gruff newsman Lou Grant, was to win three Emmys for Outstanding Performance by an Actor in a Supporting Role. The first, in 1971, "was a surprise, subject to all kinds of doubts," according to his later account of the event. "When it happened, as we say in Yiddish, I *plotzed* [burst]," he remembered.

In his acceptance speech, Asner talked about coming from three families: the one he was born into, the one he made and fostered, and the third, *The Mary Tyler Moore Show*. His second Emmy for the series was about "as thrilling as the first," Asner recalled, "because it confirmed the first."

Asner also won two Emmys for his dramatic performances in ABC's *Rich Man, Poor Man* miniseries and the same network's landmark limited series *Roots*. "Those were great elations for me because they showed I could be a switch-hitter," Asner explained, reinforcing that the onetime Shakespearean actor was certainly no stranger to drama.

He won two more statuettes for CBS' *Lou Grant* series. Emmys for starring in his own show meant to Asner that he was a "top banana." Asner keeps his seven Emmys in the den of his home. "They're nice to look at in terms of the glory days," he confides.

(Right) "Elizabeth R," a presentation of *Masterpiece Theatre*, drew strong ratings and won an Emmy for Glenda Jackson in 1972.

(Below) Peter Falk and Michael Learned picked up acting Emmys in 1976—Falk's third as the title character in *Columbo* and Learned's third for playing the mother in *The Waltons*. Julie Andrews and William Conrad were presenters.

(Opposite bottom) Mary Tyler Moore as Mary Richards and Ted Knight as Ted Baxter, the klutzy anchorman on *The Mary Tyler Moore Show*. Knight won two best supporting actor Emmys (1973, 1976) for the role.

Triple Crown

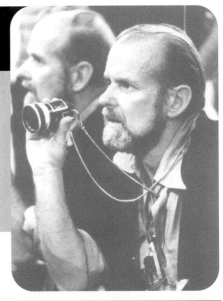

Director Bob Fosse, who won an Emmy for the NBC special "Singer Presents Liza With a 'Z'" for the 1972–73 season, also won an Oscar and a Tony during the same year. He's the only director to win all three, although actress Shirley Booth had accomplished the feat previously. Fosse won his Academy Award for directing *Cabaret* and a Tony for directing *Pippin*.

each won three Emmys. Two canceled shows—ABC's *The Ghost and Mrs. Muir* and NBC's *My World and Welcome To It*—won as well.

Dick Cavett, at Carnegie Hall in New York, and Bill Cosby, at the Century Plaza Hotel in Los Angeles, were the hosts. A special Trustees Award was presented to the heads of the news divisions of the three networks for "safeguarding" freedom of the press under an unusually

"We've come a long way since *My Friend Irma* [an early 1950s sitcom about a dumb blonde]."

—Actress Shelley Winters, appearing as a presenter at the 26th annual Emmy Awards, which were dominated by women and programs by and about them, 1974

"I don't know which of their two plots I'll miss the most."

—Johnny Carson, Emmy telecast host, commenting about the recently canceled *The FBI* series, 1974

(Above, left) Jack Klugman, who in the '60s won an Emmy for a guest shot on *The Defenders*, picked up two more in the '70s for his role as Oscar Madison in *The Odd Couple*.

(Above, right) ABC's Jim McKay and Roone Arledge won Emmys for their coverage of the Munich Olympics in 1972.

strong attack from Vice President Spiro Agnew. Special tribute was paid to the technicians and scientists who made the Apollo XI moon landing coverage possible. This was the first year the Emmy telecast concentrated solely on entertainment. Craft and technical awards were presented earlier at a nontelevised event.

For the first time since 1953, the 23rd annual Emmys was entirely a Hollywood ceremony and not split between the West and East coasts. Johnny Carson was master of ceremonies. Variety format pioneer Ed Sullivan, who spearheaded the bicoastal telecasts, was granted an honorary award. PBS' "The Andersonville Trial," from *Hollywood Television Theatre*, was honored as Program of the Year. The play also won an Emmy for dramatist Saul Levitt, who had adapted his Broadway play for TV. Lee Grant won the top actress award for her performance in "The Neon Ceiling," a Universal–NBC *World Premiere Movie*.

New shows became proud recipients that year. *The Senator* won five Emmys, *The Mary Tyler Moore Show* four, *All in the Family* three, and *The Flip Wilson Show* two. Lucille Ball and Jack Benny appeared as presenters. The most-nominated program of the year was "Hamlet," an

TV's "Murderer's Row"

The CBS-TV 1973 Saturday night lineup was one of the strongest in TV history. Each series was highly rated, long-lived, and, but for a single inexplicable exception, a big Emmy winner. The lineup was network television's equivalent to baseball's "Murderer's Row." Forget Babe Ruth, Lou Gehrig, Bob Meusel, and Tony Lazzeri of the New York Yankees in 1927—television fans remember the schedule of *All in the Family*, *M*A*S*H*, *The Mary Tyler Moore Show*, *The Bob Newhart Show*, and *The Carol Burnett Show*.

In 1973, *All in the Family* was the top-rated program on television, while *M*A*S*H*, *The Mary Tyler Moore Show*, and *The Bob Newhart Show* were among the top 20. *All in the Family* (and its sequel *Archie Bunker's Place*) lasted 13 seasons, and *M*A*S*H* and *The Carol Burnett Show* 11 seasons each. *The Mary Tyler Moore Show*, which won a total of 29 Emmys, more than any series at that time, ran for seven seasons. Three of these Emmys were for Outstanding Comedy Series. *The Carol Burnett Show* won a combined 22 program and individual Emmys. *All in the Family* won four Emmys for Outstanding Comedy Series.

The Bob Newhart Show, a favorite sitcom of viewers and critics alike over its six-season span, was completely overlooked by the Emmy voters. A comedy-variety series of the same title in the early 1960s won an Emmy for Outstanding Program Achievement in Comedy but lasted only one season. As a performer, Bob Newhart was nominated three times in the 1980s for *Newhart*, another series he fronted, but neither he nor the program was an Emmy winner. Ironically, it was the showcase of the Emmys, performing his classic stand-up telephone routine on the 1960 prime-time telecast, that first thrust Newhart into national prominence.

A Year of Specials

The 1972–73 season, television's 25th anniversary, was a time when specials—one-time-only programs pre-empting regularly scheduled series—grew in importance. The season began with ABC's more than 60 hours of coverage of the Summer Olympics and ended with the May 1973 telecast on the same network of the 25th annual Emmy Awards. In between, numerous specials provided the highlights of the season.

NBC, "Singer Presents Liza With a 'Z'," starring Liza Minnelli

ABC, "Zenith Presents a Salute to the 25th Anniversary of Television"

PBS, "Another Part of the Forest," starring Dorothy McGuire

PBS, "VD Blues," which initiated a nationwide campaign against venereal disease

NBC, "The American Experience," first in a series of specials trumpeting the American bicentennial

CBS, "Of Thee I Sing," a musical starring Carroll O'Connor and Cloris Leachman

ABC, first of three Burt Bacharach specials

NBC, Orson Welles in a new version of *The Man Who Came to Dinner*.

ABC, *The Woman I Love*, a drama about Edward VII and his future wife, Wallis Simpson, starring Richard Chamberlain and Faye Dunaway

CBS, a Marlene Dietrich special

NBC, "Jack Lemmon—Get Happy," a musical salute to songwriter Harold Arlen

NBC, "The Red Pony," *The Bell System Family Theatre*, a dramatization of John Steinbeck's short story

CBS, *Applause*, executive producer Alexander Cohen's TV version of the Broadway hit

CBS, *Once Upon a Mattress*, starring Carol Burnett, produced by her then-husband Joe Hamilton

The Emmy winner for 1972–73 for Outstanding Single Program—Variety and Popular Music was NBC's "Singer Presents Liza with a 'Z'," produced by Bob Fosse and Fred Ebb. But the most elaborate production was ABC's 90-minute "Zenith Presents a Salute to the 25th Anniversary of Television," executive produced by Bob Finkel, who went on to produce the 25th Anniversary Emmy Awards telecast. The program included some 6,700 film and videotape clips covering the first quarter-century of American television. It cost a considerable (for its time) $1.5 million.

> "It's the story of a peanut man crushed by an elephant, which had no political significance at the time."
>
> —David Lloyd, commenting on winning a writing award for the "Chuckles Bites the Dust" episode of *The Mary Tyler Moore Show*, 1976

> "I'd like to thank a lot of people at CBS—but unfortunately they're not there anymore."
>
> —*Mary Tyler Moore Show* writer Allan Burns, accepting an Emmy for the last episode of the seven-season CBS series, 1977

Oddities

At the 1972–73 Emmys, Abby Mann took the writing award for Outstanding Single Drama for "The Marcus-Nelson Murders," and Joe Sargent won the directing award for the same film. When James Garner opened the envelope and named "A War of Children"—a play about the conflict between Protestants and Catholics in Northern Ireland—the winner in the Outstanding Single Program category, the announcement came as a shock not only to producer-director George Schaefer but also to the audience.

Presenters Patty Duke Astin and John Astin stand back and let TV Academy founder Syd Cassyd do the talking. Cassyd would be the recipient in 1991 of the TV Academy's special Founder's Award, named in his honor.

NBC *Hallmark Hall of Fame* production. It won five Emmys, four of which were for technical excellence.

Carson returned as host the following year, and again the location was the Hollywood Palladium, but instead of NBC, the 24th annual Emmys were telecast on CBS. *All in the Family* won seven Emmys (out of 11 nominations) in 1971–72. Once again it was voted Outstanding Comedy Series. Three of its four cast members—Jean Stapleton, Carroll O'Connor, and Sally Struthers (she tied with Valerie Harper of *The Mary Tyler Moore Show*) received acting Emmys. Supporting Actor winner Ed Asner (*The Mary Tyler Moore Show*) kept Rob Reiner from making it a clean sweep. Glenda Jackson, a 1970 Oscar winner, took two of the five Emmys won by "Elizabeth R," a *Masterpiece Theatre*

A Road Well Traveled
Brenda Vaccaro and Lee Grant

Actress Brenda Vaccaro won an Emmy in 1974 for "The Shape of Things," an hourlong comedy-variety special that George Schlatter produced for NBC, which featured an all-female cast. The director of that special— and one of its featured performers—was Lee Grant. On the night of the Emmy telecast, Vaccaro found herself competing in the category of Best Supporting Actress in Comedy-Variety, Variety, or Music with Grant, who was also nominated for her performance in the special. Vaccaro was "thrilled to death" to win.

A year later, at the Academy Awards ceremony, Vaccaro and Grant competed again, this time for Best Actress in a Supporting Role. Vaccaro was nominated for her work in Jacqueline Susann's *Once Is Not Enough*, for which she already had won the Golden Globe. Grant was nominated for her performance in *Shampoo*. Grant won. Vaccaro remembers Grant coming to her afterward and consoling, "That's OK, I'm older."

That was not the last time Vaccaro would be nominated and not win. Most recently, it was an Emmy nomination for *The Golden Girls*. With the passing years, Vaccaro has learned to live with the disappointment of not going home with a statuette. Her philosophy on being nominated and not winning? "When you're young and you have that dress and you've been made up, and your hair is set and the flowers are right and you don't win, you go home and you cry."

The Waltons was voted best series and won five other Emmys in the 1972–73 season, including awards for leading actress Michael Learned and leading actor Richard Thomas.

Versatility
Dick Van Dyke

Like the fisherman who can't get over "the one that got away," Dick Van Dyke (right, center), a four-time Emmy winner, remembers vividly the night he didn't win an Emmy. He was nominated in 1974 for his TV dramatic debut in "The Morning After," an *ABC Wednesday Movie of the Week*. Aired February 13, 1974, it was the story of Charlie Lester, a successful public relations writer who refuses to admit that he is an alcoholic. His condition causes him to lose everything near and dear to him, and almost his life. Van Dyke's harrowing perfor-

mance earned him an Emmy nomination as Best Lead Actor in a Drama.

For the Tony Award winner (*Bye Bye Birdie*) and two-time Emmy winner (*The Dick Van Dyke Show*), being nominated as a dramatic actor was a particularly great honor. The category that year was loaded with heavyweights, including Sir Laurence Olivier, Alan Alda, and Martin Sheen. When the envelope was opened by the Emmy presenter, who happened to be Dick Van Dyke, the winner was Hal Holbrook (below, destined himself to win three more Emmys) for the *ABC Theatre* presentation of "Pueblo." "Just being nominated for a dramatic role for somebody like myself who had always been comedy or music comedy, it was a big kick," Van Dyke later related. "It was especially satisfying to be in the company of somebody like Hal Holbrook."

As a demonstration of his versatility, Van Dyke went on win two more Emmys outside the situation comedy arena. He won in 1977 for his performance in *Van Dyke and Company*, a short-lived hourlong variety series for NBC. And in a complete departure, in 1984 Van Dyke won a daytime Emmy for a children's program, *The Wrong Way Kid*, in which he played a bookworm.

"At least I tried a little bit of everything," he muses. "Everything but ballet and opera."

America's TV Sweetheart
Dinah Shore

Mary Pickford, of the big screen, was America's original "sweetheart." Dinah Shore, of the ubiquitous "black box" of television, was the second. She was dubbed "the girl with the laughing face" and was one of the first females to front a successful series.

Over a career that lasted more than five decades, Dinah, as everybody called her, was enormously popular with audiences in a number of different roles: singer, entertainer, variety and talk-show hostess, commercial spokeswoman, and golf tournament emcee. Former president Gerald Ford, one of her many friends and a Palm Springs neighbor, said of Dinah that she was "beautiful inside as well as out. She was truly a five-star person."

Dinah was also an Emmy champ. She was voted Best Female Singer in 1954 and 1955. In 1956, her Emmy was for Best Female Personality, and the next year for Best Continuing Performance by a female who plays herself. For the 1958–59 season, Dinah won for Best Performance by an Actress in a Musical or Variety Series. At the same time, her *The Dinah Shore Chevy Show* on NBC won for Best Musical or Variety Series.

The 1970s saw Dinah winning a total of three daytime Emmys for both NBC's *Dinah's Place* talk/service series, and the 90-minute syndicated talk show *Dinah!* The peak of her popularity was *The Dinah Shore Chevy Show* in the 1950s, when the jingle "See the USA in your Chevrolet" was her unofficial theme. Her signature was an end-of-the-show kiss blown to her audience. Emmy blew kisses back to her eight times.

Emmy Memories
Cloris Leachman

It was the 27th annual Emmy Awards in 1975. Actress Cloris Leachman was standing on the part of the Hollywood Palladium stage that thrust out into the audience, who were seated at tables. The versatile Leachman had already won for Best Supporting Actress in a Single Episode for *The Mary Tyler Moore Show*, tying with Zohra Lampert for *Kojak*. Leachman had previously won Emmys in 1973 and 1974. Now she was back for her second Emmy of the night, winning for a song-and-dance performance on CBS' *Cher* music/variety series.

She looked down and there was Bob Hope, literally sitting at her feet. Leachman's memory flashed back to her childhood in an Iowa country home. It was Bob Hope night on the radio, and her family was gathered around the big radio that she remembered came to a point at the top and curved all the way down. "It was a time switch," Leachman was later to remember. "For a moment I was upside down, topsy turvy." She had to get her wits about her while thinking "What's wrong with this picture? Shouldn't he be up here? And shouldn't I be down there?"

Leachman went on to win a total of eight Emmys for seven different roles, including one as Outstanding Performer in Children's Programming. Her mother would visit from Iowa once in a while and often exclaimed to her famous, much-honored daughter, "Oh, I could just pinch myself."

Later, after her mother returned home, Leachman would conclude, "That's what it is. Oh, I could just pinch myself. It's really true, and isn't it wonderful?"

The British import *Upstairs, Downstairs* won Emmys as best drama series in 1974, 1975, and 1977, but oddly, as best limited series in 1976. It aired on PBS as a taped presentation.

Ladies' Night at the Emmys

In the 1975 telecast, covering the 1974–75 season, producer Paul Keyes threw curves—10 of them. Instead of the usual host or cohosts, Keyes used 10 female stars as mistresses of ceremonies. They were Lucille Ball, Beatrice Arthur, Jean Stapleton, Carol Burnett, Cher, Teresa Graves, Mary Tyler Moore, Susan Saint James, Michael Learned, and Karen Valentine. The 11th hostess was comedian Flip Wilson (shown with Emmy winners Tony Randall and Valerie Harper), who, as he often did on his NBC series *The Flip Wilson Show*, appeared in drag as sassy Geraldine Jones. The hostesses were introduced at the top of the show to the tune of "There's No Business Like Show Business," followed, in another Emmy Awards production departure, by all of the supporting actors in every category.

production for PBS. The limited series also won both Outstanding New Series and Outstanding Drama Series awards. Another Brit, Keith Michell, took the Emmy for Outstanding Single Performance by an Actor in a CBS series, *The Six Wives of Henry VIII*. *The Carol Burnett Show* was named Outstanding Variety Series, and NBC's *Jack Lemmon in 'S Wonderful, 'S Marvelous, 'S Gershwin* was deemed Outstanding Single Program–Variety or Musical.

The Mary Tyler Moore Show and *The Waltons* won key Emmys at 1973's 25th Emmy Awards, telecast on ABC from L.A.'s Shubert Theater. The stars of the two series, Richard Thomas, Michael Learned, Mary Tyler Moore, Valerie Harper, and Ted Knight, all won acting awards. So, too, did Laurence Olivier for ABC's production of Eugene O'Neill's *Long Day's Journey Into Night*, and Cloris Leachman for "A Brand New Life," an ABC *Tuesday Movie of the Week*. "A War of Children," produced by Roger Gimbel and George Schaefer for *The New CBS Tuesday Night Movies*, was named Outstanding Single Program. *The Julie Andrews Hour*, which ABC had canceled, won seven Emmys, including the award as Outstanding Variety–Musical Series. Another musical, "Singer Presents Liza With a 'Z'," took home four awards. Three went to Bob Fosse, who directed, choreographed, and coproduced (with Fred Ebb) the special. The 25th Emmy celebration was produced by Bob Finkel and directed by Marty Pasetta.

In 1974, Mary Tyler Moore and Michael Learned were back in the winner's circle, Moore as Actress of the Year–Series, a new so-called Super Emmy category. Cicely Tyson won the counterpart Actress of the Year–Special for her work in *The Autobiography of Miss Jane Pittman* on CBS. Among the men, Alan Alda for *M*A*S*H* and Hal Holbrook for the *ABC Theatre* production of "Pueblo" won the Super Emmy honors. In the supporting actor categories, the Super Emmy winners were Michael Moriarty and Joanna Miles, both for ABC's presentation of Tennessee Williams' *The Glass Menagerie*.

The directors of the year were Robert Butler for *The Blue Knight* limited series on NBC and Dwight Hemion for a Barbra Streisand special on CBS. Writers of the year were Fay Kanin for the *GE Theater* special "Tell Me Where It Hurts" on CBS and Treva Silverman for an episode of *The Mary Tyler Moore Show*. The Best Drama Series of the year was a British import, *Upstairs, Downstairs*, on PBS. *M*A*S*H* was Outstanding Comedy Series, *The Carol Burnett Show* the Best Music–Variety Series (on its way to a total of 25 Emmys during its 12-season run), and *Columbo* the top limited series.

"Please, ladies and gentlemen, please, return to your seats. I beg you to return to your seats. Ladies and gentlemen. It does not look good for the entertainment industry if we have all these empty seats in the auditorium following a presidential speech. Do I make myself clear? Do you understand?"

—Executive producer Alexander Cohen exhorting the audience at the Pasadena Civic Auditorium after the unscheduled 1978 Emmy-interrupting broadcast from the White House with President Jimmy Carter, Anwar Sadat, and Menachem Begin, 1978

Bob Banner
Carol Burnett Meets the Velvet Hammer

Bob Banner won a 1957 Emmy, his first, for direction of a one-hour or more program. That was the last time an Emmy for directing was all-conclusive. The category covered comedy, drama, music and variety, specials, and series (there was one other category for directors that covered programs of a half hour or less). Banner's Emmy was for directing NBC's *The Dinah Shore Chevy Show*, a music-variety series. His win qualifies in Emmy annals as one of the most unexpected of all time.

His competition included four of television's greatest directors: John Frankenheimer, George Roy Hill, Arthur Penn, and George Schaefer. The first three were recognized for their work on one of television's greatest dramatic series, *Playhouse 90*: Frankenheimer for "The Comedian," Hill for "The Helen Morgan Story," and Penn for "The Miracle Worker." Schaefer, the most honored dramatic director in Emmy history, was nominated for "The Green Pastures" on *Hallmark Hall of Fame*, the dramatic anthology series that has won more Emmys than any other.

Even Banner (left), a soft-spoken man of calm temperament, was surprised. "I thought variety would be forgotten and that people would be more likely to vote for dramatic directors," he recalled. "Instead, I think they divided up the dramatic vote, and they canceled each other out. That was the last year they had only one directing award."

Beginning with the 1958–59 season, there were four different directing categories: Best Direction of a Single Dramatic Program—One Hour or Longer; Best Direction of a Single Program, Dramatic Series—Under One Hour; Best Direction of a Single Program of a Comedy Series; and Best Direction of a Single Musical or Variety Program.

In 1961, after he left *The Dinah Shore Chevy Show*, Banner was producing *The Garry Moore Show* and *Candid Camera*, both highly popular series for CBS. The network said that he was "a rare combination of showman and scholar" and pointed out his credits would amount to a virtual recitation of the history of television. His company, Bob Banner Associates, was responsible for many memorable and popular programs, including *The Carol Burnett Show* and specials starring Frank Sinatra, Perry Como, Julie Andrews, and Dionne Warwick, among others.

In all, Banner's programs won a total of 15 Emmy Awards. He helped make a star and Emmy winner out of Carol Burnett, whom he first met when she did *The Dinah Shore Chevy Show* as a guest performer. It was 1959 and Martha

Raye, scheduled as a guest on *The Garry Moore Show*, got sick. Burnett was called in on a Sunday to rehearse and went on live two nights later. That was when Banner, Joe Hamilton (producer of *The Garry Moore Show*, and one of the three founding partners of Bob Banner Associates), and Moore decided that Burnett should be a regular on the comedy-variety series. Burnett won an Emmy in 1962 for Best Performance in a Variety or Musical Program or Series for *The Garry Moore Show* (the program won as best in the field of variety or music variety). She also won the next year for her performance with Julie Andrews in the CBS special, "Julie and Carol at Carnegie Hall."

It was a crucial time in Burnett's career. The special with Julie Andrews had given her a boost. Banner was a great teacher. She later spoke of his "great taste, his quiet demeanor—never raising his voice." His calming effect was not what she had come to expect in a typical television producer. Once she got to know him, she called him "Bubba." "He can make his nos as nice as his yeses, which is a very rare quality in anybody's field, but especially in this one," she said.

When *The Carol Burnett Show* (destined to reap a harvest of Emmys) was in its sprouting period, Burnett noticed a troubled Banner. The first couple of shows had been taped but not yet aired. Burnett had come out in a yellow robe before each of the tapings to warm up the audience, but without the cameras rolling. She, Banner, and Hamilton (by then Burnett's husband, below) went to dinner to discuss the problem. Banner told them what was bothering him.

"You've got to go out there and be yourself," he said.

"I don't know how to be myself," Burnett replied. "I can only be characters in sketches like I was on Garry's show. I get nervous."

Banner didn't hesitate. "What we're going to do is tape the warm-up, the questions and answers," he said.

"Nobody will ever believe that those are not plants from the audience," Burnett shot back. "We can't tape that, Bob. It'll bomb."

Banner asked Burnett to trust him. The informal question-and-answer session with the audience became *The Carol Burnett Show*'s signature for 11 years. It was one of the most popular segments because it got the show off to an honest start.

Banner, whom Burnett thought of as a "velvet hammer," had made a strong suggestion, and Burnett had trusted him. *The Carol Burnett Show* won Emmys for best music-variety series for the 1971–72, 1973–74, and 1974–75 seasons.

Production Designers
Hazards and Hardships

Production designer and art director Jan Scott is a prime-time Emmy champ. She's been nominated 20 times, and has won 11, including honors for "Eleanor and Franklin" and its sequel, "Eleanor and Franklin: The White House Years." In all, Scott helped create 324 sets, re-creating all of Franklin Delano Roosevelt's many habitats. The TV Academy awarded these two productions a total of 17 Emmys.

Of her 11 wins, Scott is most proud of "Scarecrow," a film produced by Lewis Freedman and directed by Boris Sagal for the *NET* [National Educational Television] *Hollywood TV Playhouse*. It was "totally designed, drawn, and executed in forced perspective," Scott later remembered, meaning not only interiors but also exteriors and even farmland were built in a small studio space. The studio was public television station KCET in Hollywood, then managed by Dr. James Loper, who later became executive director of the TV Academy.

Also high on the list of Scott's achievements is *Evergreen*, a six-hour miniseries for NBC, executive produced by Edgar Scherick and Sue Pollock, produced by Phillip Barry, and directed by Fielder Cook. Scott designed various looks: Syrian army bunkers on the Golan Heights, wartime Israel, and the east coast of the United States. She covered four blocks of streets on New York's Lower East Side with dirt and gravel and installed 1914-era façades on existing buildings there, all the while dodging rocks thrown from rooftops by local drug dealers who didn't want TV cameras in the neighborhood.

In 1974, the one and only year that so-called Super Emmys were awarded, Scott, who won an Emmy that year for "The Lie," a *Playhouse 90* production for CBS, also was awarded the Super Emmy as Art Director of the Year.

It was a banner year for CBS. For the 1973–74 season, CBS took away 44 Emmys, the most won in a single year by a network, a record that still stands. The NBC telecast was from the Pacific Pantages Theatre in Hollywood. The host was Johnny Carson, and Bob Finkel was producer.

The Super Emmy concept, particularly unpopular with performers, lasted only one year. At the 27th annual awards show, the *ABC Theatre* dramatic special "Love Among the Ruins" won Emmys that year for its costars, Laurence Olivier and Katharine Hepburn, as best single performances by an actor and actress, as well as for veteran director George Cukor and writer James Costigan. But Universal Television's telefilm "The Law" for NBC surprised the audience by winning Outstanding Special—Drama or Comedy over "Love Among the Ruins." Robert Blake picked up the top award as an actor in a series for

Memorable Moments
Lucy, Groucho, and the Duck

In a scene straight out of the *I Love Lucy* series, Lucille Ball, on stage as a presenter, turned the 27th annual awards into a laugh riot. Lucy's task was to read the winners for both outstanding comedy and drama series, but she came to the podium without her glasses. "I'm in trouble," Lucy said. She couldn't find or read the card announcing the comedy series winner. Finally, she determined it was *The Mary Tyler Moore Show*. Then Milton Berle and Art Carney rushed to her aid, and she managed to read the winner of Outstanding Drama Series, *Upstairs, Downstairs*. Lucy's last chore as presenter didn't require glasses. She brought on 83-year-old Groucho Marx (right) to present the variety award. In fond remembrance of Marx's *You Bet Your Life* quiz show of the 1950s, a stuffed duck descended from the ceiling bearing the envelope with the winner's name. It turned out to be *The Carol Burnett Show*.

Baretta, and Jean Marsh won the Best Actress award for her role as the parlor maid in *Upstairs, Downstairs*. Tony Randall won for acting in a comedy series for the canceled *Odd Couple*. Valerie Harper was back again with an Emmy for *Rhoda*. The winner of Best Dramatic Series was *Upstairs, Downstairs* for the second successive year. Will Geer and Ellen Corby received Emmys as the grandpa and grandma in *The Waltons*. Betty White and Ed Asner also won Emmys for their work on *The Mary Tyler Moore Show*.

The David Susskind production of the four-hour "Eleanor and Franklin" was named Outstanding Special of the 1975–76 season. The show also garnered awards for director Daniel Petrie, writer James Costigan, and supporting actress Rosemary Murphy. The *ABC Theatre* presentation received a total of 11 Emmys, including seven in various technical categories—the most Emmys won by a made-for-TV movie to this day. Anthony Hopkins was chosen best actor for his portrayal of Bruno Richard Hauptmann in NBC's "The Lindbergh Kidnapping Case." Susan Clark won the best actress Emmy for her role as athlete Babe Didrikson Zaharias in *Babe*. NBC's *Saturday Night Live*, in its first eligible year, piled up five

Robert Blake, holding his Emmy for *Baretta*, congratulates Jean Marsh at the 27th annual awards show for winning the best actress award in a drama series for her role as a parlor maid in *Upstairs, Downstairs* on PBS.

Leading Ladies
Susan Clark Upsets the Odds

When ABC turned the cameras on for the 28th annual Emmy Awards on May 17, 1976, at the Shubert Theater in Los Angeles, the buzz had "Eleanor and Franklin" as the hot special of the 1975–76 season. Its two lead actors, Edward Herrmann, who played Franklin Delano Roosevelt, and Jane Alexander, who portrayed Eleanor Roosevelt, were heavy favorites to win.

Susan Clark (shown with presenter Telly Savalas) was a long shot among a formidable slate of nominees for Outstanding Lead Actress in a Drama or Comedy Special, including Colleen Dewhurst for *ABC Theatre*'s "A Moon for the Misbegotten" and Sada Thompson for *The Entertainer*. Clark was a contender for playing the title role in *Babe*, a CBS biographic drama about Mildred (Babe) Didrikson Zaharias, America's foremost female athlete, who won two Olympic track-and-field gold medals in 1932 and went on to become a world champion golfer.

"I was very prepared not to win," Clark remembered. "The excitement for me was in being nominated." It was a feeling reinforced when "Eleanor and Franklin" was announced as Outstanding Special—Drama or Comedy, beating out *Babe*.

But suddenly there were indications that "Eleanor and Franklin" would not sweep the awards. Surprisingly, Anthony Hopkins, not Ed Herrmann, won as Best Lead Actor for "The Lindbergh Kidnapping Case." When Clark was announced as Best Lead Actress, she couldn't believe it. "I sat there for a couple of minutes letting it sink in," she recalled. Her mother grabbed one arm and her husband and costar, Alex Karras, grabbed the other. She yelled out, "Yikes!" and ran up to the stage. "It didn't even occur to me that I was talking to millions of people who might be watching the telecast around the world," she said afterward.

In addition to an Emmy for its star and the nomination as best special, *Babe* also received nominations for director Buzz Kulik, writer Joanna Lee, cinematographer Charles Wheeler, editor Henry Berman, and makeup artist William Tuttle. Composer Jerry Goldsmith won an Emmy for Dramatic Underscore, Special Program.

The following year, 1977, Clark was nominated as Outstanding Lead Actress in a Drama or Comedy Special for another film biography, NBC's "Amelia Earhart." Ironically, her principal competition again was thought to be Jane Alexander, playing Eleanor Roosevelt once more, this time in "Eleanor and Franklin: The White House Years." The winner of the Emmy, though, was Sally Field for NBC's *The Big Event* production of "Sybil."

The Emmy for *Babe* and the nomination for "Amelia Earhart" opened doors for Clark. "It was a very exciting high point of my career," she fondly recalled.

Emmy Memories
A Hot Night in Century City for "Mary Hartman" Writer

Ann Marcus remembers going to the 28th annual Emmy Awards at Century City's Shubert Theater with her writing collaborators Jerry Adelman and Daniel Gregory Browne. They had written the first two episodes of what became the one-hour pilot for *Mary Hartman, Mary Hartman*.

Marcus remembers Emmy night as being extremely hot under the television lights. Her category was a special classification of outstanding program and individual achievement. In essence, it was for work that didn't fit into any other category. That's because *Mary Hartman*, an outrageous adult soap, was a syndicated series shown mostly in late-night time slots. The other nominees were CBS' "Bicentennial Minutes" and NBC's late-night *The Tonight Show Starring Johnny Carson*.

When Marcus, Adelman, and Browne were announced as winners it was late in a very long evening. Marcus was wearing a chiffon gown with a jacket that had ostrich feathers. Elated, she got up on stage and said, "I think I've been waiting so long that my ostrich died." The quip drew only mild laughter from the audience, but Marcus didn't mind. She felt as if she'd won the lottery and given birth.

"It's wonderful," she later said. "It's being recognized for something that you have literally poured your heart and soul into. It's a beautiful feeling. I know some people say this is silly and won't participate in these awards. I'd just love to get two or three more, and damn it, maybe I will."

nominations and four wins. *The Mary Tyler Moore Show* also received four additional Emmys, and NBC's *Police Story* won as the Outstanding Drama Series.

The big surprise of the 28th annual awards was ABC's 12-hour novel for television, *Rich Man, Poor Man*, which won four Emmys, even though it entered the competition with 23 nominations. One of the awards went to Ed Asner. It was his fourth win, but his first for dramatic work. John Moffitt directed the Emmy telecast; it was produced by Norman Rosemont, telecast on ABC, and held at the Shubert Theater in Los Angeles.

The 29th annual Emmy Awards was staged in a new venue: the Pasadena Civic Auditorium. The NBC telecast was in September, four months later than its scheduled May airdate. The telecast was postponed due to differences between the New York and Hollywood chapters of the TV Academy. In a compromise, it was decided that the Hollywood chapter—the Academy of Television Arts & Sciences—would handle the Emmys for prime-time programs exclusively.

Norman Lear's syndicated nighttime soap, *Mary Hartman, Mary Hartman*, starred Louise Lasser (below) as a befuddled housewife.

(Right) Nick Nolte and Peter Strauss starred in *Rich Man, Poor Man*, one of television's first miniseries, adapted from Irwin Shaw's novel. The show received a record 23 nominations in 1976.

(Center) Betty White and Allen Ludden both took home Emmys in 1976; he won for hosting ABC's *Password*, and she for Outstanding Supporting Actress in a Comedy Series for *The Mary Tyler Moore Show* on CBS.

(Bottom) Kristy McNichol and Gary Frank, the two youngsters from ABC's *Family*, won Emmys in 1977 for best supporting actress and actor in a drama series.

"So proud are ABC and NBC of their very own shows and stars who win Emmys on CBS tonight that they have scheduled against us a three-hour debut of the most expensive new series ever made [*Battleship Galactica*] and the conclusion of *King Kong*."

—Norman Lear, presenter (who compared the counterprogramming of the Emmys to "Dracula biting his own neck"), 1978

ABC's historic eight-day telecast of *Roots*—the most watched program in television history, with ratings in the mid-40s and shares in the mid-60s—entered the annual Emmy event with a record 37 nominations. It picked up nine awards, the most ever won by a miniseries, including acting Emmys for Louis Gossett Jr., Ed Asner, and Olivia Cole. The program also was named Outstanding Limited Series, and director David Greene and writers William Blinn and Ernest Kinoy won Emmys for specific episodes.

For the first time, there was a tie for Outstanding Special—Drama between "Eleanor and Franklin: The White House Years" and "Sybil." Daniel Petrie, an Emmy winner the previous year for the first "Eleanor

Critic's Choice
The Brits and PBS Score One for Smith

As TV critic for the *Los Angeles Times*, Cecil Smith witnessed many memorable Emmy moments. One particularly delightful memory for him was the 20th Emmy Awards in 1968, when a "squadron" (actually 10) of the writers of NBC's *Rowan and Martin's Laugh-In* paraded on stage at the Hollywood Palladium to accept awards for best writing in music or variety. The crowded stage turned into a laugh fest, with presenters Don Rickles and Sally Field joining in. The clowning continued when *Laugh-In*'s irrepressible producer, George Schlatter, won two more Emmys for Best Musical or Variety Program (for the introductory special on September 9, 1967) and Best Musical or Variety Series.

One of Smith's fondest memories was in 1977, the year of *Roots* and its author Alex Haley. Smith remembered him as not only "a very nice man" but also a "fabulous, mesmerizing" speaker. Long after the 29th annual Emmy Awards ceremony, at which *Roots* picked up six statuettes, Smith recalled Haley's involvement with the production. "The actors would all ask him what this story was all about," Smith recollected. "He went into the background, the research, and everything else, which is so rare in a movie or even a theatrical production of any kind. To have the author actually tell the actors what they are working with, to the very fiber of the roles they are playing, was quite wonderful."

Always an ardent proponent of public broadcasting, Smith experienced genuine satisfaction in 1974 when the British import *Upstairs, Downstairs* (right) won an Emmy for Best Drama Series, beating out such popular commercial network programs as CBS' *Kojak* and *The Waltons*, ABC's *The Streets of San Francisco*, and NBC's *Police Story*. In a way, he felt it was only right that *Upstairs, Downstairs* won, since in 1970 another PBS import from Britain, the 26-part "The Forsythe Saga," was nominated but didn't win.

"Roots"
Pulitzer Prize Winner
Becomes a TV Milestone

Alex Haley, a retired Coast Guardsman of gentle nature, won a Pulitzer Prize, and his creations—the miniseries *Roots* and its sequel, *Roots: The Next Generations*—received a total of 11 Emmys. The nine won by *Roots* alone is the most Emmys won by a miniseries in television history.

Haley, who helped civil rights leader Malcolm X write his autobiography, gave the world not only the best-selling hardcover book of the time but also the most-watched TV program. He won the 1977 Pulitzer for *Roots: The Saga of an American Family*, the story of his family's journey from Africa to American slavery and ultimately to freedom. Haley spent 12 years researching the book, part fact and part wonderfully imagined detail, which traced his family back six generations to Kunta Kinte, who was kidnapped from Gambia, West Africa, in 1767 and shipped to America as a slave.

The ABC 12-hour miniseries, billed as a "Novel for Television," was produced by David L. Wolper Productions, with Wolper as executive producer and Stan Margulies as producer. Some 130 million people saw all or part of *Roots* over eight nights for a Nielsen rating of 44.9. The final episode drew a 51.1 rating/71 share, making it the highest-rated program at that time. The eight episodes of *Roots*, from January 23 to January 30, 1977, averaged a 44.9 rating and a 66 share of the audience.

About five months after the telecast, 10 months since the book appeared, *Roots* was translated into 22 languages and distributed around the world. As Haley, by then the most sought-after speaker in America, stepped behind the podium on June 9, 1977, in the ballroom of the Beverly Wilshire Hotel to address a "Newsmaker" luncheon of the Hollywood Radio and Television Society, *Roots* was set for translation into Swahili and

Hebrew. "I couldn't have taken hashish and fantasized what has happened," Haley told the entertainment industry gathering. He pronounced himself "hooked" on Hollywood, noting the public's general perception that the Hollywood establishment had ruined his book. "I gained the biggest possible influence on the audience," he said. "I am just ecstatic about what was done with my book. What people equate with Hollywood creations needs to be changed."

Roots thoroughly dominated the 1977 Emmy Awards, coming into that September 11 night in Pasadena with 37 nominations and taking home the Emmy as Best Limited Series, as well as Emmys for actors Louis Gossett Jr., Ed Asner, and Olivia Cole (opposite), among others. In the category of Outstanding Lead Actor for a Single Performance in a Drama or Comedy Series, all of winner Gossett's competitors—John Amos, LeVar Burton, and Ben Vereen—were fellow *Roots* cast members.

Asner, in the Supporting Actor category, competed against fellow cast members Moses Gunn, Robert Reed, and Ralph Waite. Cole's competition for Best Supporting Actress included Sandy Duncan and Cicely Tyson, both of whom were in the first *Roots* cast. Scripts for *Roots* were written by some of TV's finest writers: William Blinn, Ernest Kinoy, James Lee, and Max Cohen. The miniseries' original music was written by Quincy Jones. Kinoy and Blinn won Emmys for Outstanding Writing in a Drama Series, and Jones and Gerald Fried received honors for Outstanding Music Composition.

Roots: The Next Generations, airing on ABC for 12 hours over seven nights in 1979, won two Emmys, including Best Limited Series, with the Emmy again going to executive producer David L. Wolper and producer Stan Margulies. *Roots* was a milestone production for television in its subject matter, casting, and unprecedented acceptance by American viewers.

After seven seasons, *The Mary Tyler Moore Show* bowed out in 1977. The 29th annual Emmy Awards audience was offered a film clip tribute to the show and responded with a standing ovation. (Left) Standing with Dick Van Dyke are cast members Betty White, Ed Asner, Mary Tyler Moore, Georgia Engel, and Ted Knight. (Below) Afterward, with past multi–Emmy winner Phil Silvers as presenter, writers Allan Burns, James L. Brooks, Ed Weinberger, Stan Daniels, David Lloyd, and Bob Ellison won Emmys for Outstanding Writing in a Comedy Series for the show's final episode.

It's a Tie!

The 29th awards at the Pasadena Civic Auditorium was the scene of a first in Emmy history. The category of Outstanding Special—Comedy or Drama not only ended in a tie, but both shows were directed by the same person. The tie, announced by Alfred Hitchcock, was between *ABC Theatre*'s "Eleanor and Franklin: The White House Years" and "Sybil," a production of NBC's *The Big Event*. Both were directed by Daniel Petrie. Fittingly, Petrie won a directorial award the previous year for "Eleanor and Franklin," the prequel to "Eleanor and Franklin: The White House Years."

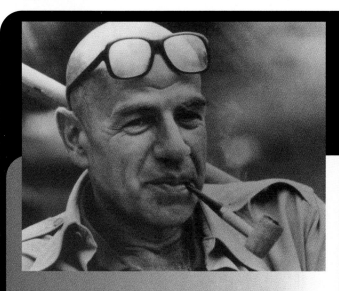

Six Emmys on a Shelf
That's Bud's Daily Reminder

Veteran sports producer Bud Greenspan won his first Emmy with his late wife, Cappy Petrash (his Cappy Productions is named after her) in 1977 for their *Olympiad* series. He has won five more Emmys since, three (out of five nominations) in 1996 for *16 Days of Glory: Lillehammer '94*.

His 1977 Emmy was the first award Greenspan ever won. He says there's no question it put him on the map. "We were on a venture as a sort of 'World at War' or 'Victory at Sea' type of series, but this one was specifically about the Olympics," he explains. The critical acclaim for the series was like getting the cake, he explained. When the Emmy was awarded, it was the icing.

"Never does it become old hat. When it becomes terrible is when you're nominated and don't win," he says. "It's as exciting an evening as any of the others, like the Tonys or the Oscars."

All six Emmys are in Greenspan's New York office—"on a shelf and the first thing you see when you come in," he assures.

(Right, above) The *Father Knows Best* team of Robert Young and Jane Wyatt present an acting Emmy to Sally Field, shown on the projection screen, for her portrayal of a woman haunted by multiple personalities in "Sybil," on NBC's *The Big Event* in the fall of 1976. (Right, below) Jean Stapleton at the podium in 1978, winning her third Emmy for *All in the Family*. Said Stapleton: "If I had one wish, it would be to relive these past eight years."

"We have been praised with faint damns all over the world."

—Producer Herbert Brodkin, accepting the Emmy for Outstanding Limited Series for *Holocaust*, 1978

and Franklin" special, won another Emmy for the sequel (he also directed "Sybil"). Concluding its seven-season run, *The Mary Tyler Moore Show* added three more awards, for a record total 29 Emmys. Sally Field picked up an Emmy for the title role of "Sybil," and 85-year-old Beulah Bondi won for a guest performance on *The Waltons*. Another veteran, 70-year-old Burgess Meredith, won for his portrayal of Joseph Welch in "Tail Gunner Joe" (the story of Senator Joseph McCarthy).

A posthumous acting award went to Diana Hyland for her role in "The Boy in the Plastic Bubble." It was an emotional moment when John Travolta, her costar, accepted for her. Produced by Don Ohlmeyer for NBC (who would later become the network's top programming executive on the West Coast), the 29th annual ceremonies clocked in at a record 3 hours and 30 minutes.

That record was broken the following year when politics and world events interrupted the Emmy proceedings. Another powerful mini-series, the nine-and-a-half-hour NBC production of *Holocaust*, was

"The best part I ever had in television was as Joe Welch [the Boston lawyer who helped discredit Senator Joseph McCarthy during the televised U.S. Senate hearings in 1954] in 'Tail Gunner Joe.' It was close to my favorite role—I don't need anything better than that in any medium. When I played Welch, I was getting a splendid revenge; I had been placed on the *Red Channels* [a paperback book published in June 1950 listing people in the entertainment industry alleged to be friendly to Communist causes] list by the McCarthy gang and this was a fine response.

"'Tail Gunner Joe' was shown on TV not too long ago on some obscure channel and the next day when I walked along the street in New York, various people stopped me to comment on it. I have seldom been happier than I was on that television show; and I was glad it 'went well,' as we say. To prepare to play him, I looked at his newsreels endless times and listened to his voice. I was fascinated by the man, and I was proud it came out well, and I was handed an Emmy."

—Burgess Meredith, in his 1994 autobiography *So Far, So Good*, on winning an Emmy in 1977 for Outstanding Performance by a Supporting Actor in a Comedy or Drama Special

"I sounded like a bumbling idiot. I had absolutely nothing prepared. Truly that's how much I didn't think I'd win. I didn't even have one of those backups, oh, just-in-case-kind-of-things. I was, like, shocked. I couldn't even feel my emotions."

—Lindsay Wagner, remembering how she felt when she scored a surprising upset over *Family*'s Sada Thompson and Michael Learned of *The Waltons* to win a 1977 Emmy as Outstanding Lead Actress in a Drama Series for ABC's *The Bionic Woman*, one of the few times a performer in the action genre was honored.

Heeeerrrres Johnny via projection screen as producer Fred DeCordova accepts an Emmy from Milton Berle at the 30th annual awards presentations in the special classification of Outstanding Program Achievement for *The Tonight Show Starring Johnny Carson.*

selected as Outstanding Limited Series and, among its eight awards, won Emmys for stars Michael Moriarty, Meryl Streep, and Blanche Baker. The telecast of the 1978 30th annual Emmys lasted 3 hours and 35 minutes. *All in the Family* was named Outstanding Comedy Series for the fifth time. Stars Carroll O'Connor and Jean Stapleton were saluted as Outstanding Lead Performers in a Comedy Series for a third time. Rob Reiner won his second Emmy for supporting actor. The show also won Emmys for director Paul Bogart and writers Bob Weiskopf, Bob Schiller, Barry Harman, and Harve Brosten.

September 17, 1978, was the night Middle East politics unexpectedly became part of the Emmy show on CBS. The prelude to this unforeseen turn of events started earlier in the day when executives worried about whether the Los Angeles Rams–Dallas Cowboys football game, also on CBS, would wind up in a regulation-time tie. Overtime in the contest would mean pushing back all programming in the East and Midwest. But that didn't happen. Instead, brought to viewers live, smack in the middle of the Emmys (as well as cutting into ABC's *Battlestar Galactica* premiere and an NBC night of specials), was a half-hour press conference in which U.S. president Jimmy Carter, Egyptian president Anwar Sadat, and Israeli prime minister Menachem Begin announced a happy ending to their peace talks at Camp David. Viewers saw Sadat and Begin embrace each other. Early in the Emmy telecast, host Alan Alda, star of *M*A*S*H*, noted that television was "a powerful world force." At that point, neither he nor the audience knew that Emmy had a date with history.

In keeping with the 1978 presidential interruption, the 31st Emmy

"These days, if a show doesn't make it in a couple of weeks, it goes out in the alley. Faith has become too expensive."

—Garry Moore, as he and Carol Burnett reminisced about the old *Garry Moore Show*, which CBS kept on the air for a year before it found an audience and became a hit, 1979

Holocaust dominated the drama category in 1978, winning eight Emmys, including Outstanding Limited Series. The cast included Michael Moriarty (left), who won as Outstanding Lead Actor in a Limited Series. Meryl Streep and Blanche Baker also won acting awards.

(Below) At the Television Academy's 30th presentation in 1978, *All in the Family* was named best comedy series for the fifth time since its introduction in the middle of the 1970–71 season, and Carroll O'Connor and Jean Stapleton (left) were among five of the shows Emmy winners. Actor Rob Reiner and producer Norman Lear were among *All in the Family*'s winners that night. To Reiner's right stands his father, Carl.

(Right) Noah Beery Jr. and James Garner as Joseph "Rocky" Rockford and Jim Rockford in NBC's *The Rockford Files*. The private-eye program was named Outstanding Drama Series in 1978. Garner won an Emmy as Outstanding Lead Actor in a Drama Series the previous year. (Far right) Gilda Radner won a 1978 Emmy as best supporting actress in a variety or music program.

Norman Lear
A "Dy-No-Mite" Decade

Norman Lear, a once only moderately successful musical comedy/variety producer-writer-director, didn't have 15 minutes of fame in the 1970s—he had a decade of it. It was, in fact, a "Dy-No-Mite" decade for Lear (to use the popular catchphrase of the character J.J. on the producer's *Good Times* sitcom).

Lear's signature series, *All in the Family*, was number one in prime-time ratings five seasons in succession, from 1971–72 through 1975–76. Over the course of three seasons, three Lear-produced shows were among the top-five ranked prime-time series. He had four in the top 10 in 1974–75, with *Sanford and Son*, *Maude*, and *The Jeffersons* joining *All in the Family*. Another Lear sitcom, *One Day at a Time*, made the top 10 in 1976–77.

Given their huge popularity, the Lear shows inevitably made a mark on the Emmys but had less of an impact than the ratings would suggest. *All in the Family* collected a strong

Emmy Memories

Happy Days for Marion Ross

Introduced in January 1974, *Happy Days* ran for 10 years and was television's number one hit by the 1976–77 season. A television icon, it was inspired by George Lucas' cult-film favorite, *American Graffiti.*

These days, *Happy Days*, according to veteran character actress Marion Ross, "is treated with awe and respect." But during its TV run, the show was all but overlooked by Emmy. "At the time we were not honored very much," confirms Ross, who throughout the long run of the ABC sitcom played Marion Cunningham, mother to Ron Howard's Richie Cunningham. Ross was nominated for best supporting actress in a comedy for the 1978–79 and 1983–84 seasons, losing to *All in the Family*'s Sally Struthers the first time and to Rhea Perlman of *Cheers* the next. But none of the other principals in *Happy Days*—not Howard, series creator Garry Marshall, Tom Bosley, not even the Fonz himself, Henry Winkler—won an Emmy for the show.

Ross went on to be nominated twice more for Emmys without a win, both for the critically popular yet low-rated *Brooklyn Bridge* on CBS. Winkler did win a 1985 daytime Emmy as coexecutive producer (with Roger Birnbaum) of "All the Kids Do It," a *CBS Schoolbreak* special.

How was it for Ross to be nominated four times for Emmys and not to win? "There's a flash of embarrassment as the camera goes by you and picks somebody else," she acknowledges. "All of us actors wish we had the nerve to make faces at the camera. Instead, we're always charming and gracious about it."

This is not to denigrate Emmy nominations, Ross takes pains to make clear. "You would kill yourself even now to get one," she says. Her Emmy nomination certificates are framed and hanging on the wall in her TV room.

Great Moments

Hearing the announcement that the 1977 best actress winner was the late Diana Hyland, costar and award accepter John Travolta threw his Emmy program into the air and leaped from his seat. "Wherever you are, Diana," he said after reaching the stage, "I love you." The award went to Hyland for her role in "The Boy in the Plastic Bubble."

"Our philosophy from the beginning—right, wrong, or indifferent—was to stage an event here in Pasadena and then to cover it for television. We did not want to do just a television show. The point is, if you're going to do an event like the Super Bowl and it ends in a tie and goes into overtime that lasts a week, then that's what you do. That's what it's about.

"When John Travolta got up there [to accept an acting award for the late Diana Hyland], that was real, that was life, that was tragedy and love, and I sat in the truck and cried. That wasn't manufactured. That's what our medium has that no other medium has."

—Producer Don Ohlmeyer, explaining in an interview why his telecast of the 29th annual Emmy Awards was the longest in history, 1977

Dear Harvey, Conway Lied

Beginning in 1973, Tim Conway won a total of four Emmys for *The Carol Burnett Show*—one for writing and three for performing (he also won a fifth in 1996 for a guest shot on *Coach*). On three occasions he found himself nominated in the category of best supporting actor in variety or music competition with Harvey Korman, his colleague from Burnett's show.

One year, knowing he wasn't going to be present for the ceremony, Conway gave Korman a note to read in case he won. The note read: "Remember when I said if you vote for me, I'll vote for you? Well, I lied." Conway won that year.

On another Emmy night, Bill Carruthers, who was producing the show, told Conway the telecast was running long and there were three more categories to go after the one in which the actor was nominated. "If you win," the producer pleaded, "just say thank you and sit down." When he won, Conway reminisces, he offered "a three-minute speech thanking everyone at the Tarzana pitch-and-putt. I described the new Mark Twain hole, and that we had baby-sitting."

In 1977, not only did Conway win as best supporting actor, but Mary Kay Place, his former secretary, won as best supporting actress for *Mary Hartman, Mary Hartman*. Asked about his reaction to having an ex-secretary win an Emmy, Conway told the press, "I was more excited about that one than mine. She's a wonderful talent. If she could only type."

Conway thinks his best year was 1976, when he didn't win. He, Korman, and *Saturday Night Live*'s Chevy Chase were the nominees. Conway went on stage to the podium as soon as his name was mentioned as a nominee. "I didn't think I was going to win that year," he later explained, "and I did want to be on television." He waited until Chevy Chase was announced as the winner and then sat down. It was the year that Chase, in his acceptance, said: "This is totally expected on my part."

It's great to joke and have fun as a winner, but is Conway a sore loser? What happens when he's nominated and doesn't win? "I just boo," he says, "and loudly, too. And then I talk to some of the other Academy members around me and ask why they didn't vote for me."

"My six children are home watching *Battlestar Galactica*. My mother-in-law is having dinner with Dwayne Hickman, and my wife is in Mexico attending the annual Kaopectate Festival."

—Tim Conway of *The Carol Burnett Show*, accepting an Emmy for Best Supporting Actor in a Variety or Musical Show, 1978

"Saturday Night Live"
The Show That Launched 1,000 Faces

The conventional wisdom in the television industry is that the value of an Emmy is more vague prestige than definite asset. Yet the eight Emmys awarded to *Hill Street Blues* in 1981, unquestionably enabling the then low-rated police drama to survive, is usually cited as an exception.

It's far from the only example, though, of Emmy's exhilarating, energizing, career-enhancing power. Authors Doug Hill and Jeff Weingrad, in *Saturday Night*, their 1986 backstage history of NBC's tumultuous live late-night series, told of the show's first year at the Emmys in 1976 when it took home four Emmys out of five nominations. The book showed how *Saturday Night Live* "accomplished a sweep that declared them, in front of the Hollywood establishment and a prime-time audience of 50 million viewers, the hottest show on television." The show won for Best Comedy-Variety Program and for Best Writing, Best Supporting Player (Chevy Chase), and Best Direction (Dave Wilson), but did not win in the graphic design category.

Also described in the book is how the attitude of Michael O'Donoghue, *Saturday Night*'s top writer and leading iconoclast, changed from having a "carefully nurtured disdain for the Emmys" to that of a believer. O'Donoghue, as quoted in the book, remembered thinking, *Why am I fighting this? This is great!* He confessed to a change of attitude, wanting "desperately" to win. "I embraced television at that moment," he told the authors.

In the 20 years since its first Emmy, *Saturday Night Live* has captured 56 more nominations and 11 additional wins for a total through 1997 of 61 nominations, 15 wins.

Emmy Memories
Mariette Hartley

Mariette Hartley's mother hated the dress her daughter wore to the 31st Emmy Awards on September 9, 1979. "Actually, it was not great-looking," Hartley remembers, describing it as "a designer dress, with circles all over it, kind of a magenta, which is not my best color."

She did her own hair for the occasion. "In those days," she said, "that stuff never occurred to me. Anyway, I never thought I would win for *The Incredible Hulk*. I thought I looked fine."

Hartley had to be tricked into the guest shot on the CBS series, which was based on a Marvel Comics character. She had recently signed with manager Arlene Dayton, who told her that she would be cast as the new wife of Dr. David Banner, played by the program's star, Bill Bixby.

"It's a wonderful script," assured Dayton.

"I have a brand-new baby and she's nursing. I'm not going to do it," responded an adamant Hartley.

About 15 minutes later, she received a call from the costumer for *The Incredible Hulk*. The woman wanted to know Hartley's size, always the first question asked of an actress after she's hired.

"No, no, you don't understand," said Hartley. "I'm not doing it."

"That's not what I hear," replied the costume lady.

Dayton had accepted the part without Hartley's approval. "She just forced me into it," Hartley explained later, adding, "She was terrific. I'm so grateful."

The role was a highly dramatic one and turned out to be a terrific experience. Kenneth Johnson, the executive producer, and Bixby became her good friends. Johnson said, as Hartley later recalled, "If the baby cries, we'll just stop the camera and you'll go into the Winnebago [portable dressing room] and nurse."

Hartley won her Emmy for an episode called "Married." In the show she marries David Banner, alias the Incredible Hulk, but then finds herself stricken by a terminal illness.

For Hartley, the best part of that 1979 Emmy night was sharing it with her family. Her mother was present, and also her husband and brother, while her nursing baby was in a nearby hotel with a nanny. At one point during the proceedings, Hartley had to leave to nurse her baby. She remembers being concerned about staining her gown.

In all, it was a glorious night for Hartley. Alan Alda, who had written the "Inga" episode of *M*A*S*H* for her, also won an Emmy for Best Writing in a Comedy or Comedy-Variety or Musical Series. To top off the night, Hartley's commercials for Polaroid ran during the Emmy telecast.

Walter Cronkite, recipient of the second annual ATAS Governors Award in 1979, started as CBS anchorman on the evening news in 1962. Among his Emmys was one in 1970 for his coverage of the journey of Apollo XI to the moon. He followed Edward R. Murrow into the Television Academy Hall of Fame. He was presented with the Governors Award at the 1979 prime-time Emmy telecast.

Awards event in 1979 featured President Carter's tribute to three television newsmen killed in Nicaragua and Guyana. The often-honored *ABC Theatre* took top honors for "Friendly Fire," a three-hour Vietnam antiwar drama. The film won a total of four Emmys. In the most predictable vote, the Outstanding Limited Series was *Roots, the Next Generations*, the 12-hour, seven-episode sequel to 1977's most-honored miniseries. ABC's *Taxi*, which debuted in the 1978–79 season, won three Emmys, including Outstanding Comedy Series. The same network's *The Jericho Mile* telefilm also won three, including one for Peter Strauss as Outstanding Lead Actor. But no other program or series took more than two Emmys. *Lou Grant* won for Best Drama Series. The Arnold Schapiro–produced *Scared Straight!*, a syndicated documentary originally created for a local L.A. television station, won as Outstanding Informational Program. (It also won an Oscar.)

Two of the top acting Emmys were big surprises. Mariette Hartley,

Distinguished Career
Hall of Famer Fred Coe

Fred Coe, a member of the Academy of Television Arts & Sciences Hall of Fame, won an Emmy in 1955 as Best Producer of a Live Series for NBC's *Producers' Showcase*. It was hardly the sum of his accomplishments. Coming out of the early days of network television as manager of new program development for NBC, Coe was the eminent producer of live plays during the era that has come to be known as the golden age of television.

As early as 1947, Coe directed an NBC Sunday prime-time half hour called *The Borden Show*, which offered a different format—dramas, films, variety shows, puppet shows—each week. From 1951 until 1955, he produced the *Goodyear TV Playhouse* for NBC. It was a showcase for the talents of young playwrights such as Paddy Chayefsky and actors such as Bette Davis, Julie Harris, Kim Stanley, Debbie Reynolds, Thelma Ritter, Roddy McDowall, Ralph Bellamy, and relative unknowns such as Ernest Borgnine, Rod Steiger, Eva Marie Saint, Paul Newman, Grace Kelly, Walter Matthau, and Martin Balsam.

Coe wrote and produced "This Time Next Year" for *Philco TV Playhouse* and produced "The Parole Chief," which starred Sidney Poitier, for *Philco-Goodyear Playhouse* and Tad Mosel's "Man in the Middle of the Ocean" for the same series. He was executive producer of the gentle, unassuming 1950s sitcom *Mr. Peepers*, which brought actors Wally Cox, Marion Lorne, and Tony Randall to prominence.

As a last hurrah, Coe produced "The Miracle Worker" in 1979 as part of the *NBC Theatre* series of dramatic specials. He died prior to the 32nd annual Emmy Awards in 1980. "The Miracle Worker" won for Outstanding Special, Drama or Comedy. The award for Outstanding Lead Actress in a Limited Series or a Special went to the play's star, Patty Duke Astin. Prestigious awards indeed, but they were not a fitting finale to a distinguished career. Coe had helped put prime-time television on the map. He produced shows that viewers talked about in supermarkets and offices the next day.

Sadly and ironically, the presentations ceremony at which he received his last and posthumous award was boycotted by actors as part of a strike against the TV networks, studios, and production companies. His star, Patty Duke Astin, was among the actors who did not show up.

previously nominated for her dramatic work, won for *The Incredible Hulk*, and Ron Liebman won for *Kaz*, a canceled CBS series. Fred DeCordova took home an award for producing *The Tonight Show Starring Johnny Carson*, and Jack Haley Jr. won for producing the 51st Academy Awards show on television. Two Oscar winners, Marlon Brando and Bette Davis, were honored, but neither was present to accept their awards. Brando won for *Roots: The Next Generations* and

Davis for a CBS drama, *Strangers: The Story of a Mother and Daughter*. Popular choices were Ruth Gordon for a role on *Taxi*, and Robert Guillaume and Esther Rolle for supporting roles, he in the ABC sitcom *Soap*, and she in the NBC telefilm *Summer of My German Soldier*.

Three legends received special awards. The Governors Award went to Walter Cronkite, who was president of the academy 25 years earlier. A special presentation was given to "Mr. Television" himself, Milton Berle. And CBS founder William S. Paley was given the Trustees Award. While humbly honoring its past, the Emmys entered the new decade of the 1980s facing the need to incorporate the new medium of cable.

In a special presentation in 1979, the TV Academy honored Milton Berle as "Mr. Television." One of the earliest Emmy winners, Berle was named Most Outstanding Kinescope (a film record of a TV program) Personality in 1949, the same year his *Texaco Star Theater*—easily the most popular of early television's offerings—was honored as Best Kinescope Show.

1980-89

n 1980, television audiences saw Cable News Network become a 24-hour news service and the "Who Shot J.R.?" episode of CBS' *Dallas* command the highest rating for any regular series program in modern TV history, with a 53.3 rating and a 76 share of the audience. Ronald Reagan became the 40th president of the United States after a landslide victory over Jimmy Carter. Republicans controlled the Senate for the first time since 1964. A boycott was conducted by more than 50 nations, including the United States, against the 1980 22nd Olympic Games in Moscow to protest the Soviet invasion of Afghanistan. Attempts made on the lives of President Reagan and Pope John Paul II were caught by TV cameras, as was the assassination of President Anwar el-Sadat of Egypt. Five Electronic News Gathering cameras were rolling

The cast of *M*A*S*H*, one of TV's most popular and honored programs. (Left to right) Mike Farrell, Alan Alda, David Ogden Stiers, Loretta Swit, Harry Morgan, Jamie Farr, and William Christopher. The show, which lasted 11 seasons and ended its run with a classic 1983 episode, also featured Larry Linville, Gary Burghoff, McLean Stevenson, and Wayne Rogers in its regular lineup.

132

(Right) Johnny Carson, an ATAS Governors Award honoree in 1980 and an inductee in the Television Academy Hall of Fame, reigned supreme over late-night comedy for more than 30 years with *The Tonight Show*.

(Below) Steve Allen, comedian, pianist, composer, writer, producer, director, actor, and first host of *The Tonight Show*, was in the third group of seven inductees to the Television Academy Hall of Fame.

(Below right) Mikhail Baryshnikov and Liza Minnelli in the ABC dance special "Baryshnikov on Broadway," choreographed by Ron Field. The special, which aired on April 26, 1980, won four Emmys, including Outstanding Variety or Music Program.

Spotlight on Powers Boothe

The 32nd annual Emmy Awards will be long remembered as the night of an actors' boycott. But it's also remembered for two profiles in courage.

Powers Boothe was a largely unknown actor. He had a supporting role in the NBC drama *Skag*, which starred Karl Malden as a steel-mill worker in Pittsburgh and aired briefly in January and February 1980. That April, Boothe played the Rev. Jim Jones in CBS' two-parter, *Guyana Tragedy: The Story of Jim Jones*, for which he earned an Emmy nomination.

By September 7, television actors were in the seventh week of a strike by the Screen Actors Guild (SAG) and the American Federation of Television and Radio Artists (AFTRA). All TV series were being affected, including the Emmy telecast. The Emmy Awards were boycotted by SAG and AFTRA members in support of their strike against the TV networks and suppliers of prime-time series programming. Powers Boothe was the only one of 52 nominated performers present for the Emmy Awards telecast on NBC. Coincidentally, he won an Emmy for Outstanding Actor in a Limited Series or a Special. After receiving a standing ovation, he said: "This either is the most courageous moment of my career, or the stupidest."

That same evening, Roger Young won a directing award for an episode of *Lou Grant* called "Cop." He looked out over the audience at the Pasadena Civic Auditorium, and saw mostly people who work behind the cameras: art directors and scenic designers, casting executives, cinematographers, costume supervisors, directors, electronic production people, graphic designers, makeup artists and hairstylists, sound editors, and writers. Other attendees included television executives, public relations people, producers, managers, lawyers, and agents. Young held his golden statuette and said, "A lot of the stars of television are here tonight."

Maybe the best way to remember the 32nd annual Emmy Awards is as the night those people who serve TV behind the scenes were not merely distant onlookers to the stars.

"The man is much better known in Hollywood today than he was 24 hours ago."

—Producer Gene Reynolds commenting about Powers Boothe, the only one of 52 nominated performers to defy the professional actors' guild strike and attend the 32nd annual Emmy Awards, 1980

Emmy Memories
Isabel Sanford

"Winning the Emmy Award as Outstanding Lead Actress in a Comedy Series for my role as Louise on *The Jeffersons* (1980–81) was a dream come true! It was a moment I will never forget. Of course, many people who saw it probably won't forget it either. I guess you could say that my entrance and acceptance speech was kind of memorable, although I hadn't planned it that way.

"I was back stage in the Green Room [at the Pasadena Civic Auditorium] with my costar Sherman Hemsley. We were set to present an award that year. I was busy socializing and visiting with my fellow actors who were also waiting to be called out to present other awards. I wasn't really paying too much attention to what else was going on. I was having a good time. Then someone in the Green Room yelled out, 'Hey, Isabel, they're calling your category.' Then I became a nervous wreck—on the inside. I wanted to appear cool about the whole thing. Never expecting to win (I had been nominated several times before and never won), I picked up a piece of cheese from the buffet table and popped it into my mouth. I figured it would help me be occupied when someone else's name was called [other nominees were Cathryn Damon and Katherine Helmond, both for *Soap*, Eileen Brennan for *Taxi*, and Lynn Redgrave for *House Calls*]. I didn't want it to be uncomfortable or awkward for me when I didn't win.

"The piece of cheese landed inside my mouth as I heard Gregory Harrison, the presenter in my category, announce 'And the winner is...' I didn't really hear much of anything else after that, except I became aware of all this commotion around me. Finally, I guess I heard someone say, 'Isabel, that's you! They called you! You won!'

"I didn't really give any thought to the cheese as I was led from the Green Room back stage onto the stage to accept my Emmy. It wasn't until I got to the podium and Gregory handed me the Emmy Award that it dawned on me that I had to speak, to say something, and what was I going to do with this cheese in my mouth? You have to understand that all of this occurred over a period of seconds, but living through it and recalling it now, it might as well have been hours.

"I swear, I never had so much trouble before or since chewing a piece of cheese. Anyway, the applause died down and there I was. Me, my Emmy, and the cheese in my mouth while the world waited for me to say something profound, something touching, something appreciative, something thankful. None of that occurred to me at that moment, only the thought of what was I going to do with this cheese in my mouth. I couldn't very well spit it out on national television. How becoming of an Emmy winner would that be? So, I just stood there, chewing. I guess whatever expression was on my face kind of summed up my situation, because while I said nothing, the audience laughed.

"Finally, with the cheese chewed and swallowed, I cleared my throat, looked out to the camera and to the audience, and said, 'At last!' It got a huge laugh.

"Later, people were never quite sure whether 'At last!' referred to my being able to swallow the cheese and speak—or if it was in reference to my winning after many years of previous Emmy nominations and losses.

"To set the record straight, the truth is my comment did refer to the cheese, at first. But it also was a remark from my heart to 'at last' have been able to thank my peers, my colleagues, and Norman Lear [producer of *The Jeffersons*] for the opportunity to be involved with a terrific hit show that ran for 11 seasons.

"My Emmy Award holds a very special place for me, in my heart and in my home. Now, I've got to get busy and try and get me a matching pair."

Trivia

Private Benjamin was a 1980 hit movie starring Goldie Hawn; it was also a 1981–83 CBS sitcom starring Lorna Patterson. Both versions featured Eileen Brennan as Captain Doreen Lewis, Private Benjamin's frustrated company commander.

Brennan, whose big break came in the 1960 off-Broadway musical *Little Mary Sunshine*, won a 1981 Emmy as best supporting actress in a comedy. Ironically, she had received an Oscar nomination the year before for the same role but lost.

when John Hinckley's shooting of Reagan became history's most heavily covered assassination attempt.

In 1980, ATAS then-President John H. Mitchell created the ATAS Television Academy Hall of Fame. Previously, the Academy had honored lifetime achievement and contributions to television at its annual Governors Ball. That same year, the TV Academy adjusted the 1979–80 Emmy Awards to reflect what appeared to be a resurgence of variety/music shows, and added three awards—for directors, writers, and art directors. Also in 1980, Johnny Carson was the recipient of the Governors Award. John Leverence, former conference administrator for the American Film Institute, was named awards administrator for the Academy in 1980.

Ken Ehrlich, writer-producer of the Grammy Awards earlier in the year, executive produced the 1980 Emmy Awards telecast on NBC. The only thing missing from the 32nd annual event were the actors and actresses, who boycotted the ceremony because it occurred during their seven-week-old strike against the television networks and major TV and film producers. After the original cohosts—Bob Newhart, Lee Remick, and Michael Landon—dropped out in support of the boycott, the show was hosted by Steve Allen and Dick Clark, who were lined up a mere two days before the event. Only one of the 52 nominated performers, Powers Boothe, was in the audience, and he won for his portrayal of Jim Jones in the CBS miniseries *The Guyana Tragedy*. He told the TV audience he had debated "long and hard" about whether to attend, finally deciding he would because "this is America and one

136

Shogun on NBC was 1981's Best Limited Series. Based on the best-seller by James Clavell, the 12-hour miniseries starred Richard Chamberlain (left) as John Blackstone, the English pilot of a wrecked Dutch ship who becomes a samurai in feudal Japan. That year, the police drama *Hill Street Blues* won a record eight Emmys. The statue for best supporting actor went to Michael Conrad (below left), who played Sgt. Phil Esterhaus (Conrad won again the following year); Barbara Bosson (below right) played Fay Furillo for five of the police drama's six years, and was nominated several times but never took home an Emmy.

(Left) Special tribute was paid to Paddy Chayefsky at the 33rd annual prime-time Emmys in 1981. One of early television's greatest writers, Chayefsky (far left) scripted such notable works as "Marty," "The Bachelor Party," and "The Tenth Man," and was among the first seven inductees into the Television Academy Hall of Fame.

(Below) The producing-directing partnership of Gary Smith and Dwight Hemion has garnered more Emmys than any other team in history.

has to do what one believes in. I believe in the Academy. I also believe in my fellow actors in their stand." The audience of nonperformers gave Boothe a standing ovation.

NBC Theatre's "The Miracle Worker," Fred Coe's last production, was named the finest dramatic special of the year. *IBM Presents Baryshnikov on Broadway* won four Emmys, including best variety show, but *Lou Grant* led all programs with six awards.

In 1981, the year of the 33rd annual Emmy Awards, the Federal Communications Commission opened the regulatory door to direct satellite-to-home television service, amid fierce objections from the broadcasting industry. Robert Montgomery (whose NBC live anthology series, *Robert Montgomery Presents,* won a 1952 Emmy as best dramatic program) died at age 77. And *Hill Street Blues,* a first-year police drama on NBC that had failed to find a large audience, received 21 nominations and won eight Emmys, including one for best drama series. No series had ever received as many nominations in one season, and none had ever won as many statuettes.

"I think she deserved this award—not only for her performance on camera but also for the performance off camera. I think she showed the same courage and determination and dignity that Golda did."

—Pia Lindstrom, accepting an Emmy as Outstanding Lead Actress in a Miniseries or a Special for *A Woman Called Golda* on behalf of her mother, Ingrid Bergman, who died the month before of cancer, 1982

Mickey Rooney
If At First You Don't Succeed...

Mickey Rooney wasn't present at the 34th annual Emmy Awards when the members of the Television Academy awarded him an Emmy for Outstanding Lead Actor in a Limited Series or a Special. Rooney was honored for playing the title role in *Bill*, a fact-based story of a retarded adult released from an institution. It aired on CBS on December 22, 1981, with Dennis Quaid costarring.

Somehow the Emmy in 1982 made up for the one he didn't win in 1957, when he was nominated for Best Single Performance by an Actor for playing the lead in Rod Serling's "The Comedian" on CBS' *Playhouse 90*. Then 37 years old, showbiz vet Rooney, having been in his share of clinkers, felt fortunate to be in a play by one of television's finest writers. But fellow nominee Peter Ustinov won the Emmy for his role in the NBC *Omnibus* production of "The Life of Samuel Johnson." Rooney was nominated two years later for his performance in the title role of "Eddie," in an *ALCOA-Goodyear Theatre* production for NBC, only to see the award go to dancer Fred Astaire.

Rooney received his third nomination in 1962 for a performance on NBC's *The Dick Powell Theatre*, but Peter Falk, for his work on the same anthology series, took home the Emmy. Maybe it was because of frustration that Rooney was not present to accept his Emmy when it was finally his turn. "It's like the old saying," he observed later, "you win a few, you lose a few. Just being in this great business is the thrill of it all."

"A lot of the stars of television are here tonight. This night is not a complete bust because the actors are not here. There are a lot of people behind the camera who also help make television roll so we don't have to feel like we're the second cousins here."
—Director Roger Young, winner of an Emmy for an episode of *Lou Grant*, commenting about actors honoring the AFTRA/SAG walkout, 1980

"I'm glad to be out of Hollywood and in the city of brotherly love, Pasadena."
—John Ritter, presenter at the creative arts Emmy Awards, held the day before the strike-plagued 32nd annual prime-time Emmy Awards, 1980

Three of the show's actors won Emmys: Barbara Babcock as Outstanding Lead Actress in a Drama Series, Daniel J. Travanti as Outstanding Lead Actor, and Michael Conrad as Outstanding Supporting Actor. Two other cast members—Betty Thomas and Barbara Bosson—were among the five nominees for Outstanding Supporting Actress, but they lost to Nancy Marchand of *Lou Grant*. *Hill Street Blues* also won Emmys for writing, directing, cinematography, and film sound editing. ABC's *Taxi* was named best comedy series and picked up a total of five awards, including Outstanding Lead Actor for Judd Hirsch and Outstanding Supporting Actor for Danny DeVito.

Danny Arnold
Personal Sacrifice, Professional Reward

Writer-actor, but mostly producer, Danny Arnold, a two-time Emmy winner, was an unforgettable television figure. A transplanted New Yorker and an ex-Marine, he never lost his Big Apple accent nor softened his tough-talking personality.

He appeared in summer stock, nightclubs, and vaudeville; acted in such motion pictures as *Scared Stiff* with Dean Martin and Jerry Lewis; performed on the team's TV show; and wrote some of their comedy sketches. A self-proclaimed "workaholic," he was arguably the hardest-working, most compulsive perfectionist ever to produce an Emmy Award–winning series.

And in fact, he produced two of them: NBC's critically acclaimed but low-rated, short-lived *My World and Welcome To It* (with ATAS Hall of Fame's Sheldon Leonard as executive producer) and the ABC smash *Barney Miller*. It was during that show's 1975–82 run, for which Arnold (and coexecutive producer Roland Kibbee) won an Emmy for Outstanding Comedy Series, that his obssession with the work at hand got the best of him. Arnold suffered a heart attack and underwent a bypass operation after he later admitted to a prolonged binge of overeating, drinking, and smoking.

What does it take to produce an Emmy Award–winning half-hour comedy? For Danny Arnold, *Barney Miller* was his life. He agonized every minute of every episode.

Highlights of the telecast included tributes to Lucille Ball, celebrating the 30th anniversary of *I Love Lucy*; TV "Golden Age" writer Paddy Chayefsky; and Lawrence Welk, whose prime-time music series ran on ABC for 16 seasons. Shirley MacLaine, who cohosted the Awards with Ed Asner, told Ball, "You're just a human national treasure." Gary Smith and Dwight Hemion, both multi–Emmy Award winners, handled producing and directing.

Actress Ingrid Bergman passed away in August 1982, a month before the 34th annual Emmy Awards. A winner in 1960 for her lead performance in NBC's production of "The Turn of the Screw" on the *Ford Startime* series, she was honored posthumously for her final performance as Israeli leader Golda Meir in *A Woman Called Golda*, which was also named Outstanding Drama Special.

Nineteen eighty-two was the year American broadcasters and the U.S. Justice Department ended restraints on the length and frequency of television commercials, and AT&T agreed to divest itself of its 23 local telephone companies after a seven-year antitrust suit. The Emmys that year were hosted by Marlo Thomas and John Forsythe. Once again,

PBS' *Creativity With Bill Moyers* won a 1982 Emmy as Outstanding Informational Series. Executive producers of the show were Merton Koplin and Charles Grinker, and the coordinating producer was Betsy McCarthy. One segment featured Carroll O'Connor and Norman Lear. Moyers also won Emmys in 1974 (as best TV news broadcaster) and in 1984 and 1993 for best informational programs.

The 10-hour *Marco Polo*, produced by the Italian TV network RAI and NBC, was voted Outstanding Limited Series for the 1981–82 season. It was filmed in Italy, Morocco, Mongolia, and China, and starred Ken Marshall and Leonard Nimoy and some 5,000 extras.

Fame, a drama about the lives and aspirations of students at a New York City school for actors, dancers, and musicians, based on a 1980 movie of the same name, won four Emmys in 1982. (Left to right) Cynthia Gibb, Debbie Allen, and Erica Gimpel.

SCTV
Life Imitates Parody

Writer/performer Dave Thomas had been with Second City since the beginning when, as *Second City TV*, it was a half-hour syndicated series. This was prior to NBC's Friday late-night series, *SCTV Network*. It seemed odd to be attending the 32nd Emmy Awards in Pasadena on September 19, 1982, because SCTV's bread and butter was doing parodies of television. This insightful and funny group of writers and performers from the Second City company in Toronto had even done a parody of the Emmys.

Now they had four of the five nominations for Outstanding Writing in a Variety or Music Program and weren't disappointed. The writers of the "Moral Majority Show" episode of the series were announced as Emmy winners.

Yet Thomas, as he later wrote in his 1996 book *SCTV Behind the Scenes* (with Robert Crane and Susan Carney), "couldn't believe it." To him it felt "that I wasn't actually in my body, that I was watching it all from some other vantage point." It reminded him of the parody of the Emmys the previous year, when *Hill Street Blues* won many awards. Standing at the back of the stage next to writer/performer Catherine O'Hara, Thomas reminded her how funny they all thought it was when the *Hill Street* people—what appeared to be 30 of them—all came up to accept their Emmys.

"With a staff and a cast that large, just by voting for themselves, they could have turned the Academy around," Thomas wrote in his book. Now, here was Thomas and his colleagues on stage in real life, and when all were counted there were 18 writers on stage. "We couldn't do that joke any more. We had become a parody of ourselves," Thomas wrote.

For the record, the talented 18-member writing staff of SCTV on stage at the Pasadena Civic Auditorium to accept Emmys in 1982, along with Thomas and O'Hara, were Jeffrey Barron, Dick Blasucci, John Candy, Chris Cluess, Bob Dolman, Joe and Paul Flaherty, Stuart Kreisman, Eugene Levy, Andrea Martin, John McAndrew, Brian McConnachie, Rick Moranis, Mert Rich, Michael Short, and Doug Steckler.

The next year, many of these same writers were on stage again, winning Emmys for the "Energy Ball/Sweeps Week" episode.

"The two Emmys were a fluke. It was an accident. The people in the business, the writers in the Academy, sensed we were on to something," says writer Doug Steckler in the Thomas book. He also noted that in 1983, *SCTV Network* had all five nominations in the Outstanding Writing in a Variety or Music Program category. "It wasn't a question of whether the show would win but which episode would take the prize," he quipped.

"More people will be aware of it and give it a try."

—Michael Kozoll, sharing an Emmy for writing the ratings-troubled series *Hill Street Blues*, NBC, 1981

"I've waited so long for this, my humility is all gone."

— Veteran actress Isabel Sanford, accepting her Emmy as lead actress in a comedy series for *The Jeffersons*, CBS, 1981

A Grand Movie Lady Passes the Torch

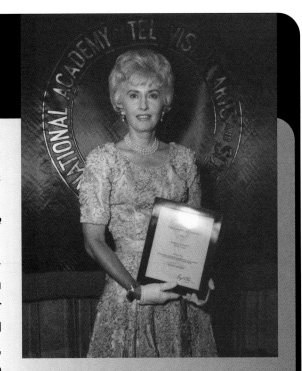

Barbara Stanwyck had a distinguished career in motion pictures. Her role as the scheming wife in the archetypical film noir of the '40s, *Double Indemnity*, is unforgettable, as is her fireball performance in the wonderful romp, *Ball of Fire*. But she also won Emmys in 1961 and 1966 for NBC's *The Barbara Stanwyck Show* and ABC's *Big Valley*.

In 1982, Stanwyck, then 75 years old, received an honorary Oscar at the Academy Awards. The next year, she won an Emmy as best actress in a limited series or special for ABC's 10-hour love story *The Thorn Birds*. Stanwyck paid tribute in her acceptance speech to one of her competitors, Ann-Margret, who had been nominated for her performance as a terminally ill mother seeking homes for her 10 kids in *Who Will Love My Children?*

"She gave us a film last season in which she gave one of the finest, most beautiful performances I have ever seen," Stanwyck said, concluding with a declaration: "Ann-Margret, you were superb."

Ann-Margret was in the audience, seated next to her husband, Roger Smith. She buried her head on his shoulder and quietly wept.

Hill Street Blues won as best drama, and two of its stars, Daniel J. Travanti and Michael Conrad, also were repeat winners. In sum, the show took home six awards. In its final season, ABC's *Barney Miller*, a comedy that took place in a police precinct, was named Outstanding Comedy Series. The NBC musical-drama series *Fame*, which was based on the successful Alan Parker film, won Emmys for directing, art direction, cinematography, choreography, and costume supervision.

For a finale, the 1982 telecast saluted Kate Smith, a favorite singer in radio days and an early musical-variety host in television. The wheelchair-bound Smith was helped onto the stage by Bob Hope. And producer-director Dwight Hemion, who, with his partner Gary Smith, was executive producer of the Emmy telecast on ABC, added to his record Emmy total by capturing a 14th for his direction of a Goldie Hawn special, *Goldie and Kids…Listen to Us*.

In 1983, ABC's *The Day After*, which depicted the aftermath of a

Emmy's All-Time Winner
Hallmark's Hall of Fame

Hallmark Cards Inc. of Kansas City, the world's biggest greeting card company, has been very good to television. The Emmys, in turn, have been very good to Hallmark.

It's a connection that has been ongoing since that day in 1951 when the company moved to what was then the new medium of television with a 15-minute weekly interview show called *Hallmark Presents Sarah Churchill*. Later that same year, Hallmark began sponsoring a program titled *Hallmark Television Playhouse*, also hosted by Sarah Churchill. Three weeks later, the company changed the title to *Hallmark Hall of Fame* and television's long-running and most-honored fully sponsored dramatic series was born.

Hallmark Hall of Fame has won 78 Emmys, more than any other dramatic series. Among this total, 12 Emmys have been for Outstanding Movie for Television. Dozens of the world's finest actors have performed in Hallmark shows over the 47-year run (and counting) of the dramatic anthology series. Many of them have won Emmys for their performances, including Dame Judith Anderson, Hume Cronyn, Ruby Dee, Maurice Evans, Lynne Fontanne, Julie Harris, Alfred Lunt, Jessica Tandy, Peter Ustinov, and James Woods.

Hallmark's 1960 presentation of "Macbeth," which was the seventh Shakespearean production offered by the series, walked away with five Emmys, and was the major award winner of that season.

The 1965 production of "The Magnificent Yankee," starring Alfred Lunt and Lynne Fontanne, also won five Emmys. "Promise," the 1986 presentation starring James Garner and James Woods, is one of the most-honored shows in television history. Its honors include five Emmys, two Golden Globes, a Christopher Award, the Humanitas Prize, and a Peabody Award.

The *Hallmark Hall of Fame* production of "Love Is Never Silent," also in 1986, broke new ground with the casting of two deaf actors, and won two Emmys including Outstanding Comedy-Drama Special.

Addressing social issues such as the problems of the hearing-impaired is one of the *Hall of Fame*'s claims to fame. In 1969, the program presented "Teacher, Teacher," an original play that told of a mentally retarded boy emerging from his isolation through the encouragement of his teacher, portrayed by David McCallum. The key role of the retarded boy was played by 13-year-old Bill Schulmann, himself mentally handicapped. His acting won him a special Emmy citation.

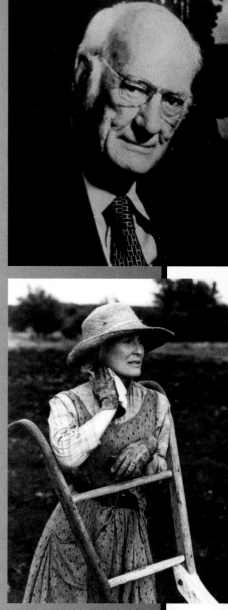

In 1961, Joyce C. Hall, founder and president of Hallmark Cards, was presented with the first Emmy ever awarded a sponsor, for the company's contribution to television through the *Hall of Fame* productions. Hall was convinced that as a sponsor Hallmark didn't need to get the largest audience on TV. "We wanted the best."

It was in 1961, too, that the two-hour production of "Macbeth" was voted the finest achievement in drama for the 1960–61 season; its stars Dame Judith Anderson and Maurice Evans were recipients of the two top acting awards; and its director, George Schaefer, was named the finest director of the year.

In 1982, the fifth annual ATAS Governors Award went to Hallmark Cards, Inc., for Hallmark Hall of Fame, for dedication to the standards of quality throughout its years on television, and for bringing to millions of Americans "an opportunity to see the classic dramas of the past and outstanding works of contemporary playwrights."

Hall was inducted posthumously into the Television Academy Hall of Fame in the spring of 1985. His son Donald pledged on that occasion "to pursue the ongoing promise of this industry to inform and entertain with consistent excellence."

(Opposite, top) Donald J. Hall, the president of Hallmark Cards Inc., and ATAS President John H. Mitchell at 1982's prime-time Emmy telecast. Hallmark, producer of *Hallmark Hall of Fame*, was presented with the Governors Award for its long history of quality television. (Top, right) Joyce C. Hall, founder of Hallmark cards. Some Hallmark landmarks include (counterclockwise from left) "The Gathering Storm," a biography of Winston Churchill starring Virginia McKenna and Richard Burton; "Peter Pan" with Mia Farrow and Danny Kaye; "Gideon's Trumpet" with Henry Fonda; "Sarah, Plain and Tall" with Glenn Close; and "The Promise" with James Garner and James Woods.

(Above) Merv Griffin (right) hosted a talk/variety show from 1962–86, which featured such guests as *The A Team*'s strong man Mr. T. (center) and comedian Don Rickles. Griffin, who cohosted the 21st prime-time Emmys in 1969 with Bill Cosby, won daytime Emmys in 1982 and 1984 for best host in a variety series, along with additional Emmys for executive producing the game show *Jeopardy!* from 1990–94.

Ed Flanders, Dr. Donald Westphall of NBC's *St. Elsewhere*, won an Emmy as the Outstanding Lead Actor in a Drama Series for the 1982–83 season.

"I can't believe we've got something up here that's bigger than the cast of *Hill Street Blues.*"
—Actor-writer Joe Flaherty, serving as spokesman for the 18-member writing staff of NBC's SCTV Comedy Network, all on stage to accept Emmys for Outstanding Writing in a Variety or Music Program, 1982

Pavarotti in Philadelphia, a PBS special starring Luciano Pavarotti, was deemed the Outstanding Classical Program in the Performing Arts for the 1982–83 season.

(Left) Jane Curtin was honored in both 1983 and 1984 as Outstanding Lead Actress in a Comedy Series for *Kate & Allie.* She costarred in the CBS sitcom with Susan Saint James.

(Below) Jean Simmons and Barbara Stanwyck display their awards for Outstanding Supporting Actress and Outstanding Lead Actress in a Limited Series or a Special for *The Thorn Birds* in 1983. The four-night ABC miniseries, based on Colleen McCullough's best-selling novel, won a total of six Emmys.

"I am one of the blessed people of the universe because I get to do work I adore, with people I adore. To have you give me this [Emmy] is almost too much, but I'll take it."

—Daniel J. Travanti accepting his second consecutive Emmy for playing precinct chief Captain Frank Furillo on NBC's *Hill Street Blues,* 1982

"I didn't think of it in those terms coming in, but obviously you're happy to see this, you're proud to see the people you have faith in do so well. I'm happy for them."

—NBC Chairman Grant Tinker, commenting about his network winning 21 of the 29 Emmys presented at the 33rd annual awards event, 1983

Three-Year War, 11-Year Series

When *M*A*S*H*, the 11-season CBS hit about the three-year Korean War, ended its run on February 28, 1983, some television-industry experts figured it was the end of an era.

Advertising agency executive Bob Igiel of N. W. Ayer, then vice president, group media director, and manager of network programming, believed so.

"It is unlikely we'll ever again see a show that will run 11 years and have that kind of grip on such a large section of the audience," he said. "Television is different today. *M*A*S*H* managed to bridge the gap between the three-network days and those of the multichoice era."

"Goodbye, Farewell, and Amen," the two-and-a-half-hour grand finale episode, brought in blockbuster ad prices and stimulated an amazing array of related programming. The television event of the '80s, it attracted a 60.2 rating, reaching an average audience per minute of 50,150,000 homes. That episode outranked the "Who Shot J.R.?" installment of the

CBS series *Dallas* as the highest-rated entertainment program of all time. "Who Shot J.R.?" produced a 53.3 rating when it aired in November 1980.

As striking evidence that mighty oaks from acorns grow, *M*A*S*H* ended its first season behind 45 other programs in audience, with a rating of 17.5 and a share of 27, when a prime-time share under 30 was considered "not likely to succeed." And *M*A*S*H* didn't succeed remarkably in the Emmy competition, despite receiving an impressive total of 99 nominations. The big Emmy year for *M*A*S*H* was 1974, when it was voted the Outstanding Comedy Series, and its star Alan Alda won for both Outstanding Lead Actor in a Comedy Series and Actor of the Year. That same year Jackie Cooper, for his *M*A*S*H* work, won an Emmy for best directing in comedy, with one of two other contenders, Gene Reynolds, for the same series (Reynolds subsequently won twice as best director).

Overall, Alda won three times for best actor for his portrayal of Hawkeye Pierce. He also won for comedy writing and directing, making him the only person to win in three separate categories. Supporting players Harry Morgan, Gary Burghoff, and Loretta Swit (twice) also won Emmys. At the 35th annual Emmy Awards, the program's last, it didn't win any Emmys, but the cast of *M*A*S*H* was ushered onstage to a standing ovation.

Richard Kiley
...Has His Say

Richard Kiley was no stranger to the Emmy spotlight in 1988 when he won as Outstanding Lead Actor in a Drama Series. His first Emmy was in 1983 when, in a surprising turn of events, he, not Richard Chamberlain, won. Both were in the cast of the ABC miniseries *The Thorn Birds*, but Chamberlain was the star and Kiley a supporting actor. While Kiley won in his category, Chamberlain, in the lead actor category, lost to Tommy Lee Jones for his performance in NBC's *The Executioner's Song*.

Five years later Kiley was being honored for his performance as Joe Gardner in the warm NBC family drama, *A Year in the Life*. The title was prophetic. A spinoff from a miniseries, *A Year in the Life* had only a year of life on the network.

It was a project near and dear to Kiley. In his acceptance, Kiley said he had "nothing but affection and admiration" for his costars, and "nothing but sadness for the corporate myopia that killed a fine show." Backstage, Kiley continued to publicly lament the demise of "a very delicate, low-key, high-class" program.

The outspoken actor was not yet finished. There are some quality programs, he acknowledged, yet "the tendency to do expedient crap is always there." They seemed words guaranteed to keep him off the Emmy stage, if not network television altogether.

Yet six years later Kiley held his third Emmy, this time for best guest actor in a drama series for the "Buried Alive" episode of the CBS series *Picket Fences*.

nuclear attack on Lawrence, Kansas, was watched by half the adult population of the United States. It was also the year *M*A*S*H* ended its run after 251 episodes. The two-and-a-half-hour final episode of the series was the most-watched program in television history, attaining a 60.2 rating and 77 percent share of the audience.

Also in 1983, actress Diana Muldaur became the Television Academy's first woman president. During her tenure, ATAS agreed to take on administration of the Daytime Emmy Awards, and joined the New York–based National Academy of Television Arts & Sciences as presenters of the Daytime Emmys.

Joan Rivers and Eddie Murphy cohosted the 35th annual Emmy Awards on NBC. Because of some risqué comments by Rivers (for example, describing the Alexis Carrington character on ABC's *Dynasty*

series as having had "more hands up her dress than the Muppets"), the NBC switchboard lit up with angry calls from viewers. The telecast was subsequently edited for the tape-delayed West Coast presentation.

NBC's rookie show *Cheers* was named best comedy series and also picked up Emmys for lead actress Shelley Long, director James Burrows, and writers Glen and Les Charles. For the third consecutive year, *Hill Street Blues* was chosen Outstanding Drama Series. Three performers from a third NBC series, *St. Elsewhere*, received Emmys as best dramatic actor, supporting actor, and supporting actress. *The Thorn Birds*, ABC's 10-hour love story set in the Australian outback, lost to the British import *Nicholas Nickleby* as Outstanding Limited Series, yet tied *Hill Street Blues* as the biggest individual program winner, with each capturing six Emmys. Acting Emmys for *The Thorn Birds* went to Barbara Stanwyck, Jean Simmons, and Richard Kiley. Tyne Daly, who played detective Mary Beth Lacy on CBS' canceled police series, *Cagney & Lacey*, won for Outstanding Lead Actress in a Drama Series.

The Governors Award for career achievement went to pioneer TV programmer and former NBC President Sylvester L. "Pat" Weaver. Credited with creating *The Tonight Show, Today*, and the concept of the TV special, Weaver accepted the statuette from Emmy telecast host Johnny Carson. The 1984 program was produced by Steve Binder.

In the presidential election of 1984, Ronald Reagan, onetime host of CBS' *General Electric Theatre*, easily defeated Walter Mondale, winning every state except Minnesota (Mondale's home) and Washington, D.C. The AIDS virus was independently discovered by research teams in both the United States and France. Michael Jackson's album *Thriller*

Q&A

Four-Time Emmy Director's "Total Adrenaline Rush"

Steve Binder, associated with comedy-variety shows since the 1960s, was producer-director of the prime-time Emmy Awards telecast from 1981 to 1984. A veteran of such programs as *The Danny Kaye Show* and *The Steve Allen Comedy Hour* for CBS, and many network specials, Binder was an Emmy Award winner as producer of "The Barry Manilow Special" for ABC, the Outstanding Special—Comedy-Variety or Music for 1976–77. Binder, in this question-and-answer interview, tells what it was like to supervise an Emmy telecast.

Q: You were producer-director of Emmy Awards shows, but Dwight Hemion and Gary Smith were executive producers. How did they find you?

A: It wasn't that they found me, we were all hired as a group by John Mitchell [then president of the Academy of Television Arts & Sciences].

Q: But didn't the network call the shots?

A: In those days [as now], the Emmys rotated. While the networks collaborated on selection, it was Mitchell who thought of and brought us in as a team. In this case, it wasn't Smith-Hemion. Dwight was out of the picture, and it was Gary and me.

Q: When you sit down for a preproduction meeting, what do you—the team—set out to do? Is there a goal? Is there a mission statement?

A: It's a problem. For the viewers, all they care about is the stars. Our goal was how do we get through the "infinite" number of "awards," and give the public as entertaining a show as possible? I think we did the last entertainment production numbers on awards shows. We did a great tribute to *Sesame Street*. We had Rod Steiger and Peter O'Toole do a tribute to Paddy Chayefsky. We had Roy Scheider doing a tribute to Edward R. Murrow. And we had a lot of what I call basic, nonawards creative ideas.

What amazes me, overall, is that (on all awards shows) the nominees, out of which will come winners, don't prepare their acceptance material. And the result is the artificial, mandated-limit (60 seconds or whatever) speeches, which are not very good. Acceptances should be the most entertaining part of the show, but because of unprepared or ill-prepared winners, it is too often boring.

Right now, awards shows are kind of a horse race, trying to get all the awards that must be given squeezed into the time allotted by the network. It's sort of foreplay without climax.

Some people describe entertainment as "the stuff between commercials," and I don't buy into that.

Q: Tell me, who is a good host? Not a name, but describe a person who is likely to do a good job hosting an awards show. In your four years you had a kind of mixed bag—Shirley MacLaine and Ed Asner, John Forsythe and Marlo Thomas, and the irreverent Eddie Murphy and Joan Rivers.

A: I think the host is incredibly important, especially in the Emmys. First, you have to appease the networks because of the revolving cycle. So you're quite limited in the "pool" of host talent to choose from because it's heavily influenced by what network is going to broadcast it.

The ideal host, in my opinion, is somebody who is of star power that the public wants to see in that role. It has to be someone who's fast on their feet, and articulate; someone comfortable in the role. That's why Bob Hope, Johnny Carson, and Billy Crystal have all been terrific hosts.

It's people, more often than not, who are out of the comedy entertainment arena. They're used to playing to live audiences, and it's a delicate line because a lot of entertainers have a real fear of getting up there for three hours and bombing.

Q: Does a good host have to be a good traffic cop or does that come from the booth?

A. It comes from the booth and from the staging. That's why the entertainment portions are so critically important because the rest of the show is formula—X number of awards, and Y number of acceptances, rules and such that viewers don't care much about. They want to see stars. They want to be entertained.

Q: Do you think there is a place for memorials at the Emmys? In 1982 there were memorials for Ingrid Bergman and for three shows, *Lou Grant*, *Barney Miller*, and *M*A*S*H*. Are these appropriate?

A: It depends on who and what is memorialized.

Q: Do you consider the four Emmy shows you did fun?

A: Absolutely. It's a total adrenaline rush. It's a lot of fun and pleasure because it goes back to "can't redo it, you can't take it back, once it happens, it happens."

I remember [in 1983] when right in the middle of his tribute to Edward R. Murrow, Roy Scheider's mike went out, and the stage manager, on his own, even before we reacted in the booth, ran out and fixed the microphone to a tremendous round of applause. And Roy, as a pro, had to get back into it with a now-functioning mike.

Q: An unplanned event lends flavor and excitement to a show such as Emmy?

A: People wait for something to go wrong. It's what was wonderful about live TV. I fear we have gotten too far away from that time. Some of the funniest moments in the history of TV have been stars improvising to get out of an "accident," an unplanned occurrence.

Those days are gone, unfortunately. Live, unplanned events and performers are exciting and wonderful, and the attitude today of "there's a boom shadow, we have to go back and fix it" is not what television was (and I hope may not be again) about. It's the spontaneous, the unexpected, the surprises that make viewers react and remember fondly.

Actor Edward James Olmos was awarded an Emmy in 1985 for his supporting role in NBC's hit show *Miami Vice*. The detective series took away a total of four awards that year.

sold more than 37 million copies, and Donald Duck celebrated his 50th birthday.

The 36th Emmy Awards on CBS saw *Hill Street Blues* become the most honored dramatic series in history with a total of 25 Emmys. The show picked up five awards, including its fourth in a row as Outstanding Drama Series, and ones for supporting actor and actress, directing, and film sound mixing. *Cheers* was named best comedy for the second year in a row.

Magnum P.I.'s Tom Selleck, who hosted the telecast, was named Outstanding Actor in a Drama Series. He seemed surprised and embarrassed and said a simple "Thank you," before continuing with his emcee duties. John Ritter of ABC's *Three's Company* won as best actor in a comedy. Cloris Leachman won her sixth Emmy, this time for Outstanding Individual Performance in a Variety or Music Program for "Screen Actors Guild 50th Anniversary Celebration" on CBS. Two Academy

The Cousteaus
Like Father, Like Son

Jean-Michel Cousteau, who won a 1985 Emmy, believes that working on TV documentaries, viewed by millions throughout the world, is a humbling experience. To him, the true value of the award concerned its validation of his goal: to provide understanding and appreciation of "the water planet."

His Emmy in the category of Outstanding Informational Special was as executive producer of Turner Broadcasting System's *Cousteau: Mississippi* (Andrew Solt, who produced, also won). After originating on Superstation WTBS Atlanta, the documentary was syndicated as two separate hours to more than 80 percent of the United States, or an estimated 71 million homes.

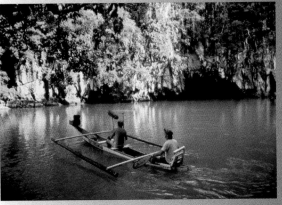

Jean-Michel has received numerous awards, including a Peabody for the *Cousteau's Amazon* series. But the Emmy was for a project that was different, one far off Cousteau's well-traveled and documented path. It was for the Cousteau family's first exploration of a U.S. mainland water system, the Mississippi and Missouri rivers.

Jean-Michel was the oldest son of Jacques-Yves Cousteau, who died in 1997 at age 87. Jean-Michel helped organize logistics for *The Undersea World of Jacques Cousteau*, which in 1972 won his father (and Marshall Flaum) an Emmy Award for Outstanding Achievement in Cultural Documentary Programming. That 13 years later he won his own Emmy made the award especially meaningful to him.

Memorable Moments
Secretary's Night Out Gets Her Emmy Spotlight

After costume designer Nolan Miller was nominated for a number of Emmys without winning, he thought of his close friend Barbara Stanwyck. "Every time she was nominated for an Academy Award she just knew that was her year, and then she would come home empty-handed," he remembered. "She got to the point where she said, 'I'm not going to get excited about it at all.'"

By 1984, Miller had reached that point, too. Although he was nominated for Outstanding Costume Design for a Series for "The Wedding" episode of ABC's *Dynasty*—a series known for its lavish sets and costumes—Miller was delighted but not overoptimistic. (He was also recovering from the flu.) His secretary, Jorjette Strumme, asked to use his tickets to the Emmy Awards presentations.

She went, and when Miller's name was called, before the folks onstage could say "the Academy is accepting the Emmy on his behalf," Strumme swept across the stage in a great ball gown. She made the acceptance with all the dignity and seriousness of a Nobel Prize winner, thanking members of the Academy for the great honor. She came to Miller's house afterward clutching the Emmy. He was lying on the sofa watching television, and couldn't have been more surprised and pleased.

His win was actually a tie, with the team of Bob Mackie (original costume concept) and Ret Turner (costumes) for *Mama's Family*.

Miller never denigrated his nominations. "When the nominations come out and you see your name among them, my gosh, it's very exciting," he said. "To be selected over all of the things that are done over a year and end up being one of the five people, it's really a great honor and quite thrilling."

Barbara Stanwyck was his closest and dearest friend for 30 years. He always dressed and escorted her to the Emmys. He was there in 1961 when she won her first Emmy for Outstanding Performance by an Actress in a Series (Lead) for *The Barbara Stanwyck Show*. In her haste to receive the kind of top honor that had eluded her in her film career, Stanwyck ripped the strap on her evening gown. It became one of Miller's fondest memories: The great lady of cinema on stage holding her gown up with one hand and holding the Emmy with the other.

Miller was also at Stanwyck's side in 1983, the year she won the last of her three Emmys (the second was in 1966 for *The Big Valley*) for her work in ABC's *The Thorn Birds* as Outstanding Lead Actress in a Limited Series or a Special.

"I was very lucky to have her as a friend," Miller said.

"So much of my work is shaped by Bill Cosby's wit and philosophy of what a family could be."

—Jay Sandrich, accepting an Emmy for outstanding directing in a comedy series, *The Cosby Show*, NBC, 1985

Costume Design
Blue-Collar Mama vs. Blue-Blooded Dynasty

The Emmy competition in 1984 for Outstanding Costume Design for a Series ended in a tie between opposites. Nolan Miller was chosen for the lavish styles of ABC's *Dynasty* series; and Bob Mackie and his colleague Ret Turner were honored for the blue-collar fashions of NBC's *Mama's Family*. One series was set among the opulent surroundings of Denver's "filthy rich," the other in the fictional Midwestern suburb of rednecked Raytown. The glamour of *Dynasty* was personified by Joan Collins, as a slinky, sensous temptress. Mama, a dowdy, gray-haired widow, was played by Vicki Lawrence.

Nobody could have been more shocked by the surprising tie than seven-time Emmy winner Mackie, renowned for working with such glamorous performers as Mitzi Gaynor and Cher. It wasn't simply that *Mama's Family* and *Dynasty* truly made for an odd couple—it was also because Mackie had little to do with the *Mama's Family* series. He had worked on *The Carol Burnett Show* for 11 seasons and never won an Emmy for his designs. *Mama's Family*, initially a series of comedy sketches within the series, was a spinoff of *The Carol Burnett Show*. Mackie established the original costumes for the sketches years before *Mama's Family* broke off on its own. Burnett's producer Joe Hamilton also produced *Mama's Family* and always put Mackie's name on the credits, even though Ret Turner was actually the costume designer for the weekly show.

"Winning for *Mama's Family* was like a present," Mackie recalled. "I hadn't put any effort into it except early on." His philosophical take on what was to him "a very funny" experience is that "so often you do a piece of work that you think is really superior and it gets nominated, or not, and then you don't win. You lose to something else that you don't think is so great. And other times I've won Emmys for things I thought were okay but weren't anything wildly special."

"We keep the violence down, we keep our car chases to a minimum. We're not doing *Starsky and Hutch* or *Dragnet.* We're a show with humor and humanity."

—Producer Barney Rosenzweig, commenting about *Cagney & Lacey* winning five Emmys, 1985

"I want to thank you for sitting down. I thought you were pulling a CBS and walking out on me. For the last 16 years I've missed you folks every Tuesday night."

—Red Skelton, after a standing ovation upon being presented with the Governors Award for his career contributions to television, referring to CBS' cancellation of his 1953–70 series, *The Red Skelton Show,* 1986

Award winners were also honored with Emmys: Jane Fonda for "The Dollmaker," her first dramatic role for TV, and Sir Laurence Olivier for the title role in *King Lear*. It was Olivier's fifth Emmy. The Governors Award went to 81-year-old Bob Hope, who first appeared on television in 1947. The Emmy was his fourth. The Academy's board of directors also paid special tribute to television producer David L. Wolper for the "international impact" achieved by the opening and closing ceremonies of the 1984 Olympic Games in Los Angeles, which he produced.

The next year was a momentous one for both network television and the TV Academy. In March 1985, Capital Cities Communications purchased ABC for $3.5 billion (as cable's Ted Turner maneuvered unsuccessfully to acquire CBS). A new corporate order was taking over

"I was never nervous about the Oscars like this. My heart was racing. I was almost in tears when I got up there."

—Jane Fonda, backstage after winning an Emmy for the *ABC Theatre* production of "The Dollmaker," 1984

network television. The same month, the TV Academy's Board of Governors voted to include national cable programming in future Emmy Awards telecasts.

At the 37th annual presentation, *Cagney & Lacey*, saved from cancellation by a successful public letter-writing campaign, ended *Hill Street Blues'* four-year reign as Outstanding Drama Series. Still, *Hill Street* won its 26th Emmy that year for Outstanding Supporting Actress in a Drama Series. *Cagney & Lacey* also won Emmys for Outstanding Lead Actress Tyne Daly (for the third consecutive year), Outstanding Writing, and Outstanding Directing. Daly, pregnant and a week overdue, looked down at her protruding stomach and thanked her husband, director Georg Stanford Brown, for "his outstanding work." NBC's innovative *Miami Vice* received 15 nominations, the most for any show that year, and captured four Emmys, one for Edward James Olmos as Outstanding Supporting Actor.

William Daniels of *St. Elsewhere*, in accepting the Emmy for Outstanding Lead Actor, told the audience that his limousine broke down on the way to the Emmys, forcing him to hitch a ride. NBC's *The Cosby Show* won for Outstanding Comedy Series, Outstanding Writing, and Outstanding Directing. Bill Cosby, generally acknowledged as the favorite for best actor in a comedy series, withdrew his name from nomination, leaving the category open for another African-American performer, Robert Guillaume, of ABC's *Benson*, to win. CBS' *Do You*

"Nothing would please us more than to write *An Early Frost: The Cure.*"

—Writer Daniel Lipman, after winning an Emmy with his cowriter Rob Cowen for *An Early Frost*, a drama about AIDS patients, 1986

At 1985's 37th annual ceremonies, David Letterman was one of 13 winners of an Emmy for Outstanding Writing in a Variety or Music Program for NBC's *Late Night with David Letterman.*

A "Hill Street Blues" Caper
Imposter Nearly Walks Off With Emmy

"I'm sorry, I never win anything."

—John Lithgow, having been nominated twice for Oscars and once for a Tony without winning, at a loss for words after accepting an Emmy as best guest performance in a drama series for his appearance in an episode of NBC's *Amazing Stories*, called "The Doll," 1986

"Somebody's going to have to go up to Trousdale [an upscale Los Angeles–area residential community] and revive our parents."

—Marlo Thomas, after both she and her brother Tony, the children of comedian Danny Thomas, won Emmys for separate programs, 1986

The announcement by presenter Peter Graves at the 1985 Emmy Awards that Betty Thomas of *Hill Street Blues* had been voted Outstanding Supporting Actress in a Drama Series was not unusual. What happened next was totally unplanned.

A smiling, dapper man in a dinner jacket bounded to the stage from a seat up front in the audience to accept the Emmy. Graves, off-mike,

asked: "Isn't she here?" The unidentified man said, "No, it was a last-minute thing." Betty Thomas, he told the audience, could not be present. He accepted the award and thanked the TV Academy in her absence. That was strange because Thomas had been seen earlier when cameras panned the crowd coming into the Pasadena Civic Auditorium. Then the audience was shocked to see Thomas herself hurrying across the stage.

The telecast broke for a commercial. The stranger was hustled off stage and arrested. Thomas was allowed to return after the break to make a brief acceptance speech.

"Well," she said in the understatement of the night, "it is definitely hard to follow an act like that." Barry Bremen, the "accepter," it was revealed later, had made a career as an imposter at sporting and other events.

Tyne Daly, of 1982–1988's *Cagney & Lacey*, won Outstanding Lead Actress Emmys for the police drama in 1983, 1984, 1985, and 1988. Her father, James Daly, won a supporting actor Emmy in 1966 for his performance in *Hallmark Hall of Fame*'s "Eagle in a Cage," and her then-husband, Georg Stanford Brown, won a 1985–86 Emmy for directing one of the *Cagney & Lacey* episodes. Daly's costar, Sharon Gless (below), was a two-time Emmy winner in 1986 and 1987.

"I'm the lucky one who gets to come up and pick up this beautiful golden girl. I want to thank the network for taking a chance on four old broads, uh, ladies."

—Betty White, accepting an Emmy as Outstanding Lead Actress in a Comedy Series for NBC's *The Golden Girls*, winning over costars Beatrice Arthur and Rue McClanahan [a fourth cast member, Estelle Getty, was a supporting actress nominee], 1986

"Bill Cosby said no."

—David Letterman, citing one of the top 10 reasons for being cohost of the 38th annual Emmy Awards with Shelley Long, 1986

> "I need this more than a working man needs a loaf of bread."
>
> —John Karlen of *Cagney & Lacey*, accepting an Emmy as Outstanding Supporting Actor in a Drama Series, 1986

> "I want to thank my wife, Linda, for making it so much fun to go home at night."
>
> —Jay Sandrich of *The Cosby Show*, winning an Emmy for Outstanding Directing in a Comedy Series, 1986

Tom Selleck, shown arriving with his wife, hosted the 36th annual awards ceremonies from the Pasadena Civic Auditorium, broadcast on CBS. After two nominations in previous years for the same role, Selleck finally captured an acting Emmy for his work in *Magnum, P.I.*

Among the honors at the 38th annual Awards in 1986 were the best actor Emmy to William Daniels (right), who had won the previous year, and the best supporting actress Emmy to Bonnie Bartlett, who would win again the following year. Daniels played Dr. Mark Craig, the brilliant but egotistical heart surgeon in NBC's medical drama *St. Elsewhere*. Bartlett was his neglected wife, Ellen Craig. The two Emmy winners are married in real life.

Phyllicia Rashad and Bill Cosby starred in the Emmy-winning best comedy of the 1984–85 season. The show was ranked number one in the ratings for the next four seasons.

"Thank you, Bill Cosby, for not being here."

—Robert Guillaume (right) after being named best actor for his role in ABC's *Benson*, referring to Bill Cosby of *The Cosby Show*, who withdrew from the category on grounds that performers should not compete against each other, 1985

"Ha, ha, Danny. I've won two and you've only got one!"

—Rhea Perlman, to her husband Danny DeVito, winner of an Emmy for his acting in *Taxi*, after she won for the second straight year as supporting actress for *Cheers*, 1985

Silence Is Golden

Marian Rees remembers looking out over the audience of more than 2,000 at the Pasadena Civic Auditorium, trying to find the Hallmark people. She was accepting an Emmy at the 38th annual awards presentation for Outstanding Drama/Comedy Special, on her own behalf and also that of her coexecutive producer Julianna Fjeld, NBC, and the executives of Hallmark Cards, Inc., of Kansas City. Also on stage was an interpreter for the deaf who used sign language to translate her remarks to hearing-impaired viewers.

It was Rees' first Emmy, but her emotions were about more than the pride and prestige of receiving a major Hollywood award. Rees remembers standing on that stage and sensing "an enormous precipice" over "a sea of faces." It was tremendously satisfying knowing that Fjeld, hearing-impaired herself, was on stage with her. Fjeld had brought "Love Is Never Silent" to Rees. It was adapted from a novel by Joanne Greenberg called *In This Sign*, about problems faced by a deaf family coping with life among those who are able to hear. Greenberg, best known for writing *I Never Promised You a Rose Garden* (produced as a 1977 theatrical) had given Fjeld an option on her book for $1.00.

Rees became passionate about the story. Most important to Fjeld was that deaf actors be cast in the principal roles. Rees agreed, but not innocently or naïvely. She knew it would be a very daunting challenge.

Then Hallmark entered the picture. Marian Rees Associates, started in 1981, was still young in corporate life. "Do you have anything you really like that you think could make a *Hallmark* presentation?" asked Richard E. Welsh, creative director for Hallmark Hall of Fame Productions. He thought "Love Is Never Silent" was a wonderful idea, and sent it to Kansas City for approval.

But Rees told the Hallmark people up front, "I have a moral and legal obligation to cast deaf people in principal roles." They considered the proviso for 24 hours, came back, and said, "Yes, we accept that condition."

Yet even with such solid support from Hallmark, the idea of deaf actors in principal roles appeared insurmountable, particularly at CBS, the network initially involved. The story itself was a tough sell. It was soon apparent that this movie was not going to be made at CBS unless Rees cast Joanne Woodward and Paul Newman as leads. When she confidently cast Mare Winningham and two hairing-impaired actors, Phyllis Frelich and Ed Waterstreet, instead, Rees and company took the project to NBC.

Cast and crew, including director Joseph Sargent, felt an obligation to be immersed in the deaf culture. Over 10 weeks they learned sign language.

The script was carefully developed by Darlene Craviotto. Much of what went into the production, from start to final edit, came from Julianna Fjeld. It was agreed that the drama would be broadcast without closed captioning;

the feeling was that captioning would be a diminution of everybody's effort. Instead, the writer found a way in which Mare Winningham could articulate what the deaf actors said. It was brilliantly done. And the project attracted an audience that hadn't really existed before—deaf people experiencing film through signing.

"Love Is Never Silent" faced serious competition from *An Early Frost*, an acclaimed TV movie about a gay man who tells his parents he's living with AIDS. Rees and her crew went to the Emmys with few expectations. She was amazed "Love Is Never Silent" was even nominated, and felt certain *An Early Frost* was going to get the Emmy. Rees also believed *Frost*'s director, John Erman, would likely take home the Outstanding Directing in a Miniseries or Special trophy, rather than Joe Sargent.

Sargent was sitting in front of Rees as his name was announced as winner. She looked up ready to acknowledge Erman. Then it dawned on her what had happened. She nudged Sargent, and said, "That's you!" She and others had to push him up on the stage.

After "Love Is Never Silent" was later named best special, Rees told an interviewer, "Never in my faintest dreams did I think we would have won. There was such an acknowledgment throughout the industry of the wonderful power of *An Early Frost*. I joined in that." It later struck her that the emotions she was experiencing when on stage to accept the Emmy were due to "the significant acknowledgment by a powerful group, the Television Academy, about a breakthrough into diversity programming."

Looking back, Rees' greatest satisfaction came not from receiving her first Emmy, but from seeing that the project's impact went beyond ratings and accolades. "Love Is Never Silent" inspired students at Gallaudet University (a school for the hearing-impaired) to successfully protest the hiring of a hearing school president. And now television accepts closed captioning, which is being provided to an audience so diverse it was virtually uncharted before the Hallmark production.

It's the hope of multi-Emmy winner Rees (her films have gone on to garner 11 Emmys) that her "memorable moment" on the Emmy Awards stage "has diminished to nonexistence in the lexicon of thinking people" the derogatory expression "deaf and dumb."

Make Proud for Daddy

"Comedy will be the hallmark of this year's show. It will be the thread that is woven through the production, setting the tone, pace, and style of the program and tying it all together."

—Don Ohlmeyer, producer of the 39th annual Emmy Awards, describing his plans for the show, 1987

"This is the shortest speech."

—Cinematographer Philip Lathrop, Emmy winner in the miniseries or special category for NBC's *Christmas Snow*, during what turned out to be the nearly four-hour telecast, 1987

Danny Thomas, one of the early inductees into the ATAS Hall of Fame, had his big nights at the Emmys, but never a prouder one than the 1986 Emmys.

Thomas, as the star of ABC's *Make Room for Daddy*, won an Emmy in 1955 as Best Actor Starring in a Regular Series. But that experience was topped 31 years later when his son Tony, coexecutive producer of *The Golden Girls*, won an Emmy for the Outstanding Comedy Series, and his daughter Marlo (an Emmy winner in 1974 for an ABC children's special she coproduced and in which she also starred) won an Emmy for Outstanding Lead Actress in a Miniseries or a Special for her depiction, on CBS' *Nobody's Child*, of an emotionally disturbed woman who overcame her illness and earned a master's degree.

Tony Thomas received the best comedy trophy for *The Golden Girls* the following year as well. And Marlo went on to coproduce yet another Emmy-winning children's program, *Free To Be...A Family*, for ABC.

"Woo-hoo! God bless America."

—Bruce Willis of ABC's *Moonlighting*, accepting an Emmy as best actor in a dramatic series, 1987

"Oh boy, I'm beginning to get slightly embarrassed by your generosity. I emphasize slightly; if you really want to embarrass me, keep this up."

—John Larroquette, winning for the third year in a row as best supporting actor in a comedy series for NBC's *Night Court*, 1987

"After almost 40 years of working in the business, it's a wonderful culmination. It means that I choose wisely people I work with."

—Producer Grant Tinker, backstage at the Pasadena Civic Auditorium, after receiving the Governors Award in recognition of his highly successful administration of NBC, when he was chairman, and previously of MTM Enterprises, 1987

Family Ties (1982–89) was nominated four times for best comedy series, and Michael J. Fox won as Outstanding Lead Actor in 1986, 1987, and 1988. Pictured with Fox are, from left, Justine Bateman, Meredith Baxter, Michael Gross, Brian Bonsall, and Tina Yothers.

Four Golden Girls
Four Emmy Women

In 1988, *The Golden Girls* was honored with Emmys for lead actress Beatrice Arthur and supporting actress Estelle Getty (below). The two wins gave the popular sitcom a clean sweep for its four actresses. Betty White and Rue McClanahan, both competing with Arthur that year, had won Emmys in 1986 and 1987, respectively.

"It's lucky, one of us gets to pick up this Golden Girl," White said about this friendly competition.

"My mother said, 'Every kick's a boost,' and over the last 27 years, I've had lot of kicks and boosts. I'm not going to run through those who gave me the kicks...you know who you are, and you'll be in the book."

—*The Golden Girls*' Rue McClanahan, Emmy winner for Outstanding Lead Actress in a Comedy Series for NBC's *The Golden Girls*, 1987

"I want to thank Norman Lear for starting me off in this crazy, wonderful, delicious medium."

—*The Golden Girls*' Beatrice Arthur, the following year

Peter the Great, an eight hour, four-part miniseries on NBC about the Russian czar, was filmed largely in the Soviet Union. Its stellar cast included Maximilian Schell, Vanessa Redgrave, Omar Sharif, and Laurence Olivier. It won three Emmys in 1986, including Outstanding Miniseries.

Remember Love?, a story about a woman's struggle with Alzheimer's disease, won three Emmys, including Outstanding Drama Special, Outstanding Lead Actress in a Limited Special for veteran Joanne Woodward, and Outstanding Writing. PBS' *Masterpiece Theatre* production of "The Jewel in the Crown," a 13-part epic about British rule in India, was voted Outstanding Limited Series.

Broadway producer Alexander Cohen and his producer-writer wife, Hildy Parks, who had teamed for many Tony Awards telecasts, produced the 37th annual Emmys. Among their innovations was opening the show with a five-minute tribute to the music of television. The Academy honored Alistair Cooke, host of the public television program *Masterpiece Theatre*, with its Governors Award for having brought to his audience "a better understanding of the classics."

In 1986, there were 25,000 diagnosed cases of AIDS in the United States. Near Kiev in the Ukraine, the world's worst nuclear accident took place in Russia when a reactor blew up at Chernobyl Power Station. Some 133,000 people were evacuated and clouds of fallout affected all of Europe.

Late Night's David Letterman and Shelley Long of *Cheers* were cohosts at the 38th Emmy Awards, which were televised by NBC. It was a big night for the peacock network. *St. Elsewhere* led all other programs with six Emmys. Outstanding Miniseries was NBC's *Peter the Great*. Best drama or comedy special was *Hallmark Hall of Fame*'s "Love Is Never Silent," an NBC movie about a young woman whose parents are deaf. NBC's first-season sitcom *The Golden Girls* was voted best comedy. It also earned Emmys for costar Betty White, for writing, and for technical direction. All four *Golden Girls* received nominations—Rue McClanahan and Beatrice Arthur for Outstanding Lead Actress in a Comedy Series and Estelle Getty for Outstanding Supporting Actress—but only White came away with a statuette. "The wonderful part," observed White, "is that all four of us were nominated."

CBS's *Cagney & Lacey* broke the NBC winning streak, receiving four Emmys, including one for Outstanding Drama Series and the first for Cagney herself, Sharon Gless. Long-retired comedian Red Skelton was presented with the ATAS Governors Award. Ron Cowen, Daniel Lipman, and Sherman Yellen, the writers of *An Early Frost*, one of the first television dramas to confront the AIDS epidemic, were Emmy winners, as was the 13-member writing team for *Late Night With David Letterman Fourth Anniversary Special*. Once again, the executive

"Brotherhood is taken very seriously in my family, as my own brother knows. I consider James Garner as my brother. I looked in his eyes for 12 hours every day and what I saw there brought me up these steps tonight."

—James Woods, speaking about his costar in the *Hallmark Hall of Fame* special "Promise," after winning an Emmy for best lead actor in a miniseries or special, 1987

"In the beginning was the word, but by the time network executives and others get through with it, sometimes it's very thin."

—Richard Friedenberg, one of three Emmy winners for Outstanding Writing in a Miniseries or a Special, "Promise" for CBS and *Hallmark Hall of Fame*, 1987

"From the bottom of my heart, I'm truly amazed my name is in the same category with the other nominees. I thank them for the inspiration they are to me. I can't be any happier than I am."

—Michael J. Fox, receiving an Emmy as lead actor in a comedy series for NBC's *Family Ties*, in reference to the other nominees in the category, Dabney Coleman, Ted Danson, Tim Reid, and John Ritter, 1988

"Before I came up here tonight, my mother said, 'Being nominated is the best.' This is better."

—Peter Douglas, executive producer of the *AT&T Presents* production of "Inherit the Wind" for NBC, Emmy winner as outstanding drama/comedy special, 1988

The Los Angeles law firm of McKenzie, Brackman, Chaney & Kuzak was the setting for NBC's hour-long dramatic series *L.A. Law*, which ended its first season with 20 nominations. The show starred (clockwise from bottom left) Blair Underwood, Susan Ruttan, Corbin Bernsen, Alan Rachins, Jimmy Smits, Richard A. Dysart, Michelle Greene, Michael Tucker, and Susan Dey. Harry Hamlin and Jill Eikenberry are in the center.

Cybill Shepherd played sexy former-model Maddie Hayes and Bruce Willis wiseguy David Addison in 1985–89's *Moonlighting*. A virtual unknown prior to the show, Willis won a 1987 Emmy as Outstanding Lead Actor in a Drama Series.

The scene outside the Pasadena Civic Auditorium before the 1988 prime-time Emmy Awards.

"I want to thank all the wonderful folks down in New Orleans who let us come in to their funeral homes and bars and restaurants and let us hear their stories."

—Hugh Wilson, Emmy winner for best writing in a comedy series, talking about his series *Frank's Place*, a CBS sitcom set in a small Creole restaurant in New Orleans with the owner of a neighborhood funeral parlor and her beautiful daughter as recurring characters, 1988

"The essence of this show is something about community. This show is made by a community of about 150 who take it very seriously. I think it shows."

—Marshall Herskovitz, coexecutive producer of ABC's *thirtysomething*, Emmy winner as best drama series, 1988

In 1987, its first year of eligibility, ABC's *thirtysomething* was voted Outstanding Drama Series. The groundbreaking show starred (clockwise from left) Mel Harris, Patricia Wettig, Polly Draper, Ken Olin, Timothy Busfield, Melanie Mayron, and Peter Horton.

The Wonder Years, one of ABC's 1987–88 mid-season entries, was one of the surprises of the 40th annual Emmy Awards when it picked up a statuette for Outstanding Comedy Series. Fred Savage starred as Kevin Arnold in the show, which was set in the 1960s.

"This is a wonderful moment, the icing on the cake."

—Larry Drake, Emmy winner as supporting actor in a drama series for his portrayal of mentally challenged office worker Benny Stulwicz on *L.A. Law*, NBC, 1988

producer of the Emmy Awards was Alexander Cohen.

In 1987, there were pronounced changes taking place in the world and on television. The U.S.S.R.'s Mikhail Gorbachev campaigned for *glasnost* (openness) and *perestroika* (reconstruction). Legendary TV star Jackie Gleason died at age 70. ATAS signed a contract to become the main tenant of a major new $350 million, 22-acre complex called The Academy in North Hollywood. Plans for the facility included a 600-seat, state-of-the-art film/tape theater, and an open-air, publicly accessible Television Academy Hall of Fame plaza area with a 25-foot replica of the Emmy Award statue.

The most surprising change concerned upstart Fox Broadcasting Co., which landed a three-year contract to telecast the annual Emmy Awards show. For more than 20 years, ABC, CBS, and NBC bid as a group for Emmy rights, then rotated the program among themselves. But in 1987, the one-year-old Fox aired the 39th annual program, bringing back 1977 executive producer Don Ohlmeyer to oversee the proceedings.

In its first eligible year, *L.A. Law* garnered 20 nominations and won

Jason Robards won a best actor Emmy in 1988 for his role as Clarence Darrow in NBC's *AT&T Presents* production of "Inherit the Wind." The show was also voted Outstanding Special.

Taxi and *Who's The Boss?* star Tony Danza acted as the "designated acceptor" at the 1988 Emmy ceremony, collecting seven statuettes for no-shows.

Emmy Memories
Paula Kaatz

"Getting yourself in a position to win an Emmy requires more than skill at your craft. First you must get the job—and it must be either a period piece or unusual enough to get attention. You must be able to convince the producing company to give you access to the tools you need to do the job well—dollars, personnel, time (actually, all of these equal dollars), a cast secure enough to wear the clothes, a cameraman to shoot them well, and a director with the same vision, or at least with enough sense to stay out of your way. The entire production must turn out good enough or have a star big enough to be promoted by the network or outlet so people see it. You, or the producers, must enter it for nomination, send tape or promotional materials, and hope that the coattails of the production are long enough to include you.

"If you've done your job, you have a chance of winning a nomination or award. I was raised in Beverly Hills. I'm not from an industry family. I had no intent to go 'into the business.' I was pretty nonchalant about the industry and all its award ceremonies—at least on the surface. The work was all, awards not required. Besides, no one was giving me any. Heidi Trotta, then publicist at Warners TV, told me one had to put oneself up for nomination. Oh, I thought, maybe that explains why scads of honors hadn't been bestowed on me.

"Warners wanted us all to enter and to join the Academy so we could vote for ourselves. Who was I to argue? It was miserably hot in Irving, Texas, even at 8:30 in the morning. We were shooting [the CBS miniseries] *Pancho Barnes*. The phone in the wardrobe department rang. It was Angie [assistant to executive producer John Sacret Young] calling to tell me that the male costumer, Darryl Levine, and I had been nominated for an Emmy for the *China Beach* pilot [cast members Marg Helgenberger, Dana Delany, Nan Woods, and Chloe Webb pictured below].

"Nonchalance evaporated. Instead, major excitement took over. Oh, sure, I got the names of the rest of the nominees in my category and from the show, but I was already dialing my mother. The thrill of being able to tell the people who know what you have been through in your career and may even have made personal sacrifices to support you is not to be denied. It may seem corny when honoree after honoree thanks their parents and family, but it is—and should be—the first response. I don't think I've ever heard my mother so excited or proud (well, there was that eighth grade Science Fair win and the Wedgewood blue cake that won the big prize at Beverly High). I wished my father were alive to see some payback. He would have loved it the most.

"I had been nominated before and had won an Emmy the previous year [for *China Beach*], but, in 1989, the stars were all in alignment for me. Well, most of them. I was working on *China Beach*, a labor of love, which satisfied the requirements I've already outlined for winning an Emmy. I had done *Pancho Barnes* during hiatus (and the writers' strike), which covered a 50-plus-year time span and was a wardrobe showcase. There were nearly 500 changes on speaking parts alone. I was nominated in both Costume Supervision categories (for Series and for Miniseries or a Special). Wow! And then I found out that meant going to both the off-air and on-air ceremonies because the Miniseries category had been chosen to be one of two Creative Arts Awards to be given live on the national telecast. I had been in charge of costumers [with Andrea Weaver, Janet Lawler, and Stephen Chudej] on *Pancho Barnes* [which was up for five nominations in the category of Costuming for a Series], and so had entered the project and was in the position to accept and speak if we won. This meant two changes of formal attire for me!

"*China Beach* didn't win that Saturday night, but the award was up second, so I didn't get as frazzled as if I had to wait all night for the outcome. And I still had another chance the next night—not that I wasn't disappointed.

"I picked the glitzy outfit for the Prime-time Awards. I hadn't been to that event before. Oscars, yes; Emmys, no. My sequined jacket made a minor splash. Our category [Outstanding Costuming for a Miniseries or Special] was up about halfway through the show. My name was mispronounced by the presenter, Kirk Cameron, an actor with whom I had done a limited series [*Two Marriages*] six years before…he mispronounced my name twice!

"All the air goes out of your lungs when your name is announced as the winner. I understand how the player feels when he has run a long way for a touchdown—the winning touchdown. Thank heavens I worked on a speech during the first half of the show. I had notes all over my program. I have my acceptance on tape, several times over, because relatives I hadn't seen in years sent me copies. I only remember that I did thank the Academy and everyone I really wanted to thank. The director was a gem. I had fabulous coverage—some unfortunately from the rear ascending the steps to the stage.

"My reaction to the announcement was seen by millions. They intercut reaction shots with actors I'd never met, but they were lovely reactions. No one else from our show was there. I didn't trip and fall. No one saw the last-minute alterations to my outfit. I particularly wanted to represent the creative arts field well and tried to speak articulately and with humor. The press rooms afterward were a blur. I worked with Ellen Gonzales, a publicist, a couple of years later who told me she had been my guide backstage. You could have fooled me.

"After calling mom—who has never really forgiven me for taking her to the Creative Arts Awards Presentations on Saturday night rather than the televised prime-time event that year—I returned to my seat feeling deservedly triumphant.

"The Governors Ball [the Emmy dinner after the telecast] was a blur as well. Somehow my date and I were seated in the hallway. I remember being

"Okay, now I am officially overwhelmed."

—John Larroquette, winning his fourth consecutive Emmy as best supporting actor in a comedy series for NBC's *Night Court*, 1988

"I never expected to be in this position tonight. My competition is so strong. I'm proud to be nominated. That would have been enough."

—Jessica Tandy, Emmy winner for "Foxfire," a *Hallmark Hall of Fame* production for CBS, talking about Ann Jillian, Mary Tyler Moore, Mary Steenburgen, and JoBeth Williams, the other nominees for Outstanding Actress in a Miniseries or a Special, 1988

served lamb. I ran into another woman dressed in the same sequined jacket, identically accessorized. She bought it at the same boutique. This is a definite no-no for the owner.

"I came up to the ball on one set of stairs as [*China Beach* star] Dana Delany was coming up the other. We spotted each other and ran across the plaza to meet in the center. Many paparazzi have a shot somewhere of Dana, who had won Outstanding Lead Actress in a Drama Series, and another woman who would remain nameless in captions running to each other waving trophies and hugging a lot.

"A rather amazing thing happened while we were waiting for our limo. I was standing with Dana and [*China Beach* executive producer] John Sacret Young and my date when a long white limo pulled to a stop and a man in a tuxedo jumped out. He congratulated Dana and John and then me. He said his wife would like to know where I had gotten my jacket. And, then, as an aside, he asked if I was interested in a career on-camera. I, of course, thought he was joking, and said, 'not really.' He told me to call him if I might be interested in series TV. I thanked him and he said John could give me his number. I found out a few days later that the man was Ted Harbert, who had just taken over drama development for ABC [and subsequently became president of ABC Entertainment]. Later that night, I went on to the party for *China Beach*. That's where my friends and supporters were.

"In 1988, I flew in from Texas for the Creative Arts Presentation ceremony. I bought a simply awful dress in Dallas—winter white wool crepe with marabou trim—and very high-heeled pumps. It was 90-plus degrees. The wool dress began to smell like sheep. I took the shoes off after successfully climbing the three flights of concrete stairs to my seat and never put them back on.

"In future years, I dressed and prepared differently for the Creative Arts Awards ceremony. In 1990, I had a tote bag and seat cushions made to match my dress. In the bag was a picnic to tide my co-nominee, Le Dawson, his wife, Karen, and my mother and me through the ceremony. We had pate and cornichons and all the trimmings. We lost that year, but were gastronomically contented.

"I am now in my second term as Governor of the Costume Designers and Supervisors Peer Group of the Academy. We get to go to all the Awards ceremonies. No more high heels. No more wool dresses. No more sequins, either. I'm more experienced, more comfortable. But should I be nominated again, and should my name be called—whether on-air or off—the wind will go out of me and I will be just as thrilled as the moment I picked up the phone in Texas and was told that I was nominated for *China Beach* that first time."

Jane Seymour
Out-of-Sync Lip Sync Nearly Blows Callas Role

Jane Seymour won an Emmy in the late '80s for her portrayal of opera diva Maria Callas in ABC's *Onassis: The Richest Man in the World*. But Callas was physically different than Seymour—the Greek singer was taller, big-boned, with bigger features. Seymour was especially "thrilled" winning an Emmy for that particular piece of work because she probably worked harder, in terms of hours devoted to mastering the role, than anything she has ever done.

Seymour had the "privilege" of having some four months notice, which gave her the time to research the part properly. Seymour listened to recorded live performances of Callas, studied her hair styles in various stage roles, and learned to lip-synch to that legendary voice. In the end, all that careful preparation, and the dedication to doing justice to Callas—the artist, as well as the woman—was partially upset.

At the last minute, the music to which Seymour was lip-synching couldn't be used. Instead, a singer was brought in to sing to Seymour's actions. The singer wasn't used to such synchronization, so that on screen it looks as if Seymour is out of sync.

"To this day it really bugs me because I had it right the first time," Seymour, still upset years later, reported.

> "I'm carrying a picture of my family. This prize is for them because they've put up with me for years and years. I'm so thrilled, I can't believe it. Thank you for letting me be an American actress."
>
> —English-born Jane Seymour, winning an Emmy as best supporting actress in a miniseries or a special for ABC's *Onassis: The Richest Man in the World*, 1988

"If it has taken one step toward making people understand what happened, and if it takes one step toward keeping it from ever happening again, then we've accomplished our mission."
—Dan Curtis, executive producer and director of the 29-hour ABC miniseries *War and Remembrance* (starring John Gielgud, right), about World War II and the Holocaust, accepting top honors for the best miniseries of the 1988–89 season, 1989

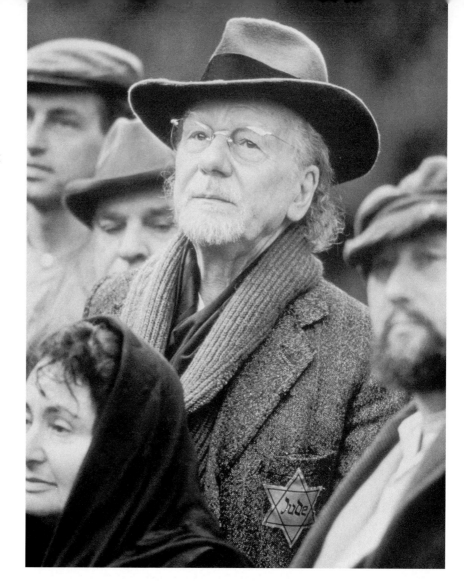

Miss Piggy and Kermit the Frog, stars of Jim Henson's large cast of imaginative puppets called "The Muppets," were lively presenters on the 1989 Prime-time Emmy telecast.

(Left) At the twilight of his distinguished career, which included Emmys in 1965, 1972, 1976, and 1987, maestro Leonard Bernstein was the subject of a *Great Performances* program on PBS, "Bernstein at 70," which won an Emmy as Outstanding Classical Program in the Performing Arts at the 1988–89 awards.

(Middle) Joe Spano was a regular on *Hill Street Blues* but he won an Emmy in 1989 for a guest appearance on NBC's *Midnight Caller*.

(Right) In December 1989, 18 years after they performed on a CBS musical-variety special from New York City's Lincoln Center, Julie Andrews and Carol Burnett did an encore—this time for ABC under the *AT&T Presents* banner—titled "Julie and Carol: Together Again."

Billy Crystal won a 1989 Emmy for hosting the 31st Annual Grammy Awards.

seven Emmys, only one less than the record set by *Hill Street Blues* for the most Emmys won by a series in its first season (a record subsequently equaled by *ER*). The NBC legal series' win as Outstanding Drama Series was its first of four in this category. Once again, *The Golden Girls* won as Outstanding Comedy Series, Sharon Gless of *Cagney & Lacey* repeated as Outstanding Lead Actress in a Drama Series, and Bonnie Bartlett of *St. Elsewhere* won another as Outstanding Supporting Actress. Rue McClanahan of *The Golden Girls* and Bruce Willis of *Moonlighting*, both nominated the previous year, took home the gold in 1987.

Delayed as a result of a 22-week strike by TV and film writers, television's production season began only a month before the 40th annual Emmy Awards. The big winners that year were ABC's freshman series *thirtysomething*, as best drama, and *The Wonder Years*, a mid-season replacement series, as best comedy. In the first year that cable television was entered into the Emmy Awards mix, Jackie Mason won for writing his Home Box Office special, *The World According to Me*. The same network's documentary, *Dear America: Letters Home From Vietnam*, won an Emmy as Outstanding Informational Special.

Two performers, John Larroquette of *Night Court* and Tyne Daly of *Cagney & Lacey*, each won their fourth Emmys, and Michael J. Fox of *Family Ties* won his third. Tony Danza (*Who's the Boss*) was given the comical title of "designated acceptor," as he picked up Emmys for seven winners who did not attend the event. The Governors Award went to animators William Hanna and Joseph Barbera for their contributions to children's programming, including Yogi Bear, *The Jetsons*, and *The Flintstones*.

In 1989, two legendary talents died. Sir Laurence Olivier, star of the stage and the silver screen, and winner of four Emmy Awards for his work in television, was 82. Lucille Ball, an early inductee in the

Lucille Ball
The Queen of Comedy

With *I Love Lucy* (1951–57), Lucille Ball "helped inaugurate the age of television just as surely as Charlie Chaplin helped inaugurate the age of movies." So said an editorial in the *New York Post* after Ball's death in 1986; so agreed many other television industry observers.

Michael McClay, in his 1995 book *The Complete Picture History of the Most Popular TV Show Ever*, declared *I Love Lucy* to be not only "the most popular situation comedy of all time, but also the most well-conceived and well-executed sitcom ever created for the small screen."

The TV Academy agreed, at least in 1952 and 1953 when the half-hour CBS series was awarded the Emmy as Best Situation Comedy. Ball's sidekick on *I Love Lucy*, Vivian Vance, was voted 1953's Best Series Supporting Actress. Ball, who during her TV career had 13 nominations, won two Emmys for *I Love Lucy*: Best Comedienne in 1952 and for Best Actress—Continuing Performance in 1955. (Later, Ball was honored for *The Lucy Show* with two successive Emmys for Outstanding Continued Performance by an Actress in a Leading Role in a Comedy Series for the 1966–67 and 1967–68 seasons.)

For three seasons, *I Love Lucy* was the top-rated program on TV, averaging a 58.8 in 1953–54, a 49.3 in 1954–55, and a 43.7 in 1956–57. Only *The $64,000 Question*, from October 1955 through April 1956, broke *I Love Lucy*'s dominance, with the difference between the two less than 2 rating points.

TV Guide, in its listing of "The 100 Greatest Episodes of All Time" ranks the May 5, 1952 , episode "Lucy Does a TV Commercial" as second only to *The Mary Tyler Moore Show*'s "Chuckles the Clown" episode. And its listing of "The 100 Most Memorable Moments in TV History" considers the candy factory episode to be topped only by the broadcast of astronaut Neil Armstrong's July 20, 1969, walk on the moon.

Lucille Ball was among the first seven stars inducted in the Television Academy Hall of Fame. And when *I Love Lucy* was inducted into the Hall in 1991 (the only TV series to receive that distinction), the Academy citation described the show as "the classic situation comedy whose worldwide popularity has been unmatched in television history." The citation also noted its wide syndication, "endearing it to millions," and its "inventive comedy" that has been "frequently imitated but rarely equaled." A virtual life-sized bronze sculpture of Ball by Ernest Shelton resides in front of the TV Academy headquarters in North Hollywood.

After Ball's death, her daughter, Lucie Arnaz, and son-in-law, Laurence Luckinbill, won an Emmy for best informational special for producing *Lucy and Desi: A Home Movie* for NBC.

Roe vs. Wade's Sweet Emmy Win

Even before it aired in May 1989, the made-for-television movie *Roe vs. Wade*, about the 1973 U.S. Supreme Court ruling that established the federal abortion law, was under heavy fire. Antiabortionists claimed it was unbalanced and mounted a campaign to discourage advertisers from buying commercial time in the NBC presentation. Some advertisers did drop out. By some estimates, the network lost about $1 million on the telecast. When *Roe vs. Wade* was named Outstanding Drama or Comedy Special for the 1988–89 season (in a tie with "Day One," an *AT&T Presents* CBS movie about the development of the atomic bomb), executive producer Michael Manheim thanked "our sponsors, each of whom stood up to be counted when it would have been easier to run and hide."

Holly Hunter, who played a character based on Norma McCorvey, whose efforts to obtain an abortion led to the court decision, won the award for Outstanding Lead Actress in a Miniseries or a Special. In her acceptance speech, Hunter thanked McCorvey for "continuing to fight to keep women from being second-class citizens" and also for "refusing to give up her right to reproductive choice." She also thanked NBC "for getting this movie on the air."

David Strathairn and Brian Dennehy were featured in "Day One," a CBS movie about the development of the atomic bomb. It was named best drama special in 1989 in a tie with the abortion-themed *Roe vs. Wade*.

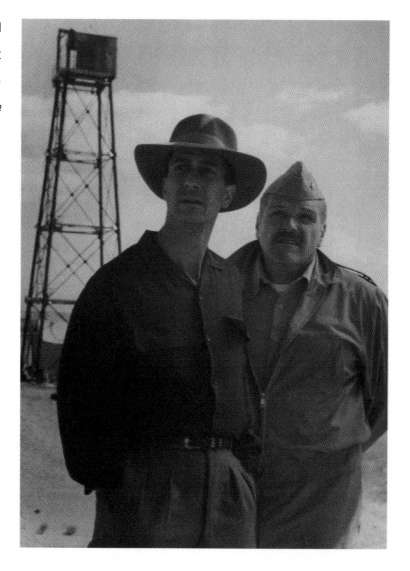

Murphy Brown
First Season Impact

Some 13 years after *Saturday Night Live*'s big night at the Emmys back in 1976, when the show won four out of five nominations, it was *Murphy Brown*'s turn to pile up nominations, if not awards themselves. Robert S. Alley and Irby B. Brown, in their 1990 Book *Murphy Brown: Anatomy of a Sitcom*, reported on how the cast and crew responded to receiving 11 nominations in their rookie season.

"Everyone in the outer office...talks and hugs at once," they wrote. "As each new office mate joins the happy melee in the room, the congratulations get repeated all around. This is the inner circle of believers in the high quality of the show, and their faith in themselves seems to have been confirmed by peers in the Academy. It's especially flattering and energizing to have your high opinion of your work confirmed by peers. *Murphy Brown* is, after all, a classic in the making. Now everybody knows it."

In what was only the beginning of the show's decade-long legacy, its Emmy recipients that year included Candice Bergen as Outstanding Lead Actress in a Comedy Series (below), Colleen Dewhurst as Outstanding Guest Actress in a Comedy Series, and the program's creator, Diane English, for Outstanding Writing in a Comedy Series.

The Tracey Ullman Show, one of the Fox network's first prime-time series, was also the first to win a major Emmy. In 1989, the program, which featured Ullman in sketch comedy (shown above with guest Steve Martin), was voted Outstanding Variety, Music, or Comedy Program. Ullman won the following year for Outstanding Individual Performance in a Variety or Music Program.

ATAS Hall of Fame, died at age 78. A four-time Emmy winner herself, her original 1950s sitcom, *I Love Lucy*, was one of television's greatest achievements. Ball, referred to as the "First Lady of Television," was posthumously given the TV Academy's Governors Award during the 41st annual Emmy Awards. It was presented by Bob Hope to her widower, Gary Morton.

At the presentation, *War and Remembrance*, ABC's 29-hour, $110 million saga about World War II, was named the best miniseries of the 1988–89 season. *Roe vs. Wade*, NBC's controversial movie about the landmark case that established a woman's right to an abortion, shared the award as Outstanding Drama/Comedy Special with Aaron Spelling's CBS production of "Day One." *L.A. Law* was voted best drama, and *Cheers* the best comedy. Fox Broadcasting, then three years old and once again telecasting the Emmy ceremonies, picked up its first four Emmys, all for *The Tracey Ullman Show*, including one as Outstanding Variety, Music, or Comedy Program. CBS' western miniseries *Lonesome Dove* was the biggest winner with seven Emmys. James Woods won an Emmy as Outstanding Lead Actor in a Miniseries or a Special for the ABC movie *My Name Is Bill W.*, and Holly Hunter was

Carroll O'Connor, Anne-Marie Johnson, and Howard Rollins in the 1988–94 NBC/CBS police drama, *In the Heat of the Night*. O'Connor, who had already won four Emmys for *All in the Family*, won another statuette in 1989 for his dramatic role as the Southern sheriff. Rod Steiger, who played the same role in the original 1968 movie, won an Academy Award for his performance.

The cast of NBC's *Empty Nest* (clockwise from left): Kristy McNichol, David Leisure, Park Overall, Dinah Manoff, and Richard Mulligan. For his role in this *Golden Girls* spinoff, Mulligan won his second Emmy as Outstanding Lead Actor in a Comedy Series. His first was for *Soap* in 1980.

named lead actress for *Roe vs. Wade*. Dana Delany took home an award for her stirring work on *China Beach*. Carroll O'Connor won as best actor in a drama series for NBC's *In the Heat of the Night* and Richard Mulligan won as best actor in a comedy series for NBC's *Empty Nest*. Colleen Dewhurst was a double winner, named Outstanding Supporting Actress in a Miniseries or a Special for the TV movie *Those She Left Behind*, and as Outstanding Guest Actress in a Comedy Series for her appearance as Candice Bergen's mother in *Murphy Brown*. John Larroquette, after winning four times as Outstanding Supporting Actor in a Comedy Series for NBC's *Night Court*, had withdrawn his name from consideration to open the category to other actors; Woody Harrelson of *Cheers* won that year.

Dana Delany was nominated four times for Outstanding Lead Actress in a Drama Series for her role as army nurse Colleen McMurphy on *China Beach*, a series set in Vietnam during the war. She won in 1989 and 1992.

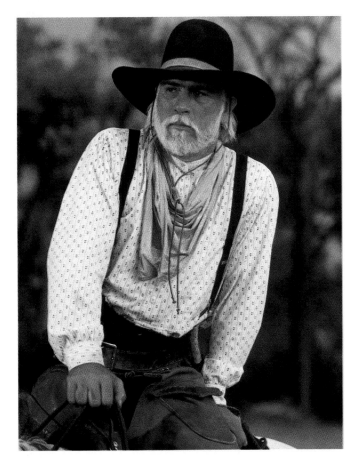

Lonesome Dove was one of the most-watched miniseries in television history. Starring Tommy Lee Jones, Robert Duvall, and Anjelica Huston, the four-parter was based on the Pulitzer Prize–winning novel by Larry McMurtry. It took home seven Emmys, one for the director, the rest in technical categories.

1990-98

Fox Broadcasting, which telecast the 42nd annual Emmy Awards on September 16, 1990, began the decade with the rights to the annual awards show for the next three years—a major coup against the Big Three networks.

That year, ABC's quirky nighttime soap *Twin Peaks* topped all shows with 14 Emmy nominations, including best drama, but it won only for costume design and editing. The award for Outstanding Drama Series was given to *L.A. Law*, which captured the category for the third time in four years. Fox's *The Tracey Ullman Show* was the top winner, with six awards; *Cheers*, *L.A. Law*, and *thirtysomething* picked up three Emmys apiece. The *Hallmark Hall of Fame* production of "Caroline?," a mystery surrounding the identity of a young woman, also won three Emmys. One of the three was the Outstanding

From 1994 to 1998, the NBC series *Frasier* won a record five consecutive Emmys as Outstanding Comedy Series. The *Cheers* spinoff stars Kelsey Grammer as psychiatrist Dr. Frasier Crane. The regular cast includes (from left to right) David Hyde Pierce, Peri Gilpin, Grammer, Jane Leeves, and Dan Butler. The series also costars John Mahoney. Grammer has won three times (1994, 1995, and 1998) for his role and Pierce has won twice (1995 and 1998).

Sherilyn Fenn was one of several newcomers in producer David Lynch's quirky prime-time serial, *Twin Peaks*, which premiered to great acclaim in April 1990. Coming in to the 42nd annual Emmy Awards as the leader in nominations (including a supporting actress nomination for Fenn), the show won a few technical awards but lost to *L.A. Law* as best drama.

Drama/Comedy Special award, for which it tied with "The Incident," an *AT&T Presents* special that starred Walter Matthau.

Ted Danson of NBC's *Cheers* and Peter Falk of *Columbo* took home outstanding lead actor statuettes (in a comedy series and a drama series, respectively). It was Danson's first-ever win after eight previous nominations—seven for his portrayal of Sam Malone on *Cheers* and one for a TV movie about incest called *Something About Amelia*. It was Falk's fourth Emmy for playing Lieutenant Columbo in the NBC police drama (he had also won an Emmy in 1962 for Outstanding Single Performance by an Actor in a Leading Role for NBC's *Dick Powell Theatre* production of "Price of Tomatoes").

Other honorees included veteran actor Hume Cronyn (whose wife, Jessica Tandy, had won a best actress Oscar earlier in the year for *Driving Miss Daisy*) for the HBO drama *Age Old Friends;* Patricia Wettig of *thirtysomething;* and *Murphy Brown*'s Candice Bergen, who was one of three hosts for the national telecast (Jay Leno and Jane Pauley were her cohosts). Wettig, who in 1988 won the supporting actress Emmy for the same role, won as lead actress this time around. Although it was the second consecutive year that Bergen had won as Outstanding Lead Actress in a Comedy Series, her show won its first Emmy as Outstanding Comedy Series that year.

Fox's new hit, *The Simpsons*, played a prominent role in the telecast, with its animated characters incorporated into the ceremony as presenters. The cartoon won an Emmy as Outstanding Animated Program during the previous night's ceremonies. The 1990 Governors Award went to ABC's Leonard H. Goldenson, one of the

"Ma, you were right. I'll never argue with you again."

—Peter Falk, accepting an Emmy as best actor in a drama series

for his detective role in NBC's *Columbo*, 1990

"I would really like to thank all the women with cancer who have shared their experiences with me. I truly salute their courage."

—Patricia Wettig, tearfully accepting an Emmy as Outstanding Lead Actress in a Drama Series for her role as cancer-stricken Nancy on ABC's *thirtysomething*, 1990

Hume Cronyn and Vincent Gardenia both won 1990 Emmys for HBO's *Age Old Friends*, Cronyn as leading actor in a miniseries or special, and Gardenia—who played Cronyn's friend in a retirement home—as outstanding supporting actor.

"This is exactly what happened to me in the drive-in. Just when I got lucky, everyone stood up and applauded."

—Ted Danson, winning an Emmy as Outstanding Lead Actor in a Comedy Series after eight previous nominations for NBC's *Cheers*, alluding to an earlier comparison of the frustration of going to a drive-in movie theater with a date who teased but didn't deliver, 1990

In 1995, after her fifth win as Best Actress in a Comedy Series for CBS' *Murphy Brown*, Candice Bergen took herself out of the competition. Her other wins were in 1989, 1990, 1992, and 1994.

"I think I'm going to mount it on the front of the Mercedes."

—Actor Burt Reynolds, honored as Outstanding Lead Actor in a Comedy Series for *Evening Shade*, 1991

key executives in the history of commercial network television. Another ABC alum, Martin Starger, was executive producer of the 1989–90 Emmy Awards, with Howard Alston as producer.

In May, the Academy of Television Arts & Sciences celebrated its move from Burbank into a new free-standing two-story ATAS building in North Hollywood and officially opened the adjacent outdoor Hall of Fame Plaza. At a gala weekend of dedication festivities for ATAS members, TV stars, and the industry in general, a nearly completed 600-seat Academy Theatre was unveiled. A 600-member star-studded black-tie audience of celebrities; industry, studio, and network executives; community dignitaries; and press attended "One More Time," which saluted memorable moments of television's past with the legendary stars who originally created them. Robert Stack served as host of the evening. Among those who recreated classic television performances from the past were Beatrice Arthur and Bill Macy (*Maude*); Jay Livingston and Alan Young (*Mr. Ed*); Milton Berle and Jack Jones (*Texaco Star Theater*); and Edie Adams, Debbie Reynolds, and Dick Van Patten (recreating the Nairobi Trio from *The Ernie Kovacs Show*).

In 1991, the 43rd annual Emmy Awards, cohosted by comics Dennis Miller and Jerry Seinfeld and actress Jamie Lee Curtis, took place in August instead of September. This was a deliberate scheduling anomaly on the part of Fox to avoid competing with new shows and season premieres on the major networks in September. That night, *Cheers* and *L.A. Law* were repeat winners as best comedy and best drama series, respectively.

African-American members of the Hollywood television community were especially honored this night. Lynn Whitfield won an Emmy for the title role in HBO's *The Josephine Baker Story*, as Outstanding Lead Actress in a Miniseries or Special (and her husband, Brian Gibson, received one for directing her in the production). Veteran actress Ruby Dee won an acting trophy for *Hallmark Hall of Fame*'s "Decoration Day." And James Earl Jones became the first performer to win two acting awards in one ceremony

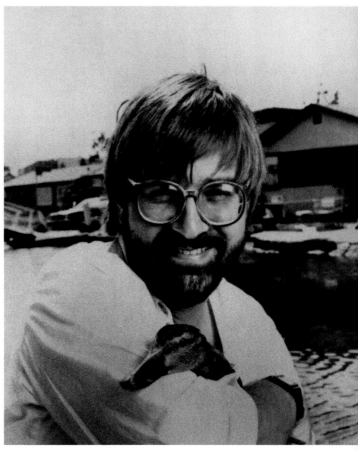

Fox Broadcasting's long-running series *The Simpsons* was created by Matt Groening (above). Beginning as vignettes on *The Tracey Ullman Show*, this television phenomenon was named best animated program in 1990, 1991, 1995, and 1998.

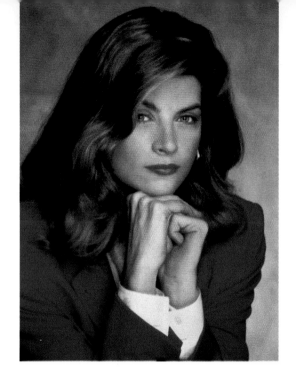

Kirstie Alley, who played opposite Ted Danson in NBC's highly popular *Cheers* after the departure of Shelley Long, was rewarded with a 1991 Emmy as best lead actress in a comedy series.

Filmmaker Ken Burns (right), with writer Shelby Foote, principal on-screen commentator, won two Emmys in 1991 for his brilliant PBS documentary *The Civil War*: one for producing, with Ric Burns, the best informational series, and the other for Outstanding Individual Achievement—Informational Programming.

since 1974, when Cicely Tyson won for her performance in *The Autobiography of Miss Jane Pittman* as both best actress in a special and best actress in a drama. Jones, however, was honored for two separate performances: one in the ABC series *Gabriel's Fire* and one in a TNT cable movie about the 1965 Watts riots titled *Heat Wave*. Thomas Carter won for Outstanding Directing in a Drama Series for an episode of *Equal Justice*.

The telecast was also notable because it was the first event to feature red ribbons, worn by those present in support of the thousands of men, women, and children living with HIV/AIDS. There were so many ribbons being worn at and on the telecast that the producers asked Jamie Lee Curtis to explain their significance.

Among the best-received features of the telecast were clips of classic sitcoms as lead-ins to commercial breaks, inserted by Steve Sohmer, the executive producer. There were tributes during the telecast to four of TV's finest actors who had passed away during the year: Michael Landon, Lee Remick, Danny Thomas, and Colleen Dewhurst, who died two days before the telecast. Dewhurst won the fourth Emmy of her distinguished career, as Outstanding Guest Actress in a Comedy Series for her portrayal of Candice Bergen's mother in *Murphy Brown*.

At the 44th annual Emmy Awards in 1992, the supposed deterioration of family values in America was in the spotlight after Vice President Dan Quayle had publicly criticized the fictitious Murphy Brown for having her baby out of wedlock. To Quayle's presumable displeasure, the Emmy for Outstanding Comedy Series went to *Murphy Brown* for the second time, and Candice Bergen won her third statuette that year. At one point, cohost Dennis Miller made the obvious more obvious by noting, "Boy, Quayle is just getting stomped tonight!"

Heat Wave, a 1990 TNT cable movie about the 1965 Watts riots, starred (left to right) Cicely Tyson, Blair Underwood, Margaret Avery, Vondie Curtis-Hall, and Glenn Plummer, along with James Earl Jones, Sally Kirkland, and Adam Arkin (not pictured).

(Clockwise from center) Kyra Sedgwick, Amanda Plummer, Maximilian Schell, Milton Selzer, and Maureen Stapleton made up the cast of "Miss Rose White," a 1991–92 *Hallmark Hall of Fame* presentation for NBC, executive produced by Marian Rees. Honored as the best film of the year, Plummer also won an Emmy as Outstanding Supporting Actress.

That year, the TV Academy Board consolidated Outstanding Guest Actor/Actress in a Drama and Comedy Series into the Outstanding Lead Actor/Actress categories, eliminating two award categories, thus permitting guest stars to participate in the televised portion of the awards rather than the off-air Creative Arts presentations.

Of the total 319 Emmy nominations that year, *Northern Exposure* led all programs with 16 nominations, while *I'll Fly Away* earned 14. Both were from the producing team of Joshua Brand and John Falsey and were nominated for Outstanding Drama Series (*Northern Exposure* won that award, plus five others). Eric Laneuville received the Outstanding Directing in a Drama Series award for an episode of *I'll Fly Away*.

Roseanne Arnold and her then-husband, Tom Arnold, presented the Emmy for Outstanding Supporting Actress in a Comedy Series to her *Roseanne* costar Laurie Metcalf. Beau Bridges received the Outstanding Lead Actor in a Miniseries or Special honors for playing the title role in HBO's *Without Warning: The James Brady Story*, and brought Brady, in a wheelchair, on stage with him. A *Hallmark Hall of Fame* presentation, "Miss Rose White," received 10 nominations and won four Emmys, including best television movie.

(Right) Among the highest rated television movies of the 1990s was "Sarah, Plain and Tall," a *Hallmark Hall of Fame* presentation. Glenn Close and Christopher Walken costarred in the 1990–91 love story based on Patricia MacLachlan's book about a New England woman answering an ad for a wife placed by a widowed Kansas father. Close, who coexecutive produced, was nominated for an Emmy, as was Walken.

Outstanding Dramatic Actor, Outstanding Sense of Humor

At the 43rd annual Emmy Awards in 1991, James Earl Jones enjoyed the rare distinction of winning two Emmys on the same night for two different acting roles. He won best actor for the ABC drama series *Gabriel's Fire* and a supporting honor for the cable film *Heat Wave* (below). Yet a lot of the newspaper publicity the next day showed an image of Jones with cream pie on his face.

The pie came before the Emmys, and it came not only with the approval of Jones but also that of his 11-year-old son. It happened because producer Steve Sohmer, sometimes known as the "P.T. Barnum of television," was looking to put more dazzle and showmanship into the Emmy Awards ceremony.

Jones was first up in what the *Los Angeles Times* was later to describe as a "down and dirty—and funny" telecast. He introduced the theme of the night, which was a tribute to television comedy. The pie in the face was both a reminder of TV comedy's primitive beginnings and a punctuation mark to his dead-serious introduction.

"I had to clear the pie in the face with my son, who was about 11 at the time," Jones was later to admit. "His dignity was all tied up with ours."

"Why would you want to do a thing like that?" his son wanted to know.

"Well," Jones took pains to explain, "because the guy I'm playing is a jerk. He says pompous things. He deserves a pie in the face. It's a bit like the green soup on Nickelodeon."

Suddenly it all became clear to his son. "If it's like Nickelodeon," he said, "it's okay."

Asked again years later why he would submit to the ignoble pie, Jones simply pointed out, "If we take ourselves too seriously, we have to stop."

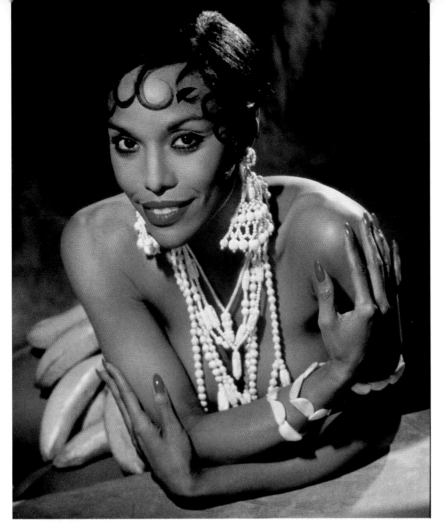

"It's about time."

—Lynn Whitfield, best actress in a miniseries or special for HBO's *The Josephine Baker Story*, asked to comment on the success of blacks in that year's Emmy competition, 1991

.

Ted Turner, recognized for his contribution to the TV industry as president of the Turner Broadcasting System and founder of the Cable News Network, was recipient of the ATAS Governors Award. Celebrated for his often outrageous and hilarious off-the-cuff remarks, Turner had his famed "motor mouth" in idle that night, making no news nor making anybody laugh. NBC's late-night *The Tonight Show Starring Johnny Carson*, which ended its 30-year run in May, won an Emmy as Outstanding Variety, Music, or Comedy Program, and also was honored with a retrospective of clips.

After six consecutive years of Emmy telecasts on Fox, ABC successfully negotiated for the next four years. The TV Academy rejected a rotating four-network bid for the Emmys in exchange for the ABC deal. The 45th annual Emmy Awards, hosted by Angela Lansbury,

"With all the proliferation of channels that are going to be available, and the new networks that are going to exist—in cable, pay, and broadcast—obviously there are going to be greater and more opportunities to do programming you're passionate about."

—Brad Grey, executive producer of *The Larry Sanders Show*, after the HBO series became the first cable entry to be nominated for either best comedy or drama series, 1993

(Right) Craig T. Nelson, star of the ABC comedy series *Coach*, hoped his 1992 Emmy as best actor would finally give his show credibility with critics.

(Below, right) With his fifth nomination for an Emmy, distinguished British actor John Gielgud finally captured the elusive lady in 1991 for his acting in "Summer's Lease" for PBS' *Masterpiece Theatre*.

(Below, left) Roseanne Barr (as she was then known) and costar John Goodman in the working class sitcom *Roseanne*. At the 45th annual prime-time Emmy Awards in 1993, Roseanne won as best lead actress in a comedy series.

What the Emmy Means to Me

"I've been lucky to receive several Emmys. Unfortunately, I was only able to be present to say thank you on one occasion. As a matter of fact, it wasn't exactly an Emmy. It was when I was inducted into the Television Academy Hall of Fame [in 1992]. At that point, I broke down and cried. Come to think of it, my emotional reaction was better than words. I've been involved in television all my adult life. To be complemented by your peers is overwhelming. Let me publicly say thank you for my Emmys. I'm truly honored."

—Dick Clark, Emmy winner, 1978–79, 1984–85, 1985–86

turned out to be a banner event for HBO, which went in with 55 nominations (combined with entries from its other channels, the cable TV sector had a total of 76 nominations, nearly 20 percent of the 367 announced by ATAS). HBO won six Emmys that night to add to the 11 it collected in nontelevised ceremonies for craft categories the previous night, for a total 17 awards. HBO had only won a total of 23 Emmys in its previous five years of eligibility. Three fact-based, made-for-cable movies were in the forefront of the HBO wins. *Stalin*, which won four Emmys, and *Barbarians at the Gate* tied as best TV movie. *The Positively True Adventures of the Alleged Texas Cheerleader-Murdering Mom* won three awards, including Emmys for Holly Hunter as lead actress, Beau Bridges as supporting actor, and Jane Anderson as writer.

Cheers, in its final season, won Emmys for star Ted Danson (his second) and for the editing of its final episode. These wins gave the NBC comedy a total of 28 Emmys over its 11-season lifespan, just behind the 29 Emmys won by *The Mary Tyler Moore Show* in its seven-season run. Moore herself received another Emmy that year, this time as best supporting actress in a miniseries or special for the Lifetime movie *Stolen Babies*. It was Moore's seventh Emmy, tying her with former costar Ed Asner. NBC's *Seinfeld*, around since the spring of 1990, finally broke through and was named Outstanding Comedy Series. Supporting actor Michael Richards was honored for his work on *Seinfeld*, as was the writing of series cocreator Larry David (his second award for the series). Not only did Laurie Metcalf win again for ABC's *Roseanne*, but the series star, Roseanne Arnold, won as well. CBS' *Picket Fences* was named Outstanding Drama Series, and its stars, Kathy Baker and Tom Skerritt, were voted top lead actor and actress in a drama.

In 1994, CBS lost its National Football League rights package to Fox

Without Warning
Thunderous Applause

James Brady, in a wheelchair, with his TV alter ego Beau Bridges clutching an Emmy, both with right thumbs up—it's that indelible image that comes to mind when recalling the 44th annual Emmy Awards. Flash back to 1981. John Hinckley shoots President Ronald Reagan and three others outside the Washington Hilton hotel. One of those three was James Brady, White House Press Secretary. Now 11 years later, Brady is up on stage at the Pasadena Civic Auditorium, unable to walk, yet triumphant, brought there by the actor who played him in HBO's *Without Warning: The James Brady Story*.

Bridges won an Emmy as Outstanding Lead Actor in a Miniseries or Special. Few expected Brady to be in attendance, but Bridges knew. When he mentioned in his acceptance speech that the subject of *Without Warning* was in the hall, the cameras sought him out at the back of the auditorium. He was urged to come forward and accept the Emmy with Bridges. To the thunderous applause of the star-studded audience, James Brady made the long journey back from the darkest day of his life.

Johnny Carson made his final appearance as host of NBC's Emmy-winning *The Tonight Show Starring Johnny Carson* on May 22, 1992, after nearly 30 years at the helm of the undisputed leader in late-night TV talk shows.

(Above, left) James Garner and Jonathan Pryce in HBO's *Barbarians at the Gate*. The film shared the prize for best made for TV movie of the 1992-93 season with *Stalin*, starring Robert Duvall (above, right).

Emmy Runs in the Family
Shari, Mallory, and "Lamb Chop"

"Lamb Chop" creator and alter-ego Shari Lewis had 11 of her 12 daytime and local Emmys in the living room of her home in Beverly Hills. The 12th went to the producer of *Shariland*, the program for which she won her first two Emmys in 1957, for being the best female performer as well as having the best show.

"My collection of them is like having a dance chorus of Emmys," she said. "They're very beautiful. Every time you win an Emmy it's a reinforcement of your value in the industry."

An accomplished actress, ventriloquist, and puppeteer, Lewis (who died in 1998) and her daughter Mallory became the first mother–daughter team to win Emmy Awards for the same show when they were honored with best writing in a children's series for PBS' *Lamb Chop's Play-Along* in 1993.

Broadcasting Co. Later, in one of the most significant developments in recent television history, Fox captured 12 major market affiliates from the Big Three networks, with CBS feeling the impact most seriously. This initiated a desperate scramble by the networks to hold on to stations and audience share. In another pivotal development, two direct broadcast satellite providers, DirecTV and USSB, launched programming services in the summer. In June, the police chase of O.J. Simpson's white Bronco was televised live by all the major networks to an estimated 95 million viewers.

By the time of the Emmys, President Clinton was seeking dismissal, for the duration of his presidency, of a lawsuit charging sexual harassment filed against him by a former Arkansas state employee, Paula Jones. Prior to 1994's annual awards event, the TV Academy confirmed a new deal to rotate the Prime-time Emmys among the Big Three networks and Fox Broadcasting. ABC, which had three years remaining on an exclusive four-year agreement, still broadcast the awards show in September and, through the random spin of a four-network wheel, in 1996. Fox would air the show in 1995, with CBS and NBC getting their turns in 1997 and 1998, respectively.

Against the background of new AIDS cases doubling in the United States the previous year, one of the major awards at the 46th annual Emmys in September was given to a movie dramatizing the early days of the AIDS crisis and those who tried to call attention to it, made by HBO after being rejected by NBC and ABC. *And the Band Played On* was chosen best made-for-TV movie. It was based on a book by Randy Shilts, a *San Francisco Chronicle* reporter who wrote about AIDS and other issues of concern to the gay community. Producer Aaron Spelling accepted the Emmy on behalf of Shilts, who had died of AIDS some six months earlier.

The Emmy Awards show also paid tribute to actress Jessica Tandy, a past Emmy winner who had died at 85 earlier that day in Connecticut. Tandy was nominated for Outstanding Lead Actress in a Miniseries or Special for "To Dance with the White Dog," a *Hallmark Hall of Fame* presentation for CBS, but that Emmy was won by Kirstie Alley for CBS' *David's Mother*. Tandy's husband, costar Hume Cronyn, was nominated for the same special as his wife, and received the award for best actor. *David's Mother* also received Emmys for writer Bob Randall and actor Michael Goorjian, who played the mentally retarded son in the program.

CBS' *Picket Fences* won the Emmy for Outstanding Drama Series for

Angela and the Elusive Emmy

She is a star of the stage and motion picture screen. She was the winner of five Golden Globes and four Tonys, and was nominated for three Oscars. In 1991, she was honored with a special British equivalent of the Academy Award, presented to her in the presence of Queen Elizabeth II. She was host of the 45th annual Emmy Awards in 1993, and also hosted the Tony Awards from 1987 to 1989.

She has been the recipient of 16 Emmy nominations during her career. Nominations included performances in the miniseries *Little Gloria...Happy at Last* (1983), the cable presentation of *Sweeney Todd* (1985), "The 1987 Tony Awards" (1987), and "The 43rd Annual Tony Awards" (1990). She was nominated 12 times as lead actress in a drama series for her performance as Jessica Fletcher in *Murder, She Wrote*. In 1995, she was inducted into the TV Academy Hall of Fame.

She's Angela Lansbury, and she's never taken home an Emmy. But don't count her out yet.

How Emmy Works
Peer Selections

So you want to win an Emmy? There are two ways to enter the annual competition: Individuals may make their entry on their own or on the behalf of their team (e.g., a writing team or a costuming team). Individuals or a program may be entered by a program's producer. In early March, entry cards are made available to both members and non-members of the Academy. Thereafter, it's out of the entrant's hands. Entries are verified as being correct and complete. To determine nominees, some entries are screened by panels, with the highest vote-getters emerging as the nominees.

Most entries are placed on separate ballots, according to type (e.g., program entries on the program ballot, performer entries on the performer ballot). Ballots are voted on by appropriate peer groups. Entrants who receive the most votes in each category are announced as the prime-time nominees, concluding the first phase of the judging.

The second phase of Emmy judging has members of the Academy gathering in panels and screening the nominated achievements in peer groups. Votes are tabulated by accountants, and the top vote-getters are announced at the Creative Arts and Prime-time Emmy Awards ceremonies. The competition takes about a year to complete from the day the Awards Committee begins its annual review of the rules and procedures to the night of the awards presentation.

The Awards Committee is comprised of two representatives from each of the Academy's peer groups. John Leverence, former conference administrator for the American Film Institute who had been with the TV Academy since 1980, is Awards Director. The Committee reviews the rules and procedures of the competition. The Committee's recommendations are sent to the TV Academy's Board of Governors for approval. After the awards presentations, the Awards Committee convenes to review the rules and procedures, and the Emmy cycle begins again.

The Academy of Television Arts & Sciences established the current structure of peer groups in 1977. This was in the wake of ATAS and the National Academy of Television Arts & Sciences separating into two entities. There are a total of 24 peer groups to ensure that all those arts, crafts, and sciences involved in creating television programming are represented in the Academy.

The groups are structured identically. Each functions under the leadership of two governors. Group meetings provide forums for individuals with similar talents and skills to discuss Academy business as well as career concerns. This system also guarantees that Emmy nominees are selected by their peers: writers vote for writers, performers vote for performers, sound editors vote for sound editors.

The programming categories, though, are different. All active members vote for nominated programs of any kind. Membership in peer groups is restricted and designed for those individuals who have contributed their creative talents to the enhancement of television.

The total national active membership of ATAS is 8,489. There are also 569 national associate members. In addition there is a total Los Angeles–area active membership of 175 and associate membership of 77. The TV Academy started in November 1946 with seven men attending a meeting at 5545 Sunset Boulevard in Hollywood. Emmy made her inaugural bow on January 25, 1949, before about

"I was blown away. I didn't think I would win. The clock was going by so quickly, and there were so many people to thank."

—Michael Richards, winning a best supporting actor award for *Seinfeld*, on why he didn't make an acceptance speech, 1994

1,000 people. A year later, in 1950, membership of the Academy totaled 576 persons engaged, in one way or another, in various disciplines of what was then generally referred to as "video." This included 497 local Los Angeles–area voting members, a few associate members, and a group in San Francisco. Today, the TV Academy, having experienced a 5 percent growth in the last year alone, has a membership totaling 9,310, excluding students (there are 165 student members).

The Peer Groups and their active membership is as follows (as of January 1998):

Animation (379)

Art Directors/Scenic Designers (237)

Casting Executives (146)

Children's Programming (88)

Cinematographers (85)

Commercials (194)

Costume Designers/Costume Supervisors (159)

Daytime Programming (216)

Directors/Choreographers (382)

Electronic Production (348)

Informational Programming (180)

Makeup Artists/Hairstylists (200)

Music (249)

Performers (1229)

Producers (797)

Production Executives (447)

Professional Representatives (270)

Public Relations (265)

Sound (304)

Sound Editors (290)

Telecommunication Executives (768)

Television Motion Picture Editors (201)

Title Design and Special Visual FX (112)

Writers (895)

(Left) Sela Ward won one of the key 1993–94 Emmys as best lead actress in a drama series for her role as Teddy Reed in NBC's family drama *Sisters*.

Kathy Baker (right) won three Emmys (1993, 1995, 1996) for her role as Dr. Jill Brock on *Picket Fences*, a CBS series created by David Kelley about life in a quirky midwestern town. After winning her third Emmy, she said "This wasn't supposed to happen again, goodness. I think it's clear by now to everybody that *Picket Fences* has been very, very good to me."

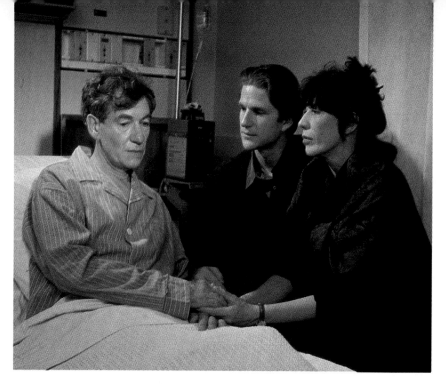

"The band is playing on, and Washington hasn't done a damn thing about it."

—Producer Aaron Spelling after winning an Emmy for his television movie on the AIDS crisis, *And the Band Played On*, 1994 (above, featuring Ian McKellen, Matthew Modine, and Lily Tomlin).

the second consecutive year. NBC's *Frasier* was named Outstanding Comedy Series, and its star, Kelsey Grammer, was named Outstanding Lead Actor in a Comedy Series. Candice Bergen won her fourth Emmy as the title character in *Murphy Brown*. *NYPD Blue* garnered a record-setting 26 nominations, more than any other series in the history of television. The ABC police drama came out of Emmy weekend with six awards, more than any other show that year. *Frasier* and *Picket Fences* were next with five each. Four awards went to the CBS miniseries *Oldest Living Confederate Widow Tells All*, including one to Cicely Tyson as Outstanding Supporting Actress in a Miniseries or a Special.

Highlights of the telecast included Bette Midler recreating moments from the musical *Gypsy*, and Jason Alexander doing a parody of theme songs from *All in the Family* to *The Brady Bunch*. Don Mischer was exec-

Cyndi Lauper won an Emmy in 1995 as Outstanding Guest Actress in a Comedy Series for a performance on NBC's *Mad About You*. The actress and pop star played Marianne Lugasso in an episode titled after one of her hit songs, "Money Changes Everything."

Jessica Tandy and Hume Cronyn
An Emmy Legacy

Jessica Tandy, who won an Oscar in 1989 for her role in *Driving Miss Daisy* and a Tony in 1978 for *The Gin Game*, was a star of television as well as of film and stage. She and her husband, Hume Cronyn, were both Emmy nominees in 1994 for the CBS special "To Dance With the White Dog." They were no strangers to Emmy. Cronyn and Tandy are among the select handful of husbands and wives who have both won the award.

In "To Dance With the White Dog," a *Hallmark Hall of Fame* production, Cronyn played a man who must adjust to being a widower after his wife of 57 years, portrayed by Tandy, dies. Then on September 11, 1994, the day of the 46th Emmys, Tandy, 85, passed away. The couple had been married for 52 years.

The awards show paid tribute to the actress. John Lithgow, as part of the tribute, noted that she was one of the few performers "to receive an Oscar, an Emmy, and a Tony." He added, "We will all miss you very much." The program then showed clips from "To Dance With the White Dog," for which Cronyn would earn his third Emmy later that evening, as Outstanding Lead Actor in a Miniseries or Special. Accepting for Cronyn was presenter Holly Hunter, who said simply, "Hume Cronyn is with his family in Connecticut tonight."

J.R. Carpenter (ATAS internship recipient in Production Management) poses with Emmy winner Laurie Metcalf of *Roseanne* outside the Pasadena Civic Auditorium after the 46th annual Prime-time Emmy Awards, September 11, 1994.

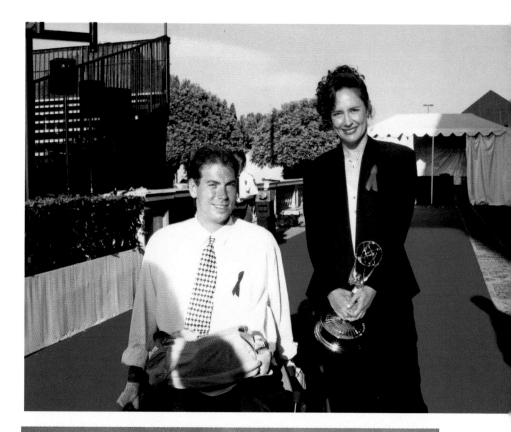

"It's flattering. Sometimes it feels like it's deserved. You work a lifetime trying to get recognition."

—Kelsey Grammer, winning for NBC's *Frasier* as Outstanding Lead Actor in a Comedy Series, 1994

Fellow *ER* cast members George Clooney (Dr. Douglas Ross), Anthony Edwards (Dr. Mark Greene), Sherry Stringfield (Dr. Susan Lewis), and Eriq LaSalle (Dr. Peter Benton) were all nominees at the 47th annual Emmy awards, but only Julianna Margulies (nurse Carole Hathaway, the sole nondoctor in the bunch) walked away with a statuette that evening.

A 30-Year Wait Gets Barbra Eight

On the night of September 10, 1995, in Pasadena, California, a 53-year-old multitalented entertainer—a singer, an actress, a producer/director—is up on stage receiving an Emmy. She had won an Emmy previously in 1965 for her first television special, "My Name Is Barbra." The audience of her peers, press, industry executives, and visiting dignitaries gives her a standing ovation. The Emmy is for Outstanding Individual Performance in a Variety or Music Program. The special, HBO's "Barbra Streisand: The Concert," would earn five Emmys that night, including one for Outstanding Variety, Music, or Comedy Program.

When the ovation quiets, Streisand tells the audience that her Emmy this time is more significant than the first one because of the self doubts she had to face while putting together the concert tour that became the basis for the television special. "Thanks to the many fans who filled those concert halls and filled my heart," she said.

Streisand's 1995 rendezvous with Emmy had a few more golden moments. She also was one of the executive producers of *Serving in Silence: The Margarethe Cammermeyer Story*, which won three Emmys. More than 30 years after her first, award-winning foray into television, her two productions at the 47th annual Emmy Awards won a total of eight Emmys. Her 30-year-old statuette suddenly had lots of company.

Glenn Close
Third Time's the Charm

At the 47th annual Emmy Awards, Glenn Close—coexecutive producer and star of *Serving in Silence: The Margarethe Cammermeyer Story*—stood at the podium and thanked the subject of this fact-based TV movie "for the privilege of trying to fill your shoes."

The NBC program, which aired in February 1995, was about an Army nurse who was discharged when she disclosed she was a lesbian. It won three Emmys: for best actress (Glenn Close), best supporting actress (Judy Davis), and best writer (Alison Cross). Although better known as a big screen actress, Close has great respect for the power of television. She thinks it's perfect for certain unusual dramatic pieces such as *Serving in Silence*. "It was just one of those fascinating stories I was hoping to do," she explained. "It was a great acting challenge."

Close went to the 1995 Emmy Awards event neither anticipating a win nor expecting not to win. She was nominated twice before for what critics agreed were superb performances, once in 1984 for *ABC Theatre*'s "Something About Amelia," and seven years later for *Hallmark*'s "Sarah, Plain and Tall" on CBS. She lost the first time to Jane Fonda for her performance in another *ABC Theatre* production, "The Dollmaker," and the second to Lynn Whitfield for *The Josephine Baker Story*. Those experiences were not at all disappointing to her, Close maintained. "I don't do what I do in order to win awards," she pointed out to an interviewer.

When the Emmys came for *Serving in Silence*, Close thought of the moment as being almost "unreal." Mostly, she was excited and grateful for the people who voted for the television film.

"I already had a fantastic time and was part of something I was very, very proud of," she said later. "Whether we won or not, it wouldn't have lessened that feeling. Yet having the entire project recognized by winning was a very happy thing."

"Thank you for the privilege of trying to fill your shoes."

—Actress Glenn Close to Margarethe Cammermeyer, an Army nurse and the subject of a fact-based TV movie about her fight with the military after she disclosed she was a lesbian, 1995

Bob Hope
"Mr. Entertainment"

On Saturday, November 23, 1996, at age 93, Bob Hope did his final special for NBC, "Laughing With the Presidents." He spent 60 years with the network, hosting his first NBC radio broadcast in 1935. He's entered into the *Guinness Book of World Records* as the entertainer with "the longest-running contract with a single network."

Hope made his television debut on Easter Sunday in 1950 on an hour-long comedy-variety program "All Star Revue." From 1948 until 1972, Hope aired an annual Christmas show; in 1966, he won an Emmy as executive producer of the best variety special for "Chrysler Presents the Bob Hope Christmas Special."

Hope never won an Emmy as a performer. But he's the only individual to win both a Television Academy Trustees Award (1966) and Governors Award (1984). He also won four special Oscars among more than 1,000 awards and citations for his humanitarian and professional efforts, and 50 honorary doctorate degrees.

Hope was inducted into the Television Academy Hall of Fame in 1987 along with Johnny Carson, Jacques-Yves Cousteau, Leonard Goldenson, Jim Henson, Ernie Kovacs, and Eric Sevareid. The inscription on the sculpture of Hope in the Hall of Fame reads: "The world's comedy legend. All generations thank 'Mr. Entertainment' for his unstinting contributions to make all our lives happier."

The original cast of NBC's gritty police/legal drama *Law & Order*, featured Richard Brooks, George Dzundza, Chris North, and Michael Moriarty, but there has been considerable cast turnover since the series started in 1990. Seven years after that start, *Law & Order* was named Outstanding Dramatic Series.

(Right) Jeffrey Tambor, Rip Torn, and Garry Shandling of *The Larry Sanders Show*. In both 1996 and 1997 HBO's comedy series amassed the most nominations of any sitcom, 12 the first year, 16 the next. Torn won an Emmy in 1996 as best supporting actor.

(Below, right) Four of the six main cast members of *Friends*, the most popular new sitcom of the 1994–95 season. (Left to right) Matthew Perry, Courteney Cox, Jennifer Aniston, and Matt LeBlanc.

(Below, left) Mandy Patinkin (at a post-Emmy party with his wife, Kathryn Grody) won a 1995 statuette as Outstanding Lead Actor in a Drama Series for his role as Dr. Jeffrey Geiger in David E. Kelley's medical drama, *Chicago Hope*.

utive producer, and cohosts were Patricia Richardson (*Home Improvement*) and Ellen DeGeneres (*Ellen*). Hank Rieger, editor-in-chief of *Emmy* magazine, received the Syd Cassyd Founders Award at the nontelevised portion of the Emmys. Rieger served as president of the Academy from 1977 to 1980. He joined past recipients ATAS founder Syd Cassyd and the late Robert F. Lewine, another former Academy president.

In January 1995, two more broadcast networks, UPN and The WB, emerged to take on what was now the Big Four. In July, the prime-time access rule, which prohibited big-market Big Three affiliates from airing off-network shows in access, was repealed. In 1995,

Leeza Gibbons
Hanging With the Winners

"The most universal image I have of interviewing Emmy winners is how tightly they clutch their statuettes. It's really an energy charge to be the first one on the scene after they've received their award and share in their excitement of being recognized by their peers. It's interesting to contrast the atmosphere from the red-carpet arrivals to the backstage interviews. When the nominees are getting out of their limos and parading in front of the fans, they are tense and many of them nervous. Once the winners' names have been announced, win or lose, that tension goes out of the air and a celebration party atmosphere engulfs the rest of the evening.

"The two most universal Emmy dilemmas based on my experience with the nominees are: 'What am I going to wear?' and 'What am I going to say if I win?' When the show starts, since it's live, it's usually hot and sunny [late afternoon on the West Coast, so that it can air during prime time on the East Coast] so the female stars are bare-shouldered with their sunglasses on, and by the end of the evening they are all fighting over wraps to keep warm.

"What's most fun for me is to watch the fan club that exists among the celebrities. That long line of arrivals gives these celebrities a chance to hang with each other. We have this feeling that they all know each other, but the fact is they're so busy working that they often don't get a chance to socialize. Forget what they say about back stabbing and fierce competition. I've witnessed genuine respect and mutual admiration."

—Leeza Gibbons, Veteran Entertainment Industry Reporter and Daytime Emmy winner

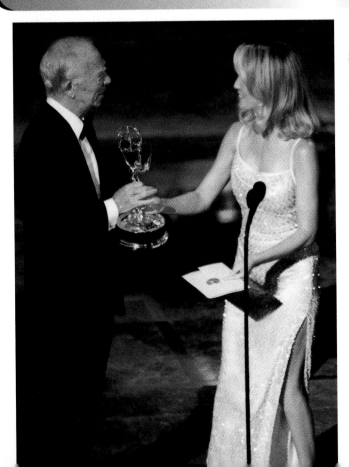

Some 30 years after he starred in *My Favorite Martian*, veteran Ray Walston received back-to-back Emmys in 1995 and 1996 for his role as Judge Henry Bone in *Picket Fences*. Here presenting him with his award is Heather Locklear. "I have 30 seconds to tell you that I've been waiting 60 years to get on this stage," said Walston.

Helen Hunt was honored three times—in 1996, 1997, and 1998—for her role as Jamie Buchman on NBC's *Mad About You*. The latter year was a lucky one for her as she also won an Academy Award and a Golden Globe for her starring role in 1997's *As Good As It Gets*. In accepting her first Emmy, Hunt said, "I'd like to thank Candice Bergen for her generosity of spirit," acknowledging five-time Emmy winner Bergen's decision to withdraw her name from competition to allow others a chance.

Frankenheimer's Comeback
Three in a Row

"It's such a great feeling," the esteemed director said as he clutched an Emmy. "It has never gotten easier," he noted about a career in directing that began with *I Remember Mama*, *You Are There*, and *Danger*. This director, who finally broke through and won an Emmy at the 46th annual Emmys in 1994, was John Frankenheimer.

Before this late-career achievement, he had directed more than 40 *Playhouse 90* dramas, and received Emmy nominations for "Portrait in Celluloid" (*Climax*, CBS, 1955), "Forbidden Area" (*Playhouse 90*, CBS, 1956), "The Comedian" (*Playhouse 90*, CBS, 1957), "A Town Has Turned to Dust" (*Playhouse 90*, CBS, 1959), and "The Turn of the Screw" (*Ford Startime*, NBC, 1960). He also directed such memorable theatrical feature films as *The Manchurian Candidate*, *Seven Days in May*, *The Birdman of Alcatraz*, and *Seconds*.

Frankenheimer's career was revived by directing for cable. That first Emmy, for Outstanding Directing in a Limited Series or a Special, was for HBO's prison drama *Against the Wall*. As he accepted it, his second Emmy was waiting in the wings, for his next cable assignment, *The Burning Season* (starring Raul Julia as murdered Brazilian activist Chico Mendes), was scheduled to premier the following week on HBO. He won a directing Emmy for that cable movie in 1995, and still another in 1996 for *Andersonville*. After waiting 40 years to win an Emmy, John Frankenheimer won three in a row.

"People love to see serious actors slip and fall on their butts."

—John Lithgow after winning his second consecutive Emmy for his leading role in NBC's *3rd Rock From the Sun*, 1997

(Clockwise from top) *ER* costars Anthony Edwards and George Clooney were presenters at the 1995 Emmys, which were domi-nated by the medical drama. Their show's eight wins tied with *Hill Street Blues* for most Emmys ever won by a series in a single season. Dennis Franz, Sharon Lawrence, Gail O'Grady, and Jimmy Smits were on hand when their series, *NYPD Blue,* picked up an Emmy as 1995's Outstanding Drama Series. For his role as Detective Andy Sipowicz in the groundbreaking show, Franz won three Emmys as lead actor in a drama series in 1994, 1996, and 1997. Steven Bochco accepted *NYPD Blue*'s Emmy for best drama series in 1995. Genuinely shocked because his show had broken *ER*'s clean sweep, Bochco said, "What a surprise. Holy mackerel." *NYPD Blue* is a truly collaborative enterprise because it is the product of four executive producers, four coexecutive producers, one line producer, three coproducers, one coordinating producer, and one consulting producer. Christine Baranski, Cybill Shepherd's costar on *Cybill*, exults in her

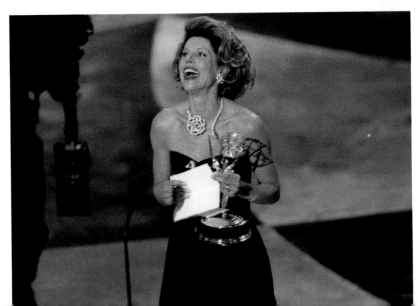

win as best supporting actress in a comedy series for the 1994–95 season. Shepherd and *Seinfeld* costar Jason Alexander hosted the 1994–95 Emmys.

(Above, left) *Truman*, a biography of the 33rd president, starring Gary Sinise, was cited as 1995–96's best movie.

(Above, right) *Saturday Night Live* alum Dennis Miller scored big at the 49th annual prime-time Emmy Awards in 1997. He won as executive producer/host and for outstanding writing for a variety or music program for HBO's weekly *Dennis Miller Live*.

Brett Butler
Back in the Game

Brett Butler was overwhelmed at the 48th annual Emmy Awards when he received a standing ovation. Yes, *he*. For it was not the female stand-up comic star of ABC's *Grace Under Fire* who attended the event, but rather the center fielder for the Los Angeles Dodgers.

"I was blown away by the response," said Butler, who, the next day, would start his fourth consecutive game after coming back from a bout with cancer. "I was kind of out of my element," he explained. "Just to go there with those people is something I'll never forget."

Butler's biggest thrill, he said, was meeting Dick Clark. He had dinner with actor David Keith, and was "awe-struck," he reported, by Milton Berle and Carol Burnett.

(Clockwise, from top) Gillian Anderson, Dana Scully in Fox's enormously successful *The X-Files*, won a best actress, drama series, Emmy at the 49th annual awards presentation in 1997. Her costar, David Duchovny, who plays Fox Mulder, being interviewed by *Daily Variety* columnist and Emmy mainstay Army Archerd at the 48th Emmys. Jay Leno won his first Emmy in 1995 for hosting *The Tonight Show*. He thanked network executives Don Ohlmeyer and Warren Littlefield "for sticking by us." After five supporting nominations playing Elaine Benes on *Seinfeld*, Julia Louis-Dreyfus won her first Emmy in 1996. The NBC show became the nation's top-rated TV comedy and a true phenomenon after it replaced *Cheers* on Thursday nights.

Worldwide Appeal
Selling the Telecast to Foreign Markets

The world's most beautiful women, wearing fabulous designer gowns and precious jewelry...Hollywood's handsomest and sexiest men...this is the stuff that sells Emmy from Asia to the Middle East, from South America to Central Europe. Among the exotic places Emmy plays are Djibouti, Honduras, Lesotho, Libya, Morocco, Saudi Arabia, Tobago, Tortola, and Tunisia.

Neve Campbell, Christine Lahti, Jayne Brook, Lisa Kudrow, Roma Downey, Kim Delaney, Kristen Johnston, Simbi Khali, Helen Hunt, and Candice Bergen in their stunning gowns at the 49th annual Emmy Awards are featured in promotional material used to sell the event to overseas broadcasters. So, too, are David Duchovny, in dress shirt and black tie, squiring Tea Leoni; Jerry Seinfeld mugging for the camera; and distinguished-looking John Lithgow greeting Christopher Reeve.

"Glamour and beauty of the people and a personal look at the stars, that's what we sell internationally," confirms Berle Adams, president of The Berle Adams Co. (BAC) in Burbank, California. BAC, a pioneer in international distribution of TV programs, has been handling foreign distribution of the yearly Emmy telecast since 1978. Adams, who was the first to take the television awards event international, celebrates a 20th anniversary at the same time Emmy celebrates her prime-time 50th.

The Emmy Awards telecast is seen in more than 90 foreign countries. This means that Emmy has the capability of reaching some 650 million potential viewers around the world. Many receive the Emmys via satellite, including Africa, Australia, Britain, Canada, Hong Kong, Israel, Latin America and the Caribbean nations, the Middle East, New Zealand, Scandinavia (Denmark, Norway, Sweden, and Finland), Singapore, and Thailand. African nations include Botswana, Egypt, Gabon, Ghana, Kenya, Lesotho, Namibia, Nigeria, Sierra Leone, and the Republic of South Africa. Among territories in the Middle East that receive the Emmy Awards telecast are Bahrain, Cyprus, Iran, Iraq, Jordan, Kuwait, Lebanon, Oman, Qatar, Saudi Arabia, Syria, United Arab Emirates (Abu Dhabi, Ajman, Dubai, Fujairah, Ras Al Khaimah, Umm Al Quwain, Sharjah), and Yemen. In North Africa, Emmy is made available to Algeria, Chad, Djibouti, Libya, Mauritania, Morocco, Somalia, Sudan, and Tunisia.

All territories (defined as the geographical area represented by the outer boundaries of the region or nation/state) except Canada (CTV Network), where the program airs live, see the show via a delayed broadcast. This allows the program to be aired into a prime-time slot, and when necessary, sufficient time to subtitle in the native language, as well as insert local commercials.

Even satellite carriers such as Sky Channel in the U.K., Canal Jimmy in France, and TNT Latin America provide the telecast on a delayed basis. The latter offers the Emmys in English, with simultaneous translation in Spanish and Portuguese. Territories under TNT Latin America coverage are Anguilla, Antigua, Argentina, Aruba, Bahamas, Barbados, Bolivia, Bonaire, Brazil, Cayman Islands, Chile, Colombia, Costa Rica, Cuba, Curacao, Dominica, Dominican Republic, El Salvador, Ecuador, French Guiana, Grenada, Guadeloupe, Guatemala, Haiti, Honduras, Jamaica, Martinique, Mexico, Netherlands Antilles, Nicaragua, Panama, Paraguay, Peru, St. Lucia, St. Kitts–Nevis, St. Maarten, St. Vincent and the Grenadines, Tortola, Trinidad and Tobago, Suriname, Uruguay, and Venezuela.

Territories not serviced by satellite receive the Emmy Awards program shipped by videocassette. A tape of the program is picked up after the telecast by IVC of Burbank and immediately duplicated. The next morning the tapes are shipped by air freight or Federal Express. "We have to deliver the scripts [of the Emmy program] to the foreign broadcasters by Wednesday preceding Emmy's Sunday broadcast," explains Adams.

Inevitable last-minute changes are his principal bugaboo, as well as having to work with different American networks each year on the TV Academy's "wheel" rotation arrangement for the annual telecasts. English-speaking territories were among the first to accept the Emmys, with Australia and Canada the initial sales, Adams recalls. The Scandinavian territories broadcast the Emmys in English with subtitles. No country dubs the show. Emmy has too large a cast of on-air personalities for dubbing to be feasible. The standard procedure is to use narrators or subtitles in the native language.

It hasn't always been an easy sell. The TV Academy requires the full telecast to be sold, with no editing permitted. With most of the prime-time presentations running three hours plus, some international buyers balk at making such a lengthy commitment. They prefer a 90-minute show, with the right to edit out American-oriented jokes and references, as well as speeches about the American television industry. "I had to persevere," Adams notes. "We had to use a lot of gimmicks to make it work."

One of the early objections to an overseas broadcast concerned winning programs that didn't air on the overseas Emmy station. In multiple-station markets, the broadcaster of the Emmys worries about promoting the competition's programs. Single-station territories do not necessarily carry a heavy load of U.S. programs.

Adams answers objections by emphasizing that the Emmy Awards is the only program on the air that promotes the general viewing of television. The Emmys add value to the programs and actors familiar to foreign audiences, says Adams, because viewers everywhere like to see the performers who play the characters "as people, as presenters and winners. They like to see them all dressed up and personal." Made-for-TV movies help considerably to sell Emmy, according to Adams, by adding recognizable film personalities to Emmy categories as nominees and winners.

The big selling point, he reports, "is the look of the show, the number of stars, and the excitement of who's going to win the Emmys." The Emmys have "turned the corner" internationally, and Adams is confident. "The Emmys will be bigger overseas as more foreign countries buy U.S. series and Movies of the Week, which is happening now. Emmy is gaining acceptance all over the world," he assures.

"It's nice that the curse is broken. We thought we were going to be the Susan Lucci [the oft-nominated-but-never-winning daytime TV actress] of prime time."

—*Law & Order* creator Dick Wolf, when the show was finally named Outstanding Drama Series after five previous nominations, 1997

"We face pressure because we hold ourselves to a high standard. With all these Emmys, I guess we're kind of a standard-bearer. We just try not to do any bad shows."

—David Lee, executive producer of NBC's *Frasier*, after the comedy series won its fourth consecutive Emmy, 1997

John Lithgow
On Winning the Emmy

John Lithgow, who won successive Emmys in 1996 and 1997 as Outstanding Lead Actor in a Comedy Series for NBC's *3rd Rock From the Sun*, says it was hard to think of the series about aliens on Earth as a mainstream success. He describes his involvement with the vehicle for his Emmy successes as "a big leap of faith." He thought *3rd Rock* would be "a really unusual failure," remembering the way people thought of the quirky British comedies *Monty Python* or *Fawlty Towers*.

By Emmy Awards time in 1996, flushed by its success in the ratings, Lithgow knew that *3rd Rock* had certainly made it big time. Nonetheless, he was a little surprised and very pleased to hear his name announced as the winner.

"It's always a shock to hear your name called, even if you're the odds-on favorite," he explained. "I knew the role was a much more virtuoso role than that of many other lead actors in comedy. I really have carte blanche as Dick Solomon [head alien visitor to Earth]. I knew from the very beginning I would be showing all my stuff. It's a huge showcase. That certainly gives me a leg up."

Lithgow joined the show with a stellar reputation as a dramatic actor. In 1986, he'd been named Outstanding Guest Performer in a Drama Series for his stint on NBC's *Amazing Stories*. Lithgow told himself prior to his win, "The award for performance in a comedy series is, after all, an award for the best actor in a series…it's a real actor's role…not necessarily the best comic." By this logic, he knew he had a good shot at the award. But *3rd Rock* was still so new he thought the best part of winning that first time was the "validation" of the series as well as of himself in a comedy role.

Lithgow's three Emmys reside on top of a sort of credenza in his dressing room. He points out that he spends half his life there so it's a totally appropriate place to keep them. "I try not to put too much importance on awards because many of them are very arbitrary," he says. "By now I feel that I've had way more than my share. In fact, it may be appropriate sometime, probably sooner than later, to recuse myself. It's almost embarrassing to win too many of these."

Lithgow also has been nominated three times for Emmys and not won. "It truly doesn't bother me not to win," he maintains. "There are always huge numbers of deserving people who aren't even nominated."

too, the TV Academy reworded its bylaws to honor programming on "telecommunications," not just television. This was the organization's way of more closely embracing cable and all future carriers on the rapidly expanding electronic superhighway. Just prior to the 47th annual Emmy Awards, the megamedia age dawned with Disney's $18.5 billion purchase of CapCities/ABC and Westinghouse's $5.4 billion deal for CBS. These striking examples of the big getting bigger were topped when media giant Time Warner acquired Turner Broadcasting System in an $8 billion stock swap.

NBC's new medical drama *ER*, which came in with 23 nominations, won eight Emmys at that year's presentations, including best supporting actress, best direction, and best writing. The eight wins tied *ER* with *Hill Street Blues* for most Emmys ever won by a series in a single season, but *NYPD Blue* won the award for Outstanding Drama Series.

Frasier, in its second season, won its second consecutive Emmy for Outstanding Comedy Series, and took four additional Emmys, including acting awards for star Kelsey Grammer and supporting actor David Hyde Pierce. *Murphy Brown* star Candice Bergen took home her fifth best actress award (and thereafter, she would elect not to enter herself in the competition).

Barbra Streisand was a winner for both her HBO special "Barbra Streisand: The Concert," which won five Emmys, and as an executive producer of *Serving in Silence: The Margarethe Cammermeyer Story,* which won three.

The Academy celebrated its golden anniversary in 1996. Dick Clark was executive producer of that year's telecast, and Paul Reiser cohosted the ceremonies with Michael J. Fox and Oprah Winfrey.

Bette Midler, whose NBC special "Ol' Red Hair Is Back" won an Emmy in 1978, won another in 1992 for her outstanding individual performance in Johnny Carson's final *Tonight Show*. Here she is backstage at the 1997 Emmys after winning again for her performance in "Diva Las Vegas," an HBO special.

Laurence Fishburne and Alfre Woodard both produced and acted in HBO's *Miss Evers' Boys*, which won the Emmy in 1997 for best television movie. The film, about a controversial government study of the effects of syphilis on a group of black men, also won a TV Academy President's Award as well as an acting Emmy for Woodard.

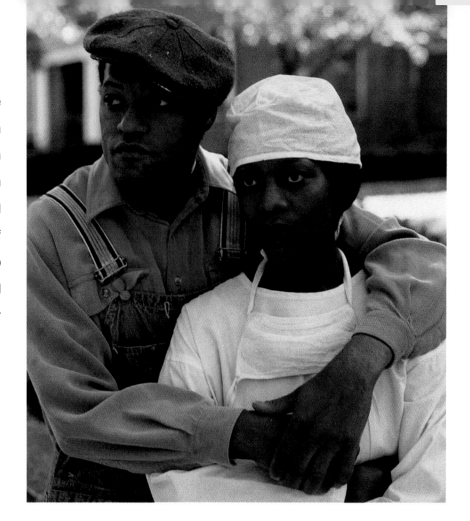

It was a year when Congress passed a landmark telecommunications measure that, among other provisions, called for installation in new TV sets of the V-chip, permitting objectionable material to be blocked electronically. The golden anniversary was commemorated throughout the year with various events and a series of exhibits under the theme "50 Years of Excellence." The 48th annual Emmy Awards featured 50 years of clips with an emphasis on the positive achievements of television. Among the features in the nostalgic broadcast were segments on television theme songs, great moments in television fiction, and a look at television families ranging from the Nelsons of *The Adventures of Ozzie and Harriet* to the Bundys of *Married...With Children*. Carroll O'Connor and Jean Stapleton, fondly remembered for *All in the Family*, got a standing ovation when they presented the night's first award, as did Milton Berle, already a performing star when the TV Academy was formed.

This Emmy telecast also featured the introduction of the President's Award, a new honor designed to recognize a program that explores social and educational issues and that "encourages and promotes...changes that help society." The first President's Award went to cable's American Movie Classics documentary *Blacklist: Hollywood on Trial*.

Ellen DeGeneres of ABC's *Ellen*, along with her writing team, took home Emmys for best writing of a comedy series at the 49th Emmy Awards in 1997. The win was a true victory for DeGeneres because the controversial episode centered on the coming out of her character. Shortly before the episode aired, DeGeneres herself publicly announced that she was a lesbian. She directed her acceptance speech to "all the people, and the teenagers especially, who think there's something wrong with them because they're gay. There's nothing wrong with you. Don't ever let anybody make you feel ashamed of who you are."

The principal awards went to NBC programs. *ER*, the most popular program with audiences that season, entered Emmy night for a second time with more nominations than any other program, and was honored with the Outstanding Drama Series award. *Frasier*, in its third season, was named Outstanding Comedy Series for a third consecutive year. For Helen Hunt, the fourth time was the charm: after being thrice nominated, the *Mad About You* star received an Emmy for Outstanding Lead Actress in a Comedy Series.

Dennis Franz was voted best actor in a drama for his portrayal of Detective Andy Sipowicz in *NYPD Blue* (it was his second Emmy during the show's first three years). Kathy Baker won her third best actress award in four years for CBS' canceled *Picket Fences*, and her castmate Ray Walston, who won his first Emmy the previous year at age 76, repeated as supporting actor in a drama. Tyne Daly was awarded her fifth Emmy (this time for a supporting role) for the short-lived CBS hour-long family drama *Christy*. Also winning a fifth Emmy was Tim Conway; and Betty White won once again for guest starring in *The John Larroquette Show*.

HBO took away 14 Emmys, including one for best movie, *Truman*. It marked the fourth consecutive year that the network took the Emmy in that category.

In 1997, television commercials were nominated for the first time. An HBO spot featuring monkeys mouthing lines from famous movies won the first such award, with the presentation at the nontelevised ceremony for creative arts categories. The TV Academy also released new criteria for what constitutes a program "producer" as it relates to prime-time Emmy Award eligibility.

The 49th annual Awards was arguably the most star-studded ever. Among the 40 presenters: Carol Burnett, Glenn Close, Demi Moore, Jay Leno, Laurence Fishburne, Mel Brooks, Michael J. Fox, Ellen DeGeneres, Gregory Hines, Bob Newhart, Carl Reiner, Jerry Seinfeld, Kelsey Grammer, Candice Bergen, Gillian Anderson, and Anthony Edwards.

In its seventh season, the New York police-and-prosecutors drama *Law & Order* was at last named Outstanding Drama Series. But the show that won the most awards that year was *NYPD Blue:* Dennis Franz, for the third time in four nominations, was named best actor; Kim Delaney was named best supporting actress; and awards were given for directing and writing. *ER*, once again going into the evening with the most nominations, won three, but in technical areas only.

On the comedy series front, the four-year-old *Frasier* was honored as best show for the fourth consecutive year. The show joined the ranks of four-time-winner sitcoms *All in the Family*, *Cheers*, and *The Dick Van Dyke Show*. John Lithgow (*3rd Rock From the Sun*) and Helen Hunt (*Mad About You*) became two-time Emmy recipients in the best lead actor and actress categories, both winning the award in back-to-back years. Lithgow's *3rd Rock* colleague Kristen Johnston won supporting actress in a comedy series with her first nomination. Michael Richards, for his performance as Kramer on *Seinfeld*, won Outstanding Supporting Actor in a Comedy Series for the third time in five nominations.

Winning a third Emmy was Bette Midler, named for Outstanding Individual Performance in a Variety or Music Program for "Diva Las Vegas."

As had become common in recent years, an HBO film, *Miss Evers' Boys*, won as best made-for-TV movie, one of its three Emmys. The pay-cable production, which had 12 nominations, also won the President's Award for socially responsible and educational programming and an acting award for Alfre Woodard, her third win out of 10 nominations. Although best actress nominee Ellen DeGeneres didn't win that award for ABC's *Ellen*, she did receive an Emmy, along with her cowriters, for scripting the highly publicized and watched "coming out" episode.

One of television's bright new stars, comic Chris Rock, who brought a great deal of energy to the telecast, took away his first two Emmys—one for his HBO special, "Chris Rock: Bring the Pain," and the second for writing the show. The Emmy telecast on CBS was executive produced by Don Mischer and, in a departure from standard practice, was hosted by a news personality, Bryant Gumbel.

Comedian Chris Rock won two Emmys at the 1997 presentation for his HBO comedy special, "Bring the Pain." Rock, who won for the best comedy special and for writing the program, said afterwards "I feel like I won for all the stand-ups."

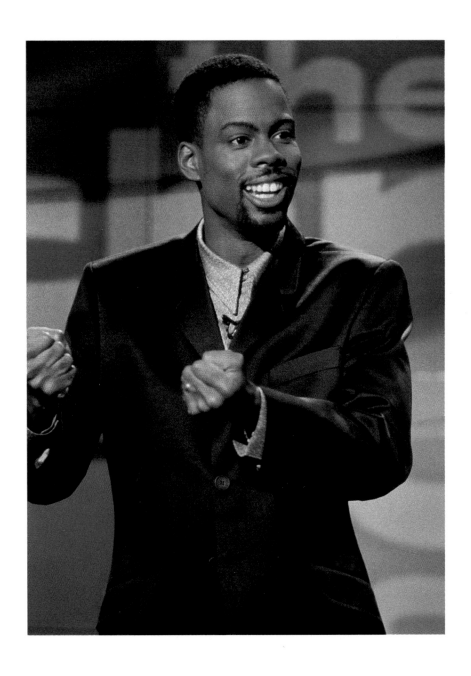

Around The Clock at the
49th Annual Prime-time Emmy Awards

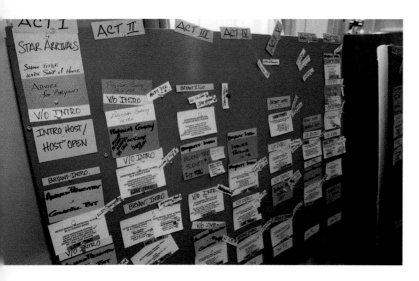

Saturday–Sunday,

September 13-14, 1997

Pasadena Civic Auditorium

Pasadena, Calif.

The 49th Annual Prime-time

Emmys will originate live on the

CBS Television Network, Sunday,

September 14, 8–11 P.M. ET, with

Bryant Gumbel as host.

SATURDAY, 4:30–7:30 P.M.

4:30 P.M.

Many red banners, emblazoned with the outstretched arms of the Emmy symbol, adorn the 67-year-old Pasadena Civic Auditorium between East Green Street and Los Robles Avenue. This is the 20th year the Italian Renaissance–style building will host the prime-time television awards.

4:35 P.M.

Inside the auditorium, the previous red-and-white color scheme has been replaced with what is said to be the original teal blue and dark brown colors. The seats, newly reupholstered, are occupied mostly by signs reserving them for nominees and possible

Emmy winners. Among the cardboard signs: one for Laurence Fishburne, another for Alfre Woodard.

5:05 P.M.

A red carpet is unrolled leading to the auditorium doors. Inside, executive producer Don Mischer, director Louis J. Horvitz, and supervising producer Michael B. Seligman are rehearsing.

5:20 P.M.

Marcus Irwin, graphics/technical director, sits in front of a giant panel with 26 individual TV screens. With pride, he points to EmmyCast '97, the official Prime-time Emmy Webcast (www.emmycast.com). This is the third year for the web site, which will feature the live Internet cybercasting of the Prime-time Emmys by using digital video cameras.

5:42 P.M.

The electric signboard outside the Pasadena Center conference building flashes on. It offers the city of Pasadena's welcome to the 49th Emmys.

5:45 P.M.

A clean-up crew begins to spruce up outside the Civic Center building. Other workers hang three additional Emmy Awards banners over light posts on Green Street.

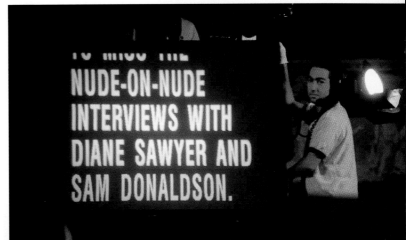

5:47 P.M.

Inside the auditorium, crews are laying cable and checking out camera vantage points.

6:05 P.M.

A credentials table is in place, with various color-keyed name badges displayed. Most impressive is a black-on-gold badge for TV Academy officials, allowing access everywhere, including the post-telecast Governors Ball. Press VIPs get a white-on-black badge, good for overall access except the post-show party. Only press badges with an escort ribbon affixed have access to the arrival area in front of the auditorium.

6:07 P.M.

Security guard William Buchanan takes up a station at Bryant Gumbel's Winnebago parked outside the auditorium. Another Winnebago nearby is for Christopher Reeve, who is scheduled as a presenter on the telecast.

6:10 P.M.

Caterers restock the Green Room with Sweet'n Low, coffee, tea, bottled water, honey, lemon, sugar, soft drinks, fresh fruit, finger sandwiches, and cookies.

6:12 P.M.

Piano tuner Mark Mandell sits quietly on stage in the auditorium, his right ear cocked to the keyboard, fingering idle notes.

6:55 P.M.

Workers from Gary's Tux, a rental company, wheel in rows of tuxedos on racks to the escort area. It's an unusual sight, like a colony of penguins waddling at the South Pole.

7:00 P.M.

An attendant empties ashtrays in the General Press Room. There are some 100 phones and five TV monitors overhead.

7:02 P.M.

Equipment and supplies are moved into the one-on-one studios. ATAS representative Sheri Goldberg supervises the *Access Hollywood*, CBS, *Good Morning America*, *ET*, *Today*, and *E!* program plaza-level rooms. Michael Salas and Janet Smith, also from ATAS, handle studios being set up for CNN and Fox News on the lower level.

7:22 P.M.

Activity in Dressing Room #3, stage left, second floor, the one to be used by Mel Brooks and Bob Newhart. Towels are brought in, along with soap, bottled water, and Pepsi.

SUNDAY, 7:00 A.M.–8:00 P.M.

7:13 A.M.

Approximately 30 people are in the bleachers. A couple of the women are sleeping with their heads on the shoulders of companions. Lots of blankets and Styrofoam coffee cups are in sight. Those who are awake look bored and sleepy-eyed.

It's a mild morning with puffy white clouds against a pale blue sky, the San Gabriel mountains etched sharply in the background. Security guards, camera crews and photographers scurry around everywhere. "I doubt they even slept," somebody comments about the camera people.

7:47 A.M.

It's a beehive outside the auditorium. A man parades in front of the bleachers pushing a baby carriage. A jogger, head down, trots by. Ushers and security people, in everyday

clothes, stream out of several close-by parking lots, uniforms in garment bags slung over their shoulders. Passengers in cars passing by stare in wonderment at the bleacher people, one of whom is now cuddling a baby. A flower delivery truck pulls up and out come baskets of table centerpieces.

"It's the quiet before the hype," a publicity guy quips. "It's like getting ready for the big game," adds a reporter.

A discussion ensues about big names at this year's event.

"George Clooney, if he shows, he's a big star," says one.

"Jerry Seinfeld, Tim Allen, they're big," adds another.

"There's no doubt Demi Moore is a big star," is a third opinion.

8:00 A.M.

The production people begin arriving for an 11:00 A.M. rehearsal.

9:00 A.M.

A janitor is sweeping the stage. Another maintenance man is polishing the piano, a giant replica of Emmy hanging over him.

9:30 A.M.

Garry Hood, stage manager, is working at a teleprompter with Bryant Gumbel's script scrolling on the screen.

10:05 A.M.

A gray-haired man, with beard and glasses, is in the balcony setting up a super crane, used for long shots. He's Ron Sheldon, a six-time Emmy Award winner for his camera work.

10:15 A.M.

As many as 80 people are in the bleachers, some sitting under umbrellas. Bright sun is what they're shielding, not rain. Several people fan themselves with folded newspapers and magazines.

10:41 A.M.

Garry Hood and Mischer talk about props for the telecast. A couple of associate directors are outlining stage setups. A P.R. executive is telling a female reporter that at this time of year "Pasadena becomes Emmy town."

11:00 A.M.

A troop of ushers in red CBS jackets, guys and gals, forms in the back of the auditorium. The telecast rehearsal begins.

11:10 A.M.

Gumbel, wearing glasses, in jeans, T-shirt, and baseball cap on backwards, is on stage doing the Emmy telecast intro, saying that television "undeniably is the most powerful medium in the world," and noting the 1997 Emmy telecast will be seen in 90 countries by an estimated 620 million people and heard in 24 languages.

11:15 A.M.–2:25 P.M.

A group of stand-ins for presenters and "hypothetical" winners goes through the telecast paces briskly.

2:30 P.M.

Led by Craig T. Mathew, ATAS staff photographers, already in formal wear, hold a brief meeting in the lobby of the nearby Holiday Inn. The escort staff meets with ATAS representative Sheri Goldberg in front of the auditorium in the red carpet area.

2:45 P.M.

ATAS reps supply each press room (deadline press, deadline photo, general photo, general press, radio, TV pool) with show programs.

3:00 P.M.

In Room 201, the Academy office, a list is posted of 1997 Prime-time Emmy Awards Presenters.

It reads:

Award #1 Ellen DeGeneres

Award #2 Chris Rock

Award #3 Michael J. Fox

Award #4 Matthew Perry

Award #5 Bob Newhart, Judd Hirsch

Award #6 Gregory Hines

Award #7 Paul Reiser

Award #8 Alan Arkin, Adam Arkin

Award #9 Dana Delany

Award #10 Christopher Reeve

Award #11 Noah Wyle, Eriq La Salle

Award #12 Roma Downey, Della Reese

Award #13 Dennis Franz

Award #14 Garry Shandling

Award #15 Jerry Seinfeld

Award #16 Richard H. Frank [outgoing ATAS president]

Award #17 Christine Lahti

Award #18 Neve Campbell

Award #19 David Duchovny, Gillian Anderson

Award #20 Jimmy Smits

Award #21 Demi Moore

Award #22 Candice Bergen

Award #23 Kelsey Grammer, David Hyde Pierce

Award #24 Jay Leno

Award #25 Helen Mirren

Award #26 Laurence Fishburne, Alfre Woodard
Award #27 Mel Brooks, Carl Reiner
Award #28 Glenn Close

4:00 P.M.

All ATAS staffers have to be in place. Squeals of excitement and applause are heard from the bleacher section as stars and other guests begin to arrive in chauffeur-driven limos and luxurious automobiles. The bleacher crowd goes crazy when Ellen DeGeneres and her partner, Anne Heche, arrive.

4:05 P.M.

Army Archerd and Joan Rivers, with mikes in hand, camera crews in attendance, greet the arrivals; photographers with badges and arrival ribbons prominently displayed scurry around in a frenzy of activity. Emmy dress is black tie for men, gowns for ladies.

4:15 P.M.

The fashion parade is led by Kim Delaney of *NYPD Blue* in violet silk, Roma Downey of *Touched by an Angel* in red and black, and Gillian Anderson of *The X-Files* in a silvery-satin gown with a velvet stole. *Seinfeld's* Julia Louis-Dreyfus is stunning in a strapless satin gown of midnight blue velvet.

4:30 P.M.

Theatre doors are closed.

5:00 P.M.

Show time. Some 2,500 dignitaries, industry executives, TV Academy officials, and world-wide media are in their seats. "CBS Special" logo/network ID comes up, center screen, at the top of the Civic Center Auditorium.

5:01 P.M.

Videotapes of star arrivals are shown, with an announcer voice-over live, followed by theme music and opening titles.

5:03 P.M.

Intro of Bryant Gumbel.

5:05 P.M.

Ellen DeGeneres is on stage presenting Award #1, Outstanding Supporting Actor in a Comedy Series.

5:10 P.M.

The second presenter of the night, comic Chris Rock, who would win two Emmys for an HBO special, jokingly notes the telecast opened "with two black men and a lesbian." As the audience

roars, the comedian adds, "Welcome home, CBS," a reference to the network's omnipresent slogan.

5:13 P.M.
First commercial.

5:39 P.M.
Award #6, Outstanding Directing for a Variety or Music Program, an interesting competition, at least for insiders. Friendly rivals and longtime colleagues, 49th Emmy director Lou Horvitz, for "The 69th Annual Academy Awards," is up against his executive producer Don Mischer, represented by his work on the opening ceremonies for the Atlanta Centennial Olympic Games. Mischer wins. It's his 13th Emmy.

6:02 P.M.
Christopher Reeve is wheeled on stage and gets a standing ovation. Predictably, it turns out to be the evening's emotional high point.

6:30 P.M.

Order is restored. Jerry Seinfeld, as a presenter, does a self-effacing, funny turn, complaining about being omitted from the nominees for lead comedy actors in favor of Michael J. Fox of *Spin City*. The one-minute, 30-second segment concludes with clever videotape clips comparing the two performers.

6:39 P.M.

ATAS President Richard H. Frank presents The President's Award to the HBO drama *Miss Evers' Boys*.

7:36 P.M.

Bryant Gumbel introduces a videotaped piece paying homage to Brandon Tartikoff, the highly respected former NBC programming whiz who passed away the previous month. It's a sad and somber moment.

7:51 P.M.

Award #28, final Emmy of the evening.

7:55 P.M.

Commercial position #12, running one minute, 32 seconds, followed by a CBS News promo.

7:57 P.M.

Bryant Gumbel says goodnight, underscored by theme music.

Approximate total program time: 3:00 hours. Off air 7:58:34 (PDT).

TV CARES

ANGELA LANSBURY
HONORARY CHAIRPERSON

DAVID MICHAELS
CHAIRMAN
DARLENE LIEBLICH
VICE-CHAIRPERSON

COMMITTEE MEMBERS

JASON ALEXANDER
JUNE BALDWIN
SCOTT BARTON
LEE PHILIP BELL
BARBARA ALLYNE BENNET
ROBERT BERGER
PETER BERGMAN
B. HARLAN BOLL
DENISE BRANCH
JANICE BRANDOW
TIM BRAUN
BARBARA CHASE
JOYCE COLEMAN
DARLENE CONLEY
JEANNE COOPER
GILBERT DEGLORIA
MAURA DUNBAR
BRENDA FELDMAN
LISA FIKE
SUSAN FINCHAM
LEEZA GIBBONS
BOB GOEN
FLORENCE HENDERSON
JOHN INGLE
MARK ITKIN
PAULA KAATZ
KELLY LANGE
VICKI LAWRENCE
KATE LINDER
LINDA LOE
DR. JAMES LOPER
PEGGY MCCAY
JOAN MESSINGER
DEBORAH MILLER
NICK MOENSSENS
JOSHUA MORROW
KAREN ANGONA NOLAN
ROBERT O'DONNELL
MELODY THOMAS SCOTT
SUSAN SIMONS
ELIZABETH SUNG
MICHAEL SUTTON
LIZ TORRES
NANCY BRADLEY WIARD
JOHN ZAK

As the Emmy Awards turn 50, a younger and exciting offspring of the Academy of Television Arts & Sciences, *TV CARES*, enters its third year. With the support of ATAS Executive Director Dr. James Loper and the ongoing mentoring and support of our dynamic ATAS President, Meryl Marshall, *TV CARES* has come a long way.

TV CARES is a committee of the Academy of Television Arts & Sciences Foundation. We promote, encourage, and publicly recognize responsible programming, raise funds, and produce Public Service Announcements (PSAs) to further educate our industry and the public regarding the challenges posed by HIV. The Office of the Mayor of Los Angeles issued a proclamation commending the Academy and *TV CARES* for its outreach.

The AIDS Awareness Ribbons (donated by Broadway Cares/Equity Fights AIDS) are distributed by the Academy at all major awards shows in the hope that this gentle reminder will inspire at least one person watching to stay safe. *TV CARES* also produces the Ribbon Of Hope Celebrations, at which we commend programs and individuals for responsible programming and deeds in the area of AIDS awareness and education. Past recipients have included *General Hospital*, *ER*, *The Young and the Restless*, Dick Clark, Michael Jeter, and Lynne Gabriel, along with Neil Tadken and Richard Jennings for their work each year with the "Day of Compassion." This year, we also honored the most effective Public Service Announcement, "Bedroom," from Streetsmart Advertising.

Currently, we have focused our efforts on the fight against complacency regarding the AIDS epidemic. Although major strides have been made with new drug therapies, the crisis is, unfortunately, far from over. Many people still need care, and there are an alarming number of new cases each day. There are people who cannot tolerate or do not have access to existing medications. Also, questions still remain regarding the long-term effectiveness of these drugs. Although the fight against AIDS is no longer new, exciting, or "hot," it is of critical importance that we remain vigilant and committed to educating the public and eliminating the life-threatening HIV virus.

The proceeds that *TV CARES* receives from the sale of this book will be used to further these efforts and will be distributed equally among Broadway Cares/Equity Fights AIDS, Caring for Babies with AIDS, and the Aileen Getty Foundation/Homestead Hospice. We thank you for your support.

As we enter into a new millennium, and begin the next 50 years of Emmy Awards, we must all—now more than ever—continue to Imagine, Demand, and Work for a Cure.

David Michaels
Chairman, *TV CARES*

TV CARES INFORMATION LINE • 818-754-2877

(Clockwise from bottom left) Bob Newhart and Judd Hirsch; Glenn Close; ATAS President Meryl Marshall, TV CARES Chairman David Michaels, and TV CARES Vice-Chairperson Darlene Lieblich; TV CARES committee member B. Harlan Böll with Dick and Kari Clark; John Lithgow; Bruce Willis, Ellen DeGeneres, and Anne Heche. (Center) Sally Field and Steven Spielberg.

(Clockwise from bottom left) Jason Priestley and Lea Thompson; Patrick Stewart; Ted Danson and Mary Steenburgen; Beau and Lloyd Bridges; Tom Skerritt; Michael J. Fox. (Center) Michael Richards and Jay Leno.

(Clockwise from bottom left) Ed Asner; Teri Hatcher; Ray Walston; Milton Berle; Steve Allen and Della Reese; Kelsey Grammer and David Hyde Pierce; Tyne Daly. (Center) Adam Arkin and Hector Elizondo.

Trivia

Most Emmys Won by a Series in its First Season:

ER - 8

Hill Street Blues - 8

Most Emmys Won by a Series in a Single Season:

ER (Premiere Season) - 8

Hill Street Blues
   (Premiere Season) - 8

Most Emmys Won as Best Drama Series:

Hill Street Blues - 4

L.A. Law - 4

Most Emmys Won as Best Comedy Series:

Frasier - 5

All in the Family - 4

Cheers - 4

The Dick Van Dyke Show - 4

Most Nominations for an Individual:

Dwight Hemion - 46

Steven Bochco - 31

Don Mischer - 31

George Stevens Jr. - 31

Michael G. Westmore - 31

Jan Scott - 30

Buz Kohan - 29

Alan Alda - 28

George Schaefer - 24

Most Nominations for a Program:

Cheers - 117

M*A*S*H - 109

Hill Street Blues - 98

Most Emmys Won by Individuals Behind the Camera:

Dwight Hemion - 17

Buz Kohan - 13

Don Mischer - 12

Ian Fraser - 11

Jan Scott - 11

Steven Bochco - 10

George Stevens Jr. - 11

Michael G. Westmore - 9

Carl Reiner - 8*

*Not including 3 Emmys for performing or 2 Emmys for writing *The Dick Van Dyke Show*

Most Emmys Won by a Male Performer:

Ed Asner - 7

Art Carney - 6

Alan Alda - 5

Billy Crystal - 5

Peter Falk - 5

Hal Holbrook - 5

Don Knotts - 5

Carroll O'Connor - 5

Laurence Olivier - 5

Dick Van Dyke - 5

Harvey Korman - 4

John Larroquette - 4

Bob Hope - 4

Peter Ustinov - 4

Most Emmys Won by a Female Performer:

Mary Tyler Moore - 8

Dinah Shore - 8

Cloris Leachman - 8

Candice Bergen - 5

Carol Burnett - 5

Tyne Daly - 5

Lily Tomlin - 5

Tracey Ullman - 5

Lucille Ball - 4

Valerie Harper - 4

Michael Learned - 4

Rhea Perlman - 4

Betty White - 4*

*Not including a Hollywood Area Emmy won in 1952 for *Life With Elizabeth*, a sitcom

Most Emmys Won by a Performer, Same Role, Same Series:

Candice Bergen - 5

Most Emmys Won by a Male Art Director:

Roby Christopher - 5

Most Emmys Won by a Female Art Director:

Jan Scott - 11

Most Emmys Won by a Male Writer in Variety-Music Programming:

Herb Sargent - 6

Most Emmys Won by a Female Writer in Variety-Music Programming:

Merrill Markoe - 3

Marilyn Suzanne Miller - 3

Most Emmys Won by a Series:

The Mary Tyler Moore Show - 29
Cheers - 28
Hill Street Blues - 26
The Carol Burnett Show - 25

Most Emmys Won by a Miniseries:

Roots (1977) - 9

Most Emmys Won by a Movie of the Week:

Eleanor and Franklin
(1986) - 11

Most Emmys Won in a Single Year by a Network:

CBS (1973–74) - 44

MOST PROGRAM NOMINATIONS IN A SINGLE AWARDS YEAR

Comedy Series:

The Larry Sanders Show
(1996–97) - 16
The Cosby Show (1985–86) - 15
The Golden Girls (1985–86) - 15

Drama Series:

NYPD Blue (1993–94) - 27
ER (1996–97) - 22

Miniseries:

Roots (1976–77) - 37

Drama-Comedy Specials:

Eleanor and Franklin
(1976–77) -17

Variety:

Motown Returns to the Apollo
(1984–85) - 11

Informational:

The Undersea World of Jacques
Cousteau (1971–72) - 8

First-run Syndication:

Fame (1983–84) -11

Husbands and Wives Who Have Both Won Emmys:

Bonnie Bartlett and
    William Daniels
Colleen Dewhurst and
    George C. Scott
Lynn Fontanne and Alfred Lunt
Jessica Tandy and Hume Cronyn
Marlo Thomas and Phil Donahue
Betty White and Allen Ludden
Lynn Whitfield and Brian Gibson

Parents and Children Who Have Both Won Emmys:

James and Tyne Daly
Carl and Rob Reiner
Danny and Marlo Thomas
Grant and John and Mark Tinker

Emmy Winners Who Have Also Won Oscars (Performers Only):

Jack Albertson
Ingrid Bergman
Shirley Booth
Marlon Brando
Art Carney
Bette Davis
Melvyn Douglas
Patty Duke
Faye Dunaway
Sally Field
Jane Fonda
Lee Grant
Helen Hayes
Katharine Hepburn
Dustin Hoffman
William Holden
Helen Hunt
Holly Hunter
Glenda Jackson
Cloris Leachman
Karl Malden
Thomas Mitchell
Rita Moreno
Laurence Olivier
Geraldine Page
Vanessa Redgrave
Jason Robards
Cliff Robertson
Eva Marie Saint
George C. Scott
Paul Scofield
Simone Signoret
Maureen Stapleton
Meryl Streep
Barbra Streisand
Jessica Tandy
Claire Trevor
Peter Ustinov
Robin Williams
Shelley Winters
Joanne Woodward
Loretta Young

Nominee List-1998

OUTSTANDING COMEDY SERIES

Ally McBeal–Fox
David E. Kelley Productions in association with
20th Century Fox

***Frasier–NBC**
Grub Street Productions in association with
Paramount

The Larry Sanders Show–HBO
Brillstein/Grey Entertainment, Partners with
Boundaries Productions

Seinfeld–NBC
Castle Rock Entertainment

3rd Rock From the Sun–NBC
Carsey-Werner Productions, LLC

OUTSTANDING DRAMA SERIES

ER–NBC
Constant c Productions, Amblin Television in
association with Warner Bros. Television

Law & Order–NBC
Wolf Films in association with Universal Television

NYPD Blue–ABC
Steven Bochco Productions

***The Practice–ABC**
David E. Kelley Productions in association with
20th Century Fox

The X-Files–Fox
Ten Thirteen Productions in association with
20th Century Fox

OUTSTANDING MINISERIES

More Tales of the City–Showtime
Productions La Fete (More Tales) Inc.

***From the Earth to the Moon–HBO**
HBO Programming in association with
Imagine Entertainment and Clavius Base

George Wallace–TNT
A Mark Carliner Production

Merlin–NBC
Hallmark Entertainment

Moby Dick–USA
Hallmark Entertainment

OUTSTANDING MADE FOR TELEVISION MOVIE

A Bright Shining Lie–HBO
A Bleecker Street Films Production

***Don King: Only in America–HBO**
A Thomas Carter Company production in
association with HBO Pictures

Gia–HBO
A Marvin Worth Production in association with
Citadel Entertainment/Kahn Power Pictures and
HBO Pictures

12 Angry Men–Showtime
MGM Worldwide Television

What the Deaf Man Heard [Hallmark Hall of Fame Presentation]–CBS
Hallmark Hall of Fame

*Denotes winner

OUTSTANDING VARIETY, MUSIC, OR COMEDY SERIES

*Dennis Miller Live–HBO
Happy Family Productions

Late Show With David Letterman–CBS
Worldwide Pants Incorporated

Politically Incorrect With Bill Maher–ABC
Brillstein-Grey Communications, HBO
Downtown Productions

The Tonight Show With Jay Leno–NBC
Big Dog Productions in association with
NBC Studios, Inc.

Tracey Takes On...–HBO
Takes On Productions, Inc.

OUTSTANDING VARIETY, MUSIC, OR COMEDY SPECIAL

The 70th Annual Academy Awards–ABC
Academy of Motion Pictures Arts and Sciences

Christopher Reeve: A Celebration of Hope–ABC
Don Mischer Productions in association with the
Christopher Reeve Foundation

Garth Live From Central Park–HBO
Picture Vision

Rodgers & Hammerstein's Cinderella
[The Wonderful World of Disney]–ABC
Citadel Entertainment, Storyline Entertainment,
Brownhouse Productions in association with Walt
Disney Television

*The 1997 Tony Awards–CBS
Tony Award productions

OUTSTANDING LEAD ACTOR IN A COMEDY SERIES

Michael J. Fox as Michael Flaherty
Spin City–ABC

*Kelsey Grammer as Dr. Frasier Crane
Frasier–NBC

John Lithgow as Dr. Dick Solomon
3rd Rock from the Sun–NBC

Paul Reiser as Paul Buchman
Mad About You–NBC

Garry Shandling as Larry Sanders
The Larry Sanders Show–HBO

OUTSTANDING LEAD ACTOR IN A DRAMA SERIES

*Andre Braugher as Frank Pembleton
Homicide: Life on the Street–NBC

David Duchovny as Fox Mulder
The X-Files–Fox

Anthony Edwards as Dr. Mark Greene
ER–NBC

Dennis Franz as Andy Sipowicz
NYPD Blue–ABC

Jimmy Smits as Bobby Simone
NYPD Blue–ABC

OUTSTANDING LEAD ACTOR IN A MINISERIES OR MOVIE

Jack Lemmon as Juror #8
12 Angry Men–Showtime

Sam Neill as Merlin
Merlin–NBC

*Denotes winner

Ving Rhames as Don King
Don King: Only in America–HBO

*Gary Sinise as George Wallace
George Wallace–TNT

Patrick Stewart as Captain Ahab
Moby Dick–USA

OUTSTANDING LEAD ACTRESS IN A COMEDY SERIES

Kirstie Alley as Veronica Chase
Veronica's Closet–NBC

Ellen DeGeneres as Ellen Morgan
Ellen–ABC

Jenna Elfman as Dharma Montgomery
Dharma & Greg–ABC

Calista Flockhart as Ally McBeal
Ally McBeal–Fox

*Helen Hunt as Jamie Buchman
Mad About You–NBC

Patricia Richardson as Jill Taylor
Home Improvement–ABC

OUTSTANDING LEAD ACTRESS IN A DRAMA SERIES

Gillian Anderson as Dana Scully
The X-Files–Fox

Roma Downey as Monica
Touched by an Angel–CBS

*Christine Lahti as Dr. Kate Austin
Chicago Hope–CBS

Julianna Margulies as Carol Hathaway
ER–NBC

Jane Seymour as Dr. Michaela Quinn
Dr. Quinn, Medicine Woman–CBS

OUTSTANDING LEAD ACTRESS IN A MINISERIES OR MOVIE

*Ellen Barkin as Glory Marie
Before Women Had Wings
[Oprah Winfrey Presents]–ABC

Jamie Lee Curtis as Maggie Green
Nicholas' Gift–CBS

Judy Davis as Gladwyn
The Echo of Thunder [Hallmark Hall
of Fame Presentation]–CBS

Olympia Dukakis as Anna Madrigal
More Tales of the City–Showtime

Angelina Jolie as Gia
Gia–HBO

Sigourney Weaver as Claudia Hoffman
Snow White: A Tale of Terror–Showtime

OUTSTANDING SUPPORTING ACTOR IN A COMEDY SERIES

Jason Alexander as George Costanza
Seinfeld–NBC

Phil Hartman as Bill McNeal
NewsRadio–NBC

*David Hyde Pierce as Dr. Niles Crane
Frasier–NBC

Jeffrey Tambor as Hank Kingsley
The Larry Sanders Show–HBO

Rip Torn as Arthur
The Larry Sanders Show–HBO

**Denotes winner

OUTSTANDING SUPPORTING ACTOR IN A DRAMA SERIES

*Gordon Clapp as Detective Greg Medavoy
NYPD Blue–ABC

Hector Elizondo as Dr. Phillip Watters
Chicago Hope–CBS

Steven Hill as District Attorney Adam Schiff
Law & Order–NBC

Eriq La Salle as Dr. Peter Benton
ER–NBC

Noah Wyle as Dr. John Carter
ER–NBC

OUTSTANDING SUPPORTING ACTOR IN A MINISERIES OR MOVIE

Hume Cronyn as Juror #9
12 Angry Men–Showtime

Gregory Peck as Father Mapple
Moby Dick–USA

*George C. Scott as Juror #3
12 Angry Men–Showtime

Martin Short as Frik
Merlin–NBC

J.T. Walsh as Ray Perc
Hope–TNT

OUTSTANDING SUPPORTING ACTRESS IN A COMEDY SERIES

Christine Baranski as Maryann Thorpe
Cybill–CBS

Kristen Johnston as Sally Solomon
3rd Rock from the Sun–NBC

*Denotes winner

*Lisa Kudrow as Phoebe Buffay
Friends–NBC

Jane Leeves as Daphne Moon
Frasier–NBC

Julia Louis-Dreyfus as Elaine Benes
Seinfeld–NBC

OUTSTANDING SUPPORTING ACTRESS IN A DRAMA SERIES

Kim Delaney as Diane Russell
NYPD Blue–ABC

Laura Innes as Dr. Kerry Weaver
ER–NBC

*Camryn Manheim as Ellenor Frutt
The Practice–ABC

Della Reese as Tess
Touched by an Angel–CBS

Gloria Reuben as Jeanie Boulet
ER–NBC

OUTSTANDING SUPPORTING ACTRESS IN A MINISERIES OR MOVIE

Helena Bonham Carter as Morgan
Merlin–NBC

Julie Harris as Leonora
Ellen Foster [Hallmark Hall of Fame Presentation]–CBS

Judith Ivey as Lucille
What the Deaf Man Heard [Hallmark Hall of Fame Presentation]–CBS

Angelina Jolie as Cornelia Wallace
George Wallace–TNT

*Mare Winningham as Lurleen Wallace
George Wallace–TNT

OUTSTANDING GUEST ACTOR IN A COMEDY SERIES

Hank Azaria as Nat
Mad About You–NBC

Lloyd Bridges as Izzy Mandelbaum
Seinfeld–NBC

*Mel Brooks as Uncle Phil
Mad About You–NBC

John Cleese as Dr. Neesam
3rd Rock From the Sun–NBC

Nathan Lane as Professor Twilley
Mad About You–NBC

OUTSTANDING GUEST ACTOR IN A DRAMA SERIES

Bruce Davison as Jake
Touched by an Angel–CBS

Vincent D'Onofrio as John Lange
Homicide: Life on the Street–NBC

Charles Durning as Thomas Finnegan
Homicide: Life on the Street–NBC

*John Larroquette as Joey Heric
The Practice–ABC

Charles Nelson Reilly as Jose Chung
Millennium–Fox

OUTSTANDING GUEST ACTRESS IN A COMEDY SERIES

Carol Burnett as Theresa Stemple
Mad About You–NBC

Jan Hooks as Vicki Dubcek
3rd Rock From the Sun–NBC

Patti LuPone as Zora
Frasier–NBC

Bette Midler as Caprice Feldman
Murphy Brown–CBS

*Emma Thompson as Herself
Ellen–ABC

OUTSTANDING GUEST ACTRESS IN A DRAMA SERIES

Veronica Cartwright as Cassandra Spender
The X-Files–Fox

Swoosie Kurtz as Tina-Marie Chambliss
ER–NBC

*Cloris Leachman as Aunt Mooster
Promised Land–CBS

Lili Taylor as Marty Glenn
The X-Files–FOX

Alfre Woodard as Dr. Roxanne Turner
Homicide: Life on the Street–NBC

OUTSTANDING PERFORMANCE IN A VARIETY OR MUSIC PROGRAM

Garth Brooks
Garth Brooks Live From Central Park–HBO

Michael Crawford
Michael Crawford in Concert–PBS

*Billy Crystal
The 70th Annual Academy Awards–ABC

Jay Leno
The Tonight Show With Jay Leno–NBC

*Denotes winner

David Letterman
Late Show With David Letterman–CBS

Tracey Ullman
Tracey Takes On...–HBO

OUTSTANDING DIRECTING FOR A COMEDY SERIES

Ally McBeal, Cro-Magnon–Fox
Allan Arkush, Director

Ally McBeal, Pilot–Fox
James Frawley, Director

Dharma & Greg, Pilot–ABC
James Burrows, Director

*The Larry Sanders Show, Flip–HBO
Todd Holland, Director

3rd Rock From the Sun, Dick and
the Other Guy–NBC
Terry Hughes, Director

OUTSTANDING DIRECTING FOR A DRAMA SERIES

*Brooklyn South, Pilot–CBS
Mark Tinker, Director

Chicago Hope, Brain Salad Surgery–CBS
Bill D'Elia, Director

ER, Ambush–NBC
Thomas Schlamme, Director

NYPD Blue, Lost Israel, Part 2–ABC

Paris Barclay, Director

The X-Files, The Post-Modern Prometheus–Fox
Chris Carter, Director

OUTSTANDING DIRECTING FOR A VARIETY OR MUSIC PROGRAM

*The 70th Annual Academy Awards–ABC
Louis J. Horvitz, Director

Fleetwood Mac "The Dance"–MTV
Bruce Gowers, Director

Garth Live From Central Park–HBO
Marty Callner, Director

Rodgers & Hammerstein's Cinderella
[The Wonderful World of Disney]–ABC
Robert Iscove, Director

Stomp Out Loud–HBO
Luke Cresswell, Steve McNicholas, Directors

Tracey Takes On...Smoking–HBO
Don Scardino, Director

OUTSTANDING DIRECTING FOR A MINISERIES OR MOVIE

Don King: Only in America–HBO
John Herzfeld, Director

From the Earth to the Moon, Can We Do This?
(Part 1)–HBO
Tom Hanks, Director

*George Wallace–TNT
John Frankenheimer, Director

Merlin–NBC
Steve Barron, Director

12 Angry Men–Showtime
William Friedkin, Director

*Denotes winner

Bibliography

Alley, Robert S. and Irby B. Brown. *Murphy Brown: Anatomy of a Sitcom.* New York: Dell Publishing, 1990.

Barabas, SuzAnne, and Gabor Barabas. *Gunsmoke, A Complete History.* Jefferson, N.C.: McFarland & Col., Inc., 1990.

Barnouw, Erik. *The History of Broadcasting in the United States*, vol. 1-3. New York: Oxford University Press, 1966-1970.

Bilby, Kenneth. *The General: David Sarnoff and the Rise of the Communications Industry.* New York: Harper and Row, 1986.

Brooks, Tim, and Earle Marsh. *The Complete Directory to Prime Time Network and Cable TV Shows*, Sixth Edition. New York: Ballantine Books, 1995.

Brown, Les. *The New York Times Encyclopedia of Television.* New York: Times Books, 1977.

Castleman, Harry, and Walter J. Podrazik. *Watching TV: Four Decades of American Television.* New York: McGraw-Hill Book Co., 1982.

Cronkite, Walter. *A Reporter's Life.* New York: Alfred A. Knopf, 1996.

Cronyn, Hume. *A Terrible Liar: A Memoir.* New York: William Morrow & Co., 1991.

Fortune magazine. "Television! Boom! (May 1948): 79-83; 191-97.

Gelman, Morrie. "75 Years of Pioneers." *Broadcasting & Cable Magazine.* (November 6, 1995): 80-96, 117.

————. "Feature Films and Television." *Television* magazine. (April 1968): 46-51, 73-80.

————. "Hollywood and TV." *Television* magazine. (September 1963): 27-53, 66-82.

————. "The Young Lions Take Over Hollywood." *Television* magazine. (July 1967): 20-25, 44-45.

Hill, Doug and Jeff Weingrad. *Saturday Night.* New York: Beech Tree Books/William Morrow, 1986.

Jaffe, Alfred J. "A Broadcast History: 30 years full of Drama, Change and Controversy." *Television/Radio Age.* (November 21, 1983): 23-39.

Leamer, Laurence. *King of the Night.* New York: William Morrow and Co., Inc., 1989.

Lyons, Eugene. *David Sarnoff.* New York: Harper and Row, 1966.

Manchester, William. *The Glory and the Dream*, vol. 1 and 2. Boston and Toronto: Little, Brown and Co., 1973-1974.

Mayer, Martin. *Madison Avenue, U.S.A.* New York: Harper & Brothers, 1958.

McClay, Michael. *I Love Lucy, The Complete Picture History of the Most Popular TV Show Ever.* New York: Warner Books, 1995.

McNeil, Alex. *Total Television*, Fourth Edition. New York: Penguin Books USA Inc., 1996.

Meredith, Burgess. *So Far, So Good*. Boston: Little, Brown and Co., 1994.

Minow, Newton. *Equal Time*. New York: Atheneum, 1964.

Moore, Mary Tyler. *After All*. New York: Dell Publishing, 1995.

O'Neil, Thomas. *The Emmys*. New York: Penguin Books, 1992.

Osborne, Robert. *65 Years of the Oscar: The Official History of the Academy Awards*. New York: Abbeville Press, 1989.

Paper, Lewis J. *Empire: William S. Paley and the Making of CBS*. New York: St. Martin's Press, 1987.

Parish, James Robert. *The Unofficial Murder She Wrote Casebook, The Definitive Unauthorized Companion to TV's Most Popular Whodunit!* New York: Kensington Books, 1997.

Rowen, Beth, editor. The A&E Entertainment Almanac. Boston: Information Please LLC, 1997.

Sheuer, Steven H. *Who's Who in Television and Cable*. New York: Facts On File Publications, 1983.

Tartikoff, Brandon and Charles Leerhsen. *The Last Great Ride*. New York: Random House, Turtle Bay Books, 1992.

Thomas: Bob. *King Cohn: The Life and Times of Harry Cohn*. New York: G.P. Putnam's Sons, 1967.

Tinker, Grant and Bud Bukeyser. *Tinker In Television: From General Sarnoff to General Electric*. New York: Simon & Schuster, 1994.

TV Guide Book of Lists, The. From the Editors of TV Guide. New York: HarperCollins Publishers, 1998.

Waldron, Vince. *The Official Dick Van Dyke Show Book, The Definitive History and Ultimate Viewer's Guide to Television's Most Enduring Comedy*. New York: Hyperion, 1994.

World Almanac, The. Mahwah, N.J.: World Almanac Books, 1998.

Writers Guild of America. *The Writers Guild of America Present the Prize Plays of Television and Radio 1956*. New York: Random House, 1957.

Young, Alan with Bill Burt. *Mister Ed and Me*. New York: St. Martin's Press, 1994.

Index

Photo Credits

All photographs courtesy of the Academy of Television Arts & Sciences except the following: